Effective Shipping and Port Management

Effective Shipping and Port Management

Medwin Gale

RANDOM PUBLICATIONS
NEW DELHI (INDIA)

Effective Shipping and Port Management

ISBN 978-93-5111-938-8

Published in 2016 in India by

RANDOM PUBLICATIONS

4376-A/4B, Gali Murari Lal, Ansari Road
New Delhi-110 002
Phone : +9111-43580356, 011-23289044, 011-43142548
e-mail: sales@randompublications.com,
info@randompublications.com, randomexports@gmail.com

Reprinted 2021

Type Setting by : Friends Media, Delhi-110089
Digitally Printed at: Replika Press Pvt. Ltd.

Preface

Shipping and Port management which plays a crucial role in international trade and commerce, falls in the department of logistics. As almost 90% of world's overall trade is done through sea route, these ports need to be managed well. When trade across countries flourished, movement of freight by means of ships was considered the most cost effective means of transport. Port Management is a mishmash of transportation, materials and goods handling and storage, ship operations and safety and health management.

The Shipping and Logistics vertical is among the key sectors of the economy. It plays a major role as a backbone of supply chain for all other sectors such as manufacturing, retail, pharmaceutical, hospitality, energy, engineering and utilities and others. This sector has a significant role in playing a balancing act between the supply and demand cycles of any vertical and impacting the economy. However, the shipping and logistics has its own challenges such as warehousing operations, supply and management operations, consignment tracking and timely deliveries, identification of consignments and bill authentication for payments, workforce management and many more.

Ports usually deal with a number of disparate activities like the movement, loading and unloading of ships, containers, and other cargo; customs activities as well as human resources.

Port management is a necessary position required to keep ports organized, supervised, and functioning. Managing ports is a combination of material handling, road transport, storage, safe ship operations, health and safety. In other words, Port management include overseeing all commercial and technical components of the shipping industry. Duties in port management may also include cooperating with other ports, coordinating deliveries with ships, overseeing port development, advertising and promoting the port, and enforcing security and environmental protection initiatives.

Paramatrix offers major benefits and advantages to businesses and organizations since it focuses on pre and post processes of warehousing operations including the back end processes of data related to sales, inventory, orders, payments as well as integration with enterprise class supply chain management applications and data flow. This helps the shipping and logistics companies to have full view of the business cycle and operation managements.

After observing and understanding these challenges and issues for over many years, Paramatrix has developed wide range of IT services and software solutions to addresses the core processes involved in the warehouse operations and supply chain management. We provide effective IT solutions, software applications and support services for the warehouse operations to bring a better coordination, integration and efficiency in the whole supply chain process. Using the domain knowledge and expertise,

Paramatrix offers customization of IT applications and software solutions for the shipping and logistics companies as per their business models and requirements. In addition, we also offer point of sales (POS) solutions based on hand held devices using the scanning and infrared methods for businesses, which help in the sales process including inventory management, orders, billing, transaction and payments. Moreover, Paramatrix also addresses to niche demand of mobile based applications required for tracking and identification of consignments and goods. Our software development teams in past have developed niche mobile based applications as well as its web integration for organizations that helps the customers with greater transparency to the logistics and shipping processes.

– Author

Contents

1

Introduction to Shipping

SHIP

A ship is a large buoyant watercraft. Ships are generally distinguished from boats based on size, shape and cargo or passenger capacity. Ships are used on lakes, seas, and rivers for a variety of activities, such as the transport of people orgoods, fishing, entertainment, public safety, and warfare. Historically, a "ship" was a sailing vessel with at least three square-rigged masts and a full bowsprit. In armed conflict and in daily life ships have become an integral part of modern commercial and military systems. Fishing boats are used by millions of fishermen throughout the world. Military forces operate vessels for naval warfare and to transport and support forces ashore. Commercial vessels, nearly 35,000 in number, carried 7.4 billion tons of cargo in 2007. As of 2011, there are about 104,304 ships with IMO numbers in the world.

Ships were always a key in history's great explorations and scientific and technological development. Navigators such as Zheng He spread such inventions as the compass and gunpowder. Ships have been used for such purposes as colonizationand the slave trade, and have served scientific, cultural, and humanitarian needs. After the 16th century, new crops that had come from and to the Americas via the European seafarers significantly contributed to the world population growth. Ship transport has shaped the world's economy into today's energy-intensive pattern.

NOMENCLATURE

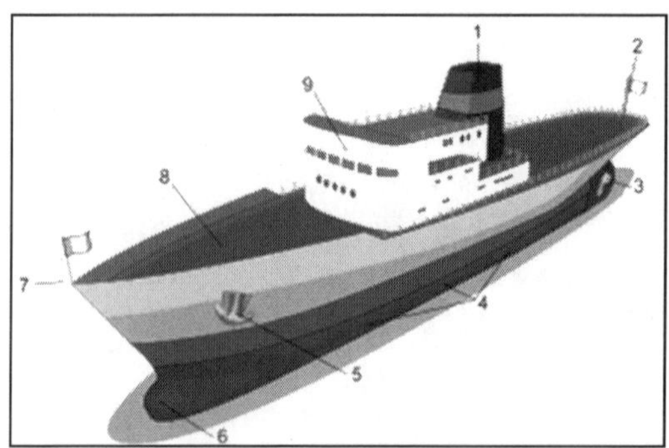

Fig. Main Parts of Ship. 1: Smokestack or Funnel; 2: Stern;3: Propeller and Rudder; 4: Portside (the Right Side is known as Starboard); 5: Anchor; 6: Bulbous Bow; 7: Bow;8: Deck; 9: Superstructure.

Ships can usually be distinguished from boats based on size and the ship's ability to operate independently for extended periods. A commonly used rule of thumb is that if one vessel can carry another, the larger of the two is a ship. Dinghiesare carried on sailing yachts as small as 35 feet (10.67 m), clearly not ships; this rule of thumb is not foolproof.

In the age of sail, a "ship" was a sailing vessel with at least three square-rigged masts and a full bowsprit; other types of vessel were also defined by their sailplan, *e.g.* barque, brigantine, etc. A number of large vessels are usually referred to as boats. Submarines are a prime example. Other types of large vessel which are traditionally called boats are Great Lakes freighters, riverboats, and ferryboats. Though large enough to carry their own boats and heavy cargoes, these vessels are designed for operation on inland or protected coastal waters. In most maritime traditions ships have individual names, and modern ships may belong to a ship class often named after its first ship. In English, a ship is traditionally referred to as "she", even if named after a man, but this is not universal usage; some journalistic style guides advise using "it" as referring to ships with female pronouns can be seen as offensive and outdated.

HISTORY

Prehistory and Antiquity

The first known vessels date back about 10,000 years ago, but could not be described as ships. The first navigators began to use animal skins or woven fabrics as sails. Affixed to the top of a pole set upright in a boat, these sails gave early ships range. This allowed men to explore widely, allowing for the settlement of Oceania for example (about 3,000 years ago).

By around 3000 BC, Ancient Egyptians knew how to assemble wooden planks into a hull. They used woven straps to lash the planks together, and reeds or grass stuffed between the planks helped to seal the seams. The Greek historian and geographer Agatharchideshad documented ship-faring among the early Egyptians: "During the prosperous period of the old Kingdom, between the 30th and 25th centuries B. C., the river-routes were kept in order, and Egyptian ships sailed the Red Sea as far as the myrrh-country." Sneferu's ancient cedar wood ship Praise of the Two Lands is the first reference recorded (2613 BC) to a ship being referred to by name.

Fig. A Raft is Among the Simplest Boat Designs.

The ancient Egyptians were perfectly at ease building sailboats. A remarkable example of their shipbuilding skills was the Khufu ship, a vessel 143 feet (44 m) in length entombed at the foot of the Great Pyramid of Giza around 2500 BC and found intact in 1954.

It is known that ancient Nubia/Axum traded with India, and there is evidence that ships from Northeast Africa may have sailed back and forth between India/Sri Lanka and Nubia trading goods and even to Persia, Himyar and Rome. Aksum was known by the Greeks for having seaports for ships from Greece and Yemen. Elsewhere in Northeast Africa, the Periplus of the Red Sea reports that Somalis, through their northern ports such as Zeila and Berbera, were trading frankincense and other items with the inhabitants of the Arabian Peninsula well before the arrival of Islam as well as with then Roman-controlled Egypt.

A panel found at Mohenjodaro depicted a sailing craft. Vessels were of many types; their construction is vividly described in the Yukti Kalpa Taru, an ancient Indian text on shipbuilding. This treatise gives a technical exposition on the techniques of shipbuilding. It sets forth minute details about the various types of ships, their sizes, and the materials from which they were built. The Yukti Kalpa Taru sums up in a condensed form all the available information. The Yukti Kalpa Taru gives sufficient information and dates to prove that, in ancient times, Indian shipbuilders had a good knowledge of the materials which were used in building ships. In addition to describing the qualities of the different types of wood and their suitability for shipbuilding, the Yukti Kalpa Taru gives an elaborate classification of ships based on their size. The oldest discovered sea faring hulled boat is the Egyptian Uluburun shipwreck off the coast of Turkey, dating back to 1300 BC.

The Phoenicians, the first to sail completely around Africa, and Greeks gradually mastered navigation at sea aboard triremes, exploring and colonizing the Mediterranean via ship. Around 340 BC, the Greek navigator Pytheas of Massalia ventured from Greece to Western Europe and Great Britain. In the course of the 2nd century BC, Rome went on to destroy Carthage and subdue the Hellenistic kingdoms of the eastern Mediterranean, achieving complete mastery of the inland sea, that they called Mare Nostrum. Themonsoon wind system of the Indian Ocean was first sailed by Greek navigator Eudoxus of Cyzicus in 118 BC. In China, by the time of the Zhou Dynasty ship technologies such as stern mounted rudders were developed, and by the Han Dynasty, a well kept naval fleet was an integral part of the military. Ship technology advanced to the point where by the medieval period, water tight compartments were developed.

Fig. Roman Trireme Mosaic from Carthage, Bardo Museum, Tunis.

The Swahili people had various extensive trading ports dotting the coast of medieval East Africa and Great Zimbabwe had extensive trading contacts with Central Africa, and likely also imported goods brought to Africa through the Southeast African shore trade of Kilwa in modern-day Tanzania. It is known by historians that at its height the Mali Empire built a large naval fleet under Emperor Mansa Musa in the late 13th and early 14th century. Arabic sources describe what some consider to be visits to the New World by a Mali fleet in 1311. Before the introduction of the compass, celestial navigation was the main method for navigation at sea. In China, early versions of themagnetic compass were being developed and used in navigation between 1040 and 1117. The true mariner's compass, using a pivoting needle in a dry box, was developed in Europe no later than 1300.

Renaissance

Until the Renaissance, navigational technology remained comparatively primitive. This absence of technology did not prevent some civilizations from becoming sea powers. Examples include the maritime republics of Genoa and Venice, Hanseatic League, and the Byzantine navy. The Vikings used theirknarrs to explore North America, trade in the Baltic Sea and plunder many of the coastal regions of Western Europe.

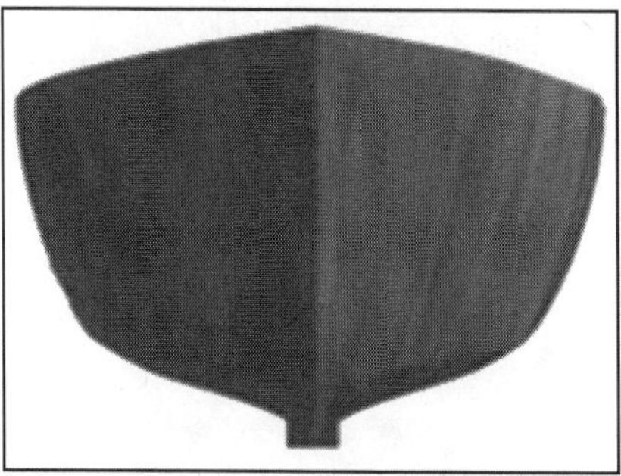

Fig. A 3D Model of the Basic Hull Structure of a Venetian "Galley of Flanders", a Large Mediterranean Trading Vessel of the 15th Century. The Reconstruction by Archaeologist Courtney Higgins is Based on Measurements Given in Contemporary Ship Treatises.

Towards the end of the 14th century, ships like the carrack began to develop towers on the bow and stern. These towers decreased the vessel's stability, and in the 15th century, the caravel, designed by thePortuguese, based on the Arabic qarib which could sail closer to the wind, became more widely used. The towers were gradually replaced by the forecastle and sterncastle, as in the carrack Santa María ofChristopher Columbus. This increased freeboard allowed another innovation: the freeing port, and the artillery associated with it.

Fig. A Japanese Atakebune from the 16th Century.

In the 16th century, the use of freeboard and freeing ports became widespread on galleons. The English modified their vessels to maximize their firepower and demonstrated the effectiveness of their doctrine, in 1588, by defeating the Spanish Armada.

At this time, ships were developing in Asia in much the same way as Europe. Japan used defensive naval techniques in the Mongol invasions of Japan in 1281. It is likely that the Mongols of the time took advantage of both European and Asian shipbuilding techniques. During the 15th century, China's Ming Dynastyassembled one of the largest and most powerful naval fleets in the world for the diplomatic and power projection voyages of Zheng He. Elsewhere in Japan in the 15th century, one of the world's first iron-clads, "Tekkosen", literally meaning "iron ships", was also developed. In Japan, during the Sengoku erafrom the fifteenth to 17th century, the great struggle for feudal supremacy was fought, in part, by coastal fleets of several hundred boats, including the atakebune.

Fig. Model of a MedievalMogadishan Ship.

During the Age of the Ajuran, the Somali sultanates and republics of Merca, Mogadishu, Barawa, Hobyo and their respective ports flourished, enjoying a lucrative foreign commerce with ships sailing to and coming from Arabia, India, Venetia,Persia, Egypt, Portugal and as far away as China. In the 16th century, Duarte Barbosa noted that many ships from the Kingdom of Cambaya in what is modern-day India sailed to Mogadishu with cloth and spices, for which they in return received gold, wax and ivory. Barbosa also highlighted the abundance of meat, wheat, barley, horses, and fruit on the coastal markets, which generated enormous wealth for the merchants.

Middle Age Swahili Kingdoms are known to have had trade port bullship and trade routes with the Islamic world and Asia and were described by Greek historians as "metropolises". Famous African trade ports such as Mombasa, Zanzibar, and Kilwa were known to Chinese sailors such as Zheng He and medieval Islamic historians such as the Berber Islamic voyager Abu Abdullah ibn Battua. In the 14th century AD, King Abubakari I, the brother of King Mansa Musa of the Mali Empire, is thought to have had a great armada of ships sitting on the coast of West Africa. This is corroborated by ibn Battuta himself who recalls several hundred Malian ships off the coast. This has led to great speculation, with historical evidence, that it is possible that Malian sailors may have reached the coast of Pre-Columbian America under the rule of Abubakari II, nearly two hundred years before Christopher Columbus and that black traders may have been in the Americas before Columbus.

Fig. Replica of Magellan's Victoria.Ferdinand Magellan led the First Expedition that Circumnavigated the Globe in 1519-1522.

Fifty years before Christopher Columbus, Chinese navigator Zheng He traveled the world at the head of what was for the time a huge armada. The largest of his ships had nine masts, were 130 metres (430 ft) long and had a beam of 55 metres (180 ft). His fleet carried 30,000 men aboard 70 vessels, with the goal of bringing glory to the Chinese emperor.

The carrack and then the caravel were developed in Iberia. After Columbus, European explorationrapidly accelerated, and many new trade routes were established. In 1498, by reaching India, Vasco da Gama proved that the access to the Indian Ocean from the Atlantic was possible. These explorations in the Atlantic and Indian Oceans were soon followed by France,England and the Netherlands, who explored the Portuguese and Spanish trade routes into the Pacific Ocean, reaching Australia in 1606 and New Zealand in 1642. In the 17th century Dutch explorers such as Abel Tasman explored the coasts of Australia, while in the 18th century it was British explorer James Cook who mapped much of Polynesia.

Specialization and Modernization

Parallel to the development of warships, ships in service of marine fishery and trade also developed in the period between antiquity and the Renaissance. Still primarily a coastal endeavor, fishing is largely practiced by individuals with little other money using small boats. Maritime trade was driven by the development of shipping companies with significant financial resources. Canal barges, towed by draft animals on an adjacent towpath, contended with the railway up to and past the early days of the industrial revolution. Flat-bottomed and flexible scow boats also became widely used for transporting small cargoes.

Mercantile trade went hand-in-hand with exploration, self-financed by the commercial benefits of exploration.

Fig. The British HMS Sandwich Fires at the French Flagship Bucentaure(Completely Dismasted) at the Battle of Trafalgar (1805). The Bucentaure also Fights HMS Victory (Behind Her) andHMS Temeraire (Left Side of the Picture). In fact, HMS Sandwich Never Fought at Trafalgar, it's a Mistake from Auguste Mayer, the Painter.

During the first half of the 18th century, the French Navy began to develop a new type of vessel known as a ship of the line, featuring seventy-four guns. This type of ship became the backbone of all European fighting fleets. These ships were 56 metres (184 ft) long and their construction required 2,800 oak trees and 40 kilometres (25 mi) of rope; they carried a crew of about 800 sailors and soldiers.

Fig. RMS Titanic Departs from Southampton. Her Sinking Would Tighten safety Regulations.

During the 19th century the Royal Navy enforced a ban on the slave trade, acted to suppress piracy, and continued to map the world. A clipper was a very fast sailing ship of the 19th century. The clipper routesfell into commercial disuse with the introduction of steam ships with better fuel efficiency, and the opening of the Suez and Panama Canals. Ship designs stayed fairly unchanged until the late 19th century. The industrial revolution, new mechanical methods of propulsion, and the ability to construct ships from metal triggered an explosion in ship design. Factors including the quest for more efficient ships, the end of long running and wasteful maritime conflicts, and the increased financial capacity of industrial powers created an avalanche of more specialized boats and ships. Ships built for entirely new functions, such as firefighting, rescue, and research, also began to appear.

In light of this, classification of vessels by type or function can be difficult. Even using very broad functional classifications such as fishery, trade, military, and exploration fails to classify most of the old ships. This difficulty is increased by the fact that the terms such as sloop and frigate are used by old and new ships alike, and often the modern vessels sometimes have little in common with their predecessors.

Today

Fig. The Colombo Express, one of the Largest Container Ships in the World, Owned and Operated by Hapag-Lloyd ofGermany.

In 2007, the world's fleet included 34,882 commercial vessels with gross tonnage of more than 1,000 tons, totaling 1.04 billion tons.These ships carried 7.4 billion tons of cargo in 2006, a sum that grew by 8 per cent over the previous year. In terms of tonnage, 39 per cent of these ships are tankers, 26 per cent are bulk carriers, 17 per cent container ships and 15 per cent were other types.

In 2002, there were 1,240 warships operating in the world, not counting small vessels such as patrol boats. The United States accounted for 3 million tons worth of these vessels, Russia 1.35 million tons, the United Kingdom 504,660 tons and China 402,830 tons. The 20th century saw many naval engagements during the two world wars, the Cold War, and the rise to power of naval forces of the two blocs. The world's major powers have recently used their naval power in cases such as the United Kingdom in the Falkland Islands and theUnited States in Iraq.

The size of the world's fishing fleet is more difficult to estimate. The largest of these are counted as commercial vessels, but the smallest are legion. Fishing vessels can be found in most seaside villages in the world. As of 2004, the United Nations Food and Agriculture Organization estimated 4 million fishing vessels were operating worldwide.The same study estimated that the world's 29 million fishermen caught 85,800,000 tonnes (84,400,000 long tons; 94,600,000 short tons) of fish and shellfish that year.

TYPES OF SHIPS

Because ships are constructed using the principles of naval architecture that require same structural components, their classification is based on their function such as suggested by Paulet and Presles., which requires modification of the components.

The categories accepted in general by naval architects are:

- *High-speed craft* - Multihulls including wave piercers, small-waterplane-area twin hull (SWATH), surface effect ships and hovercraft, hydrofoil, wing in ground effect craft (WIG).
- *Off shore oil vessels* - Platform supply vessel, pipe layers, accommodation and crane barges, non and semi-submersible drilling rigs, production platforms, floating production storage and offloading units.
- Fishing vessels

Motorised fishing trawlers, trap setters, seiners, longliners, trollers factory ships. Traditional sailing and rowed fishing vessels and boats used for handline fishing

Cable layers

Tugboats, dredgers, salvage vessels, tenders, Pilot boats.

Floating dry docks, floating cranes, lightership.

- Dry cargo ships - tramp freighters, bulk carriers, cargo liners, container vessels, barge carriers, Ro-Ro ships, refrigerated cargo ships, timber carriers, livestock and light vehicle carriers.
- Liquid cargo ships - Oil tankers, liquefied gas carriers, chemical carriers.
- Passenger vessels

Liners, cruise and Special Trade Passenger (STP) ships

Cross-channel, coastal and harbour ferries.

Luxury and cruising yachts

Sail training and multi-masted ships

- Recreational boats and craft - rowed, masted and motorised craft
- Special-purpose vessels - weather and research vessels, deep sea survey vessels, and icebreakers.
- Submersibles - industrial exploration, scientific research, tourist and hydrographic survey.
- Warships

Surface combatant- deep and shallow draft

Submarines

Some of these are discussed in the following sections.

Inland and Coastal Boats

Many types of boats are designed for inland and coastal waterways. These are the vessels that trade upon the lakes, rivers and canals.

Fig. Passenger Ship of Köln-Düsseldorfer on the River Rhine.

Barges are a prime example of inland vessels. Flat-bottomed boats built to transport heavy goods, most barges are not self-propelled and need to be moved by tugboats towing or towboats pushing them. Barges towed along canals by draft animals on an adjacenttowpath contended with the railway in the early industrial revolution but were out competed in the carriage of high value items because of the higher speed, falling costs, and route flexibility of rail transport.

Lake freighters, also called lakers, are cargo vessels that ply the Great Lakes. The most well-known is the SS Edmund Fitzgerald, the latest major vessel to be wrecked on the Lakes. These vessels are traditionally called boats, not ships. Visiting ocean-going vessels are called "salties." Because of their additional beam, very large salties are never seen inland of the Saint Lawrence Seaway. Because the smallest of the Soo Locks is larger than any Seaway lock, salties that can pass through the Seaway may travel anywhere in the Great Lakes. Because of their deeper draft, salties may accept partial loads on the Great Lakes, "topping off" when they have exited the Seaway. Similarly, the largest lakers are confined to the Upper Lakes (Superior,Michigan, Huron, Erie) because they are too large to use the Seaway locks, beginning at the Welland Canal that bypasses the Niagara River.

Since the freshwater lakes are less corrosive to ships than the salt water of the oceans, lakers tend to last much longer than ocean freighters. Lakers older than 50 years are not unusual, and as of 2005, all were over 20 years of age. The SS St. Marys Challenger, built in 1906 as the William P Snyder, was the oldest laker still working on the Lakes until its conversion into a barge starting in 2013. Similarly, theE.M. Ford, built in 1898 as the Presque Isle, was sailing the lakes 98 years later in 1996. As of 2007 the Ford was still afloat as a stationary transfer vessel at a riverside cement silo in Saginaw, Michigan.

Seagoing Commercial Vessels

Commercial vessels or merchant ships can be divided into four broad categories: fishing, cargo ships, passenger ships, and special-purpose ships. Modern commercial vessels are typically powered by a single propeller driven by a diesel or, less usually, gas turbine engine., but until the mid-19th century they were predominantly square sail rigged. The fastest vessels may use pump-jet engines. Most commercial vessels have full hull-forms to maximize cargo capacity. Hulls are usually made of steel, although aluminum can be used on faster craft, and fibreglass on the smallest service vessels. Commercial vessels generally have a crew headed by a captain, with deck officers and marine engineers on larger vessels. Special-purpose vessels often have specialized crew if necessary, for example scientists aboard research vessels.

Fig. Two Modern Container Ships in San Francisco.

Fishing boats are generally small, often little more than 30 meters (98 ft) but up to 100 metres (330 ft) for a large tuna or whaling ship. Aboard a fish processing vessel, the catch can be made ready for market and sold more quickly once the ship makes port. Special purpose vessels have special gear. For example, trawlers have winches and arms, stern-trawlers have a rear ramp, and tuna seiners have skiffs. In 2004, 85,800,000 tonnes (84,400,000 long tons; 94,600,000 short tons) of fish were caught in the marine capture fishery. Anchoveta represented the largest single catch at 10,700,000 tonnes (10,500,000 long tons; 11,800,000 short tons). That year, the top ten marine capture species also included Alaska pollock, Blue whiting,Skipjack tuna, Atlantic herring, Chub mackerel, Japanese anchovy, Chilean jack mackerel, Largehead hairtail, and Yellowfin tuna. Other species including salmon, shrimp,lobster, clams, squid and crab, are also commercially fished. Modern commercial fishermen use many methods. One is fishing by nets, such as purse seine, beach seine, lift nets, gillnets, or entangling nets. Another is trawling, including bottom trawl. Hooks and lines are used in methods like long-line fishing and hand-line fishing. Another method is the use of fishing trap.

Cargo ships transport dry and liquid cargo. Dry cargo can be transported in bulk by bulk carriers, packed directly onto a general cargo ship in break-bulk, packed in intermodal containers as aboard a container ship, or driven aboard as in roll-on roll-off ships. Liquid cargo is generally carried in bulk aboard tankers, such as oil tankers which may include both crude and finished products of oil, chemical tankers which may also carry vegetable oils other than chemicals and LPG/LNG tankers, although smaller shipments may be carried on container ships in tank containers.

Passenger ships range in size from small river ferries to very large cruise ships. This type of vessel includes ferries, which move passengers and vehicles on short trips; ocean liners, which carry passengers from one place to another; and cruise ships, which carry passengers on voyages undertaken for pleasure, visiting several places and with leisure activities on board, often returning them to the port of embarkation. Riverboats and inland ferries are specially designed to carry passengers, cargo, or both in the challenging river environment. Rivers present special hazards to vessels. They usually have varying water flows that alternately lead to high speed water flows or protruding rock hazards. Changing siltation patterns may cause the sudden appearance of shoal waters, and often floating or sunken logs and trees (called snags) can endanger the hulls and propulsion of riverboats. Riverboats are generally of shallow draft, being broad of beam and rather square in plan, with a low freeboard and high topsides. Riverboats can survive with this type of configuration as they do not have to withstand the high winds or large waves that are seen on large lakes, seas, or oceans.

Fig. The Albatun Dos, a Tuna Boat at Work Near Victoria, Seychelles.

Fishing vessels are a subset of commercial vessels, but generally small in size and often subject to different regulations and classification. They can be categorized by several criteria: architecture, the type of fish they catch, the fishing method used, geographical origin, and technical features such as rigging. As of 2004, the world's fishing fleet consisted of some 4 million vessels. Of these, 1.3 million were decked vessels with enclosed areas and the rest were open vessels. Most decked vessels were mechanized, but two-thirds of the open vessels were traditional craft propelled by sails and oars. More than 60 per cent of all existing large fishing vessels were built in Japan, Peru, the Russian Federation, Spain or the United States of America.

Special purpose vessels

Fig. The Weather Ship MS Polarfront at Sea.

A weather ship was a ship stationed in the ocean as a platform for surface and upper air meteorological observations for use in marine weather forecasting. Surface weather observations were taken hourly, and four radiosonde releases occurred daily. It was also meant to aid in search and rescue operations and to support transatlantic flights. Proposed as early as 1927 by the aviationcommunity, the establishment of weather ships proved to be so useful during World War II that the International Civil Aviation Organization (ICAO) established a global network of weather ships in 1948, with 13 to be supplied by the United States. This number was eventually negotiated down to nine.

The weather ship crews were normally at sea for three weeks at a time, returning to port for 10 day stretches. Weather ship observations proved to be helpful in wind and wave studies, as they did not avoid weather systems like other ships tended to for safety reasons. They were also helpful in monitoring storms at sea, such as tropical cyclones. The removal of a weather ship became a negative factor in forecasts leading up to the Great Storm of 1987. Beginning in the 1970s, their role became largely superseded by weather buoys due to the ships' significant cost. The agreement of the use of weather ships by the international community ended in 1990. The last weather ship was Polarfront, known as weather station M ("Mike"), which was put out of operation on 1 January 2010. Weather observations from ships continue from a fleet of voluntary merchant vessels in routine commercial operation.

Naval Vessels

Naval vessels are those used by a navy for military purposes. There have been many types of naval vessel. Modern naval vessels can be broken down into three categories: surface warships, submarines, and support and auxiliary vessels. Modern warships are generally divided into seven main categories:

aircraft carriers, cruisers, destroyers, frigates, corvettes, submarinesand amphibious assault ships. The distinction between cruisers, destroyers, frigates, and corvettes is not rigourous; the same vessel may be described differently in different navies. Battleships were used during the Second World War and occasionally since then (the last battleships were removed from the U.S. Naval Vessel Register in March 2006), but were made obsolete by the use of carrier-borne aircraft and guided missiles.

Fig. American Aircraft Carrier Harry S. Truman and a Replenishment Ship.

Most military submarines are either attack submarines or ballistic missile submarines. Until the end of World War II the primary role of the diesel/electric submarine was anti-ship warfare, inserting and removing covert agents and military forces, and intelligence-gathering. With the development of the homing torpedo, better sonar systems, and nuclear propulsion, submarines also became able to effectively hunt each other.

The development ofsubmarine-launched nuclear and cruise missiles gave submarines a substantial and long-ranged ability to attack both land and sea targets with a variety of weapons ranging from cluster munitions to nuclear weapons. Most navies also include many types of support and auxiliary vessel, such as minesweepers, patrol boats, offshore patrol vessels, replenishment ships, and hospital ships which are designated medical treatment facilities. Fast combat vessels such as cruisers and destroyers usually have fine hulls to maximize speed and maneuverability. They also usually have advanced marine electronicsand communication systems, as well as weapons.

ARCHITECTURE

Some components exist in vessels of any size and purpose. Every vessel has a hull of sorts. Every vessel has some sort of propulsion, whether it's a pole, an ox, or a nuclear reactor. Most vessels have some sort of steering system. Other characteristics are common, but not as universal, such as compartments, holds, a superstructure, and equipment such as anchors and winches.

Hull

For a ship to float, its weight must be less than that of the water displaced by the ship's hull. There are many types of hulls, from logs lashed together to form a raft to the advanced hulls of America's Cup sailboats. A vessel may have a single hull (called a monohull design), two in the case of catamarans, or three in the case of trimarans.

Vessels with more than three hulls are rare, but some experiments have been conducted with designs such as pentamarans. Multiple hulls are generally parallel to each other and connected by rigid arms.

Fig. A ship's hull endures harsh conditions at sea, as illustrated by thisreefer ship in bad weather.

Hulls have several elements. The bow is the foremost part of the hull. Many ships feature a bulbous bow. The keel is at the very bottom of the hull, extending the entire length of the ship.

The rear part of the hull is known as the stern, and many hulls have a flat back known as a transom. Common hull appendages include propellers for propulsion, rudders for steering, and stabilizers to quell a ship's rolling motion. Other hull features can be related to the vessel's work, such as fishing gear and sonar domes.

Hulls are subject to various hydrostatic and hydrodynamic constraints. The key hydrostatic constraint is that it must be able to support the entire weight of the boat, and maintain stability even with often unevenly distributed weight. Hydrodynamic constraints include the ability to withstand shock waves, weather collisions and groundings.

Older ships and pleasure craft often have or had wooden hulls. Steel is used for most commercial vessels. Aluminium is frequently used for fast vessels, and composite materials are often found in sailboats and pleasure craft. Some ships have been made with concrete hulls.

Propulsion Systems

Fig. A Ship's Engineroom.

Main article: Marine propulsion

Propulsion systems for ships fall into three categories: human propulsion, sailing, and mechanical propulsion. Human propulsion includesrowing, which was used even on large galleys. Propulsion by sail generally consists of a sail hoisted on an erect mast, supported by stays and spars and controlled by ropes. Sail systems were the dominant form of propulsion until the 19th century. They are now generally used for recreation and competition, although experimental sail systems, such as the turbosails, rotorsails, and wingsails have been used on larger modern vessels for fuel savings.

Mechanical propulsion systems generally consist of a motor or engine turning a propeller, or less frequently, an impeller or wave propulsion fins. Steam engines were first used for this purpose, but have mostly been replaced by two-stroke or four-stroke diesel engines, outboard motors, and gas turbine engines on faster ships. Nuclear reactors producing steam are used to propel warships andicebreakers, and there have been attempts to utilize them to power commercial vessels. In addition to traditional fixed and controllable pitch propellers there are many specialized variations, such as contra-rotating and nozzle-style propellers. Most vessels have a single propeller, but some large vessels may have up to four propellers supplemented with transverse thrusters for maneuvring at ports. The propeller is connected to the main engine via a propeller shaft and, in case of medium- and high-speed engines, a reduction gearbox. Some modern vessels have a diesel-electric powertrain in which the propeller is turned by an electric motor powered by the ship's generators.

Steering Systems

For ships with independent propulsion systems for each side, such as manual oars or some paddles, steering systems may not be necessary. In most designs, such as boats propelled by engines or sails, a steering system becomes necessary. The most common is a rudder, a submerged plane located at the rear of the hull. Rudders are rotated to generate a lateral force which turns the boat. Rudders can be rotated by a tiller, manual wheels, or electro-hydraulic systems. Autopilot systems combine mechanical rudders with navigation systems. Ducted propellers are sometimes used for steering.

Fig. The Rudder and Propeller on a Newly Built Ferry.

Some propulsion systems are inherently steering systems. Examples include the outboard motor, the bow thruster, and the Z-drive.

Holds, Compartments, and the Superstructure

Larger boats and ships generally have multiple decks and compartments. Separate berthings and heads are found on sailboats over about 25 feet (7.6 m). Fishing boats and cargo ships typically have one or more cargo holds. Most larger vessels have an engine room, agalley, and various compartments for work. Tanks are used to store fuel, engine oil, and fresh water. Ballast tanks are equipped to change a ship's trim and modify its stability. Superstructures are found above the main deck. On sailboats, these are usually very low. On modern cargo ships, they are almost always located near the ship's stern. On passenger ships and warships, the superstructure generally extends far forward.

Equipment

Shipboard equipment varies from ship to ship depending on such factors as the ship's era, design, area of operation, and purpose.

Some types of equipment that are widely found include:

- Masts can be the home of antennas, navigation lights, radar transponders, fog signals, and similar devices often required by law.
- Ground tackle includes equipment such as mooring winches, windlasses, and anchors. Anchors are used to moor ships in shallow

water. They are connected to the ship by a rope or chain. On larger vessels, the chain runs through a hawsepipe.

- Cargo equipment such as cranes and cargo booms are used to load and unload cargo and ship's stores.
- Safety equipment such as lifeboats, liferafts, and survival suits are carried aboard many vessels for emergency use.

DESIGN CONSIDERATIONS

Hydrostatics

Some vessels, like the LCAC, can operate in a non-displacement mode.

Boats and ships are kept on (or slightly above) the water in three ways:

- For most vessels, known as displacement vessels, the vessel's weight is offset by that of the water displaced by the hull.
- For planing ships and boats, such as the hydrofoil, the lift developed by the movement of the foil through the water increases with the vessel's speed, until the vessel is foilborne.
- For non-displacement craft such as hovercraft and air-cushion vehicles, the vessel is suspended over the water by a cushion of high-pressure air it projects downwards against the surface of the water.

A vessel is in equilibrium when the upwards and downwards forces are of equal magnitude. As a vessel is lowered into the water its weight remains constant but the corresponding weight of water displaced by its hull increases. When the two forces are equal, the boat floats. If weight is evenly distributed throughout the vessel, it floats without trim or heel.

A vessel's stability is considered in both this hydrostatic sense as well as a hydrodynamic sense, when subjected to movement, rolling and pitching, and the action of waves and wind. Stability problems can lead to excessive pitching and rolling, and eventually capsizing and sinking.

Hydrodynamics

Fig. Fishing Boat Dona Delfina.

The advance of a vessel through water is resisted by the water. This resistance can be broken down into several components, the main ones being the friction of the water on the hull and wave making resistance. To reduce resistance and therefore increase the speed for a given power, it is necessary to reduce the wetted surface and use submerged hull shapes that produce low amplitude waves. To do so, high-speed vessels are often more slender, with fewer or smaller appendages. The friction of the water is also reduced by regular maintenance of the hull to remove the sea creatures and algae that accumulate there. Antifouling paint is commonly used to assist in this. Advanced designs such as the bulbous bow assist in decreasing wave resistance.

A simple way of considering wave-making resistance is to look at the hull in relation to its wake. At speeds lower than the wave propagation speed, the wave rapidly dissipates to the sides. As the hull approaches the wave propagation speed, however, the wake at the bow begins to build up faster than it can dissipate, and so it grows in amplitude. Since the water is not able to "get out of the way of the hull fast enough", the hull, in essence, has to climb over or push through the bow wave. This results in an exponential increase in resistance with increasing speed.

This hull speed is found by the formula:

$$\text{knots} \approx 1.34 \times \sqrt{\text{Lft}}$$

or, in metric units:

$$\text{knots} \approx 2.5 \times \sqrt{\text{Lm}}$$

where L is the length of the waterline in feet or meters.

When the vessel exceeds a speed/length ratio of 0.94, it starts to outrun most of its bow wave, and the hull actually settles slightly in the water as it is now only supported by two wave peaks. As the vessel exceeds a speed/length ratio of 1.34, the hull speed, the wavelength is now longer than the hull, and the stern is no longer supported by the wake, causing the stern to squat, and the bow rise. The hull is now starting to climb its own bow wave, and resistance begins to increase at a very high rate. While it is possible to drive a displacement hull faster than a speed/length ratio of 1.34, it is prohibitively expensive to do so. Most large vessels operate at speed/length ratios well below that level, at speed/length ratios of under 1.0.

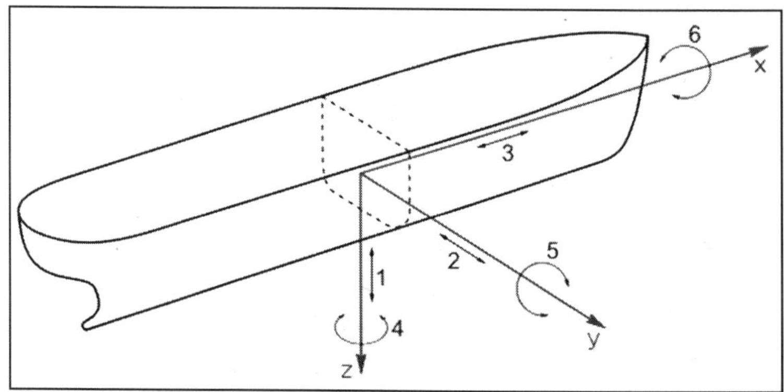

Fig. Vessels Move Along the Three Axes: 1. Heave, 2. Sway, 3. Surge, 4. Yaw, 5. Pitch, 6. Roll.

For large projects with adequate funding, hydrodynamic resistance can be tested experimentally in a hull testing pool or using tools ofcomputational fluid dynamics.

Vessels are also subject to ocean surface waves and sea swell as well as effects of wind and weather. These movements can be stressful for passengers and equipment, and must be controlled if possible. The rolling movement can be controlled, to an extent, by ballasting or by devices such as fin stabilizers. Pitching movement is more difficult to limit and can be dangerous if the bow submerges in the waves, a phenomenon called pounding. Sometimes, ships must change course or speed to stop violent rolling or pitching.

How it has been convincingly shown in scientific studies of the 21st century, controllability of some vessels decreases dramatically in some cases that are conditioned by effects of the bifurcation memory. This class of vessels includes ships with high manoeuvring capabilities, aircraft and controlled underwater vehicles designed to be unstable in steady-state motion that are interesting in terms of applications. These features must be considered in designing ships and in their control in critical situations.

LIFECYCLE

A ship will pass through several stages during its career. The first is usually an initial contract to build the ship, the details of which can vary widely based on relationships between the shipowners, operators, designers and the shipyard.

Then, the design phase carried out by a naval architect. Then the ship is constructed in a shipyard. After construction, the vessel is launched and goes into service. Ships end their careers in a number of ways, ranging from shipwrecks to service as a museum ship to the scrapyard.

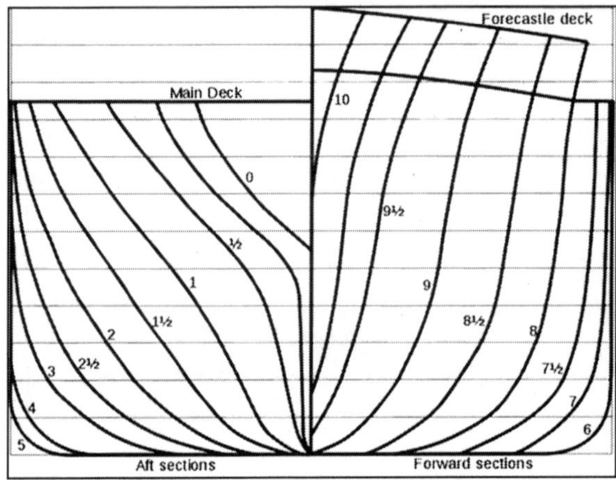

Fig. Lines Plan for the Hull of a Basic Cargo Ship.

Design

A vessel's design starts with a specification, which a naval architect uses to create a project outline, assess required dimensions, and create a basic layout of spaces and a rough displacement. After this initial rough draft, the architect can create an initial hull design, a general profile and an initial overview of the ship's propulsion. At this stage, the designer can iterate on the ship's design, adding detail and refining the design at each stage.

Fig. MS Freedom of the Seasunder Construction in a Shipyard in Turku.

The designer will typically produce an overall plan, a general specification describing the peculiarities of the vessel, and construction blueprints to be used at the building site. Designs for larger or more complex vessels may also include sail plans, electrical schematics, and plumbing and ventilation plans. As environmental laws are becoming more strict, ship designers need to create their design in such a way that the ship, when it nears its end-of-term, can be disassembled ordisposed easily and that waste is reduced to a minimum.

Construction

Ship construction takes place in a shipyard, and can last from a few months for a unit produced in series, to several years to reconstruct a wooden boat like the frigate Hermione, to more than 10 years for an aircraft carrier. During World War II, the need for cargo ships was so urgent that construction time for Liberty Ships went from initially eight months or longer, down to weeks or even days. Builders employed production line and prefabrication techniques such as those used in shipyards today.

Hull materials and vessel size play a large part in determining the method of construction. The hull of a mass-produced fibreglass sailboat is constructed from a mold, while the steel hull of a cargo ship is made from large sections welded together as they are built.

Fig. A Ship Launching at the Northern Shipyard in Gdansk, Poland.

Fig. A Shipyard at Kerala, Southern India.

Generally, construction starts with the hull, and on vessels over about 30 meters (98 ft), by the laying of the keel. This is done in a drydock or on land.

Once the hull is assembled and painted, it is launched. The last stages, such as raising the superstructure and adding equipment and accommodation, can be done after the vessel is afloat.

Once completed, the vessel is delivered to the customer. Ship launching is often a ceremony of some significance, and is usually when the vessel is formally named. A typical small rowboat can cost under US$100, $1,000 for a small speedboat, tens of thousands of dollars for a cruising sailboat, and about $2,000,000 for a Vendée Globe class sailboat. A 25 meters (82 ft) trawler may cost $2.5 million, and a 1,000-person-capacity high-speed passenger ferry can cost in the neighbourhood of $50 million. A ship's cost partly depends on its complexity: a small, general cargo ship will cost $20 million, a Panamax-sized bulk carrier around $35 million, a supertanker around $105 million and a large LNG carrier nearly $200 million. The most expensive ships generally are so because of the cost of embedded electronics: a Seawolf-class submarine costs around $2 billion, and an aircraft carrier goes for about $3.5 billion.

Repair and Conversion

An able seaman uses a needlegun scaler while refurbishing a mooring winch at sea Ships undergo nearly constant maintenance during their career, whether they be underway, pierside, or in some cases, in periods of reduced operating status between charters or shipping seasons.

Most ships, however, require trips to special facilities such as a drydock at regular intervals. Tasks often done at drydock include removing biological growths on the hull, sandblasting and repainting the hull, and replacing sacrificial anodes used to protect submerged equipment from corrosion. Major repairs to the propulsion and steering systems as well as major electrical systems are also often performed at dry dock. Vessels that sustain major damage at sea may be repaired at a facility equipped for major repairs, such as a shipyard. Ships may also be converted for a new purpose: oil tankers are often converted into floating production storage and offloading units.

Fig. A Ship Graveyard in France.

End of Service

Most ocean-going cargo ships have a life expectancy of between 20 and 30 years. A sailboat made of plywood or fibreglass can last between 30 and 40 years. Solid wooden ships can last much longer but require regular maintenance. Carefully maintained steel-hulled yachts can have a lifespan of over 100 years. As ships age, forces such as corrosion, osmosis, and rotting compromise hull strength, and a vessel becomes too dangerous to sail. At this point, it can be scuttled at sea or scrapped by shipbreakers. Ships can also be used as museum ships, or expended to construct breakwaters orartificial reefs. Many ships do not make it to the scrapyard, and are lost in fires, collisions, grounding, or sinking at sea. The Allies lost some 5,150 ships during World War II.

Measuring Ships

One can measure ships in terms of overall length, length of the ship at the waterline, beam (breadth), depth (distance between the crown of the weather deck and the top of the keelson), draft (distance between the highest waterline and the bottom of the ship) and tonnage. A number of different tonnage definitions exist and are used when describing merchant ships for the purpose of tolls, taxation, etc.

In Britain until Samuel Plimsoll's Merchant Shipping Act of 1876, ship-owners could load their vessels until their decks were almost awash, resulting in a dangerously unstable condition. Anyone who signed on to such a ship for a voyage and, upon realizing the danger, chose to leave the ship, could end up in jail. Plimsoll, a Member of Parliament, realised the problem and engaged some engineers to derive a fairly simple formula to determine the position of a line on the side of any specific ship's hull which, when it reached the surface of the water during loading of cargo, meant the ship had reached its maximum safe loading level. To this day, that mark, called the "Plimsoll Line", exists on ships' sides, and consists of a circle with a horizontal line through the centre. On the Great Lakes of North America the circle is replaced with a diamond. Because different types of water (summer, fresh, tropical fresh, winter north Atlantic) have different densities, subsequent regulations required painting a group of lines forward of the Plimsoll mark to indicate the safe depth (or freeboard above the surface) to which a specific ship could load in water of various densities. Hence the "ladder" of lines seen forward of the Plimsoll mark to this day. This is called the "freeboard mark" or "load line mark" in the marine industry.

Ship Pollution

Ship pollution is the pollution of air and water by shipping. It is a problem that has been accelerating as trade has become increasingly globalized, posing an increasing threat to the world's oceans and waterways as globalization continues. It is expected that, "...shipping traffic to and from the USA is projected to double by 2020." Because of increased traffic in ocean ports, pollution from ships also directly affects coastal areas. The pollution produced affects biodiversity, climate, food, and human health. However, the degree to which humans are polluting and how it affects the world is highly debated and has been a hot international topic for the past 30 years.

Oil Spills

The Exxon Valdez spilled10,800,000 US gallons (8,993,000 imp gal; 40,880,000 L) of oil into Alaska's Prince William Sound. Oil spills have devastating effects on the environment. Crude oil contains polycyclic aromatic hydrocarbons (PAHs) which are very difficult to clean up, and last for years in the sediment and marine environment. Marine species constantly exposed to PAHs can exhibit developmental problems, susceptibility to disease, and abnormal reproductive cycles.

By the sheer amount of oil carried, modern oil tankers must be considered something of a threat to the environment. An oil tanker can carry 2 million barrels (318,000 m3) of crude oil, or 84,000,000 US gallons (69,940,000 imp gal; 318,000,000 L). This is more than six times the amount spilled in the widely known Exxon Valdez incident. In this spill, the ship ran aground and dumped 10,800,000 US gallons (8,993,000 imp gal; 40,880,000 L) of oil into the ocean in March 1989. Despite efforts of scientists, managers, and volunteers, over 400,000 seabirds, about 1,000 sea otters, and immense numbers of fish were killed. The International Tanker Owners Pollution Federation has researched 9,351 accidental spills since 1974. According to this study, most spills result from routine operations such as loading cargo, discharging cargo, and taking on fuel oil. 91 per cent of the operational oil spills were small, resulting in less than 7 tons per spill. Spills resulting from accidents like collisions, groundings, hull failures, and explosions are much larger, with 84 per cent of these involving losses of over 700 tons. Following the Exxon Valdez spill, the United States passed the Oil Pollution Act of 1990 (OPA-90), which included a stipulation that all tankers entering its waters be double-hulled by 2015. Following the sinkings of the Erika (1999) and Prestige (2002), the European Union passed its own stringent anti-pollution packages (known as Erika I, II, and III), which require all tankers entering its waters to be double-hulled by 2010. The Erika packages are controversial because they introduced the new legal concept of "serious negligence".

Ballast Water

When a large vessel such as a container ship or an oil tanker unloads cargo, seawater is pumped into other compartments in the hull to help stabilize and balance the ship. During loading, this ballast water is pumped out from these compartments.

One of the problems with ballast water transfer is the transport of harmful organisms. Meinesz believes that one of the worst cases of a single invasive species causing harm to an ecosystem can be attributed to a seemingly harmless jellyfish. Mnemiopsis leidyi, a species of comb jellyfish that inhabits estuaries from the United States to the Valdés peninsula in Argentina along the Atlantic coast, has caused notable damage in theBlack Sea. It was first introduced in 1982, and thought to have been transported to the Black Sea in a ship's ballast water. The population of the jellyfish shot up exponentially and, by 1988, it was wreaking havoc upon the local fishing industry.

Fig. A cargo ship pumps ballast water over the side.

"The anchovy catch fell from 204,000 tonnes(225,000 short tons; 201,000 long tons) in 1984 to 200 tonnes (220 short tons; 197 long tons) in 1993; sprat from 24,600 tonnes (27,100 short tons; 24,200 long tons) in 1984 to 12,000 tonnes (13,200 short tons; 11,800 long tons) in 1993; horse mackerel from 4,000 tonnes (4,410 short tons; 3,940 long tons) in 1984 to zero in 1993." Now that the jellyfish have exhausted the zooplankton, including fish larvae, their numbers have fallen dramatically, yet they continue to maintain a stranglehold on the ecosystem. Recently the jellyfish have been discovered in theCaspian Sea. Invasive species can take over once occupied areas, facilitate the spread of new diseases, introduce new genetic material, alter landscapes and jeopardize the ability of native species to obtain food. "On land and in the sea, invasive species are responsible for about 137 billion dollars in lost revenue and management costs in the U.S. each year." Ballast and bilge discharge from ships can also spread human pathogens and other harmful diseases and toxins potentially causing health issues for humans and marine life alike. Discharges into coastal waters, along with other sources of marine pollution, have the potential to be toxic to marine plants, animals, and microorganisms, causing alterations such as changes in growth, disruption of hormone cycles, birth defects, suppression of the immune system, and disorders resulting in cancer, tumors, and genetic abnormalities or even death.

Exhaust Emissions

Exhaust emissions from ships are considered to be a significant source of air pollution. "Seagoing vessels are responsible for an estimated 14 percent of emissions of nitrogen from fossil fuels and 16 percent of the emissions of sulfur from petroleum uses into the atmosphere." In Europe ships make up a large percentage of the sulfur introduced to the air, "...as much sulfur as all the cars, lorries and factories in Europe put together." "By 2010, up to 40 per cent of air pollution over land could come from ships." Sulfur in the air creates acid rain which damages crops and buildings. When inhaled sulfur is known to cause respiratory problems and increase the risk of a heart attack.

Fig. Exhaust Stack on a Container Ship.

Ship Breaking

Ship breaking or ship demolition is a type of ship disposal involving the breaking up of ships for scrap recycling, with the hulls being discarded in ship graveyards. Most ships have a lifespan of a few decades before there is so much wear that refitting and repair becomes uneconomical. Ship breaking allows materials from the ship, especially steel, to be reused.

Fig. Ship Breaking Near Chittagong, Bangladesh.

In addition to steel and other useful materials, however, ships (particularly older vessels) can contain many substances that are banned or considered dangerous in developed countries. Asbestos and polychlorinated biphenyls (PCBs) are typical examples. Asbestos was used heavily in ship construction until it was finally banned in most of the developed world in the mid 1980s. Currently, the costs associated with removing asbestos, along with the potentially expensive insurance and health risks, have meant that ship-breaking in most developed countries is no longer economically viable. Removing the metal for scrap can potentially cost more than the scrap value of the metal itself. In most of the developing world, however, shipyards can operate without the risk of personal injury lawsuits or workers' health claims, meaning many of these shipyards may operate with high health risks. Furthermore, workers are paid very low rates with no overtime or other allowances. Protective equipment is sometimes absent or inadequate. Dangerous vapors and fumes from burning materials can be inhaled, and dusty asbestos-laden areas around such breakdown locations are commonplace.

Aside from the health of the yard workers, in recent years, ship breaking has also become an issue of major environmental concern. Many developing nations, in which ship breaking yards are located, have lax or no environmental law, enabling large quantities of highly toxic materials to escape into the environment and causing serious health problems among ship breakers, the local population and wildlife. Environmental campaign groups such as Greenpeace have made the issue a high priority for their campaigns.

BUOYANCY

A floating boat displaces its weight in water. The material of the boat hull may be denser than water, but if this is the case then it forms only the outer layer. If the boat floats, the mass of the boat (plus contents) as a whole divided by the volume below the waterline is equal to the density of water (1 kg/l). If weight is added to the boat, the volume below the waterline will increase to keep the weight balance equal, and so the boat sinks a little to compensate.

SHIPPING

Shipping, initially derived from the word relationship, is the desire by fans for two or more people, either real-life celebrities or fictional characters, to be in a relationship, romantic or otherwise. It is considered a general term for fans' emotional involvement with the ongoing development of a relationship in a work of fiction. Shipping often takes the form of creative works, including fanfiction and fan art, most often published on the internet. Shipping can involve virtually any kind of relationship: from the well-known and established, to the ambiguous or those undergoing development, and even to the highly improbable or blatantly impossible. Though "shipping" usually refers to romantic relationships, it can also refer to simple friendships; this subset is sometimes known as "friendshipping", or a "BrOTP" (a portmanteau of the terms bromance and one true pairing). Shipping in fan fiction between a same-sex couple is also known as slash fiction, an older term and concept that dates to the late 1970s. In anime/manga communities, shipping is more commonly referred to as pairing(s); in Filipino pop culture, it is frequently called loveteam(s). In East Asian contexts, the practice is also referred to as coupling or CP.

ETYMOLOGY

The activity of fans creating relationships for fictional characters far predates the term. Though the word "ship" is a truncation of "relationship", where and when it was first used to indicate involvement with fictional relationships is unclear. The first "ship" that became widely popular and accepted was the characters Kirk and Spock from the television show Star Trek. This began in the mid-1970s, and was often referred to as Kirk/Spock, and later "K/S". This is why relationships between two men are now often referred to as "slash".

The actual term "shipping" was originated in the mid-1990s by internet fans of the TV show The X-Files, who believed the two main characters, Fox Mulder and Dana Scully, should be or were engaged in a romantic relationship. They called themselves "relationshippers," at first; then R'shipper, 'shipper, and finally just shipper. The oldest uses of the nouns ship and shipper, as recorded by the Oxford English Dictionary, date back to 1996 postings on the Usenet group alt.tv.x-files; shipping is first attested slightly later, in 1997. Its earliest attestation of the verb to ship, on the other hand, comes from 2005, from the printed version of the Urban Dictionary.

NOTATION AND TERMINOLOGY

"Ship" and its derivatives in this context have since come to be in wide and versatile use. "Shipping" refers to the phenomenon; a "ship" is the concept of a fictional couple; to "ship" a couple means to have an affinity for it in one way or another; a "shipper" is somebody significantly involved with such an affinity, and so forth. There are a wide number of terms used among fans who practice shipping. In addition to popular terms used among shippers in general, there are other terms that only specific fandoms use, such as giving special names to the ships in question. For example, a "Sailed Ship" is a pairing that has been established as canonically true. Another common term is an "OTP", an abbreviation of "One True Pairing". To deem a ship OTP, one is declaring their deep emotional investment in it. On occasion, though, a person may not be able to decide on an OTP in a single fandom. This is when the uncommon term "TTP" is used. It simply stands for Two True Pairings.

Various naming conventions have developed in different online communities to refer to prospective couples, likely due to the ambiguity and cumbersomeness of the "Character 1 and Character 2" format. The most widespread appears to be putting the slash character (/) between the two names ("Character1/Character2"). Other methods of identifying relationships between characters often create hybrid terms such as portmanteaus and clipped compounds to abbreviate character pairings. For example, Drarry forms a clipped compound, abbreviated from the complete names Draco and Harry. Another form of hybrid naming is to place an exclamation point (!) between the two names being compounded (*i.e.*: Draco!Harry). These combinations often follow systematic phonological principles.

Many fandom-specific variants exist and often use fandom-specific terminology. These often employ words that describe the relationship between characters in the context of the fictional universe and simply add the word "Shipping" to the end. For example, MartyrShipping refers to the relationship between Ivypool and Hollyleaf from the Warriorsseries, because both suffered a great deal for their beliefs. Other terminology is more vague, consisting of codes for the character names. For example, according to Japanese wordplay, Takeshi Yamamoto can be represented by the number 80 and Hayato Gokudera by the number 59, thus the Reborn! pairing is referred to as "8059".

SLASH AND NON-CONVENTIONAL RELATIONSHIPS

Within shipping, homosexual pairings are popular; they are known as "slash and femslash", or by borrowed Japanese terms, yaoi for male homosexuality and yuri for female homosexuality. A person who supports homosexual pairings and reads or writes slash fiction may be referred to as a "slasher". The term "slash" predates the use of "shipping" by at least some 20 years. It was originally coined as a term to describe a pairing of Kirk and Spock of Star Trek, Kirk/Spock (or "K/S"; sometimes spoken "Kirk-slash-Spock", whence "Slash") homosexual fan fiction. For a time in the late 1970s and early 1980s, "K/S" was used to describe such fan fiction, regardless of whether or not they were related to Star Trek, and eventually "slash" became a universal term to describe all homosexual themed fan works.

Parallel to this development, the term "Slash" was also being used in some fandoms to denote fan fiction or other fan works depicting sexual acts with an implied rating of NC-17, whether homosexual or heterosexual. It is likely that this is the same "Slash" term born of the Star Trek fandom, but adapted to the pornographic focus that commonly dominates fanfiction and fan works in the Kirk/Spock ship, as well as the ships of other homosexual couples, (Harry/Louis, Dan/Phil, Derek/Stiles, Dean/Castiel, John/Sherlock, Merlin/Arthur, Erik/Charles, RinHaru, MakoHaru, Draco/Harry, Hannibal/Will, Frank/Gerard, Ray/Mikey, Ash/Gary) allowing the use of the term to spread to heterosexual ships. However, pornographic content is now referred to as "smut", or, in anime, "lemon". "Slash" now refers only to male/male pairings, while "femmeslash" or "femslash" is for female/female pairings. Shipping may defy social standards and taboos. Some online groups support ships which constitute incest or bestiality. Characters of any age, even adults and children, may be paired together in romantic fan fiction. Such pairings are often controversial, however. Another example of non-conventional shipping is in the Homestuck fandom, which introduced three new shipping categories: "Kismesissitude" or "hatelove" (a deep-rooted rivalry), "Moirallegiance" (a deep, very powerful platonic friendship), and "Auspisticism" (a three-person relationship created between two would-be rivals and a peer mediator). Those in the Homestuck fandom refer to the usual romantic relationship as "matespritship".

CASE STUDIES

Daria Fandom

Daria fandom was marked through its entire run by shipper debate. From the series' first season, the main conflict was over whether the title character, Daria Morgendorffer, should have a relationship with Trent Lane, a slacker rock-band frontman, whom Daria met through his sister, Jane. A common argument against this possible outcome was that such a development would signal a turn away from the more subversive aspects of Daria's character, and thus the show. The show's writers responded by having Daria develop a crush on Trent. Trent, however, remained involved with his off-and-on girlfriend Monique, who immediately became a target of shipper ire. The crush ended in the third season's finale, "Jane's Addition", when Daria realized that Trent could never satisfy her in the long run.

That same episode introduced Tom Sloane, a charming and intellectual son of privilege. Although Tom became Jane's boyfriend, threatening Daria and Jane's friendship in the process, Daria and Tom warmed up to each other throughout the fourth season, leading up to its finale, "Dye! Dye! My Darling," broadcast August 2, 2000. With Jane and Tom's relationship in crisis, a heated argument between Daria and Tom led up to a kiss in Tom's car. In the TV movie Is it Fall Yet?, Daria decided to begin a relationship with Tom, and Daria and Jane patched up their friendship.

This caused an instant uproar, and conversation now turned to whether Tom was more appropriate than Trent had been. The debate was satirized by the show's writers in a piece on MTV's web site. In interviews done after the series' run, series co-creator Glenn Eichler revealed that "any viewer who really thought that Daria and Trent could (have) a relationship was just not watching the show we were making," Tom came about because "going into our fourth year... I thought it was really pushing credibility for Daria to have only had one or two dates during her whole high school career," and "teaser" episodes like "Pierce Me" were "intended to provide some fun for that portion of the audience that was so invested in the romance angle. The fact that those moments were few and far between should have given some indication that the series was not about Daria's love life."

Harry Potter Fandom

The Harry Potter series' most contentious ship debates came from supporters of the prospective relationship between Harry Potter and his close female friend Hermione Granger, and supporters of Hermione ending up instead with Ron Weasley, close friend of both. Author J.K. Rowling appeared to try to tamp down the possibility, stating at one point that Harry and Hermione "are very platonic friends".

Another alternative was of Harry ending up with Ginny Weasley, Ron's younger sister, whose obvious crush on him served as a comical plot-line starting in Harry Potter and the Chamber of Secrets. In Harry Potter and the Order of the Phoenix, Hermione informs Harry that Ginny has "given up" on him. In the subsequent Harry Potter and the Half-Blood Prince, however, Harry develops a crush on Ginny, convinced that he has missed his opportunity with her. In the end Ginny turns out to never have given up on Harry after all, but merely taken Hermione's advice to try to date other boys to boost her self-confidence. Though their romantic relationship becomes one of the few sources of comfort in Harry's difficult life, he makes a decision to end it for fear that Voldemort would learn of it and target Ginny. Rowling later commented that she had planned Ginny as Harry's "ideal girl" from the very beginning.

An interview with J.K. Rowling conducted by fansite webmasters Emerson Spartz (MuggleNet) and Melissa Anelli (The Leaky Cauldron) shortly after the release of Half-Blood Prince caused significant controversy within the fandom. In the interview, Spartz stated that Harry/Hermione fans were delusional, to which Rowling responded that they were "still valued members of her readership", but that there had been "anvil-sized hints" for future Ron/Hermione and Harry/Ginny relationships, and that Harry/Hermione shippers needed to re-read the books. This incident resulted in an uproar among Harry/Hermione shippers, some of whom announced that they would return their copies of Harry Potter and the Half-Blood Prince and boycott future Harry Potter books, leveling criticism at Spartz, Anelli, and Rowling herself. Many of them complained that both sites had a Ron/Hermione bias and criticized Rowling for not including a representative of their community. The uproar was the subject of an article in the San Francisco Chronicle.

Rowling's attitude towards the shipping phenomenon has varied between amused and bewildered to frustrated. In that same interview, she stated:

" Well, you see, I'm a relative newcomer to the world of shipping, because for a long time, I didn't go on the net and look up Harry Potter. A long time. Occasionally I had to, because there were weird news stories or something that I would have to go and check, because I was supposed to have said something I hadn't said. I had never gone and looked at fan sites, and then one day I did and oh – my – god. Five hours later or something, I get up from the computer shaking slightly [all laugh]. 'What is going on?' And it was during that first mammoth session that I met the shippers, and it was a most extraordinary thing. I had no idea there was this huge underworld seething beneath me. ”

The release of Harry Potter and the Deathly Hallows in July 2007 saw an epilogue, nineteen years after the events at the focus of the series, where Harry and Ginny are married and have three kids, Lily Luna, James Sirius, and Albus Severus, and Ron and Hermione are also married and have two, Rose and Hugo. This has been received negatively by some fans, especially those who ship non-canon pairings. A result has been the "EWE" tag added to the summaries of fan-fiction, meaning "Epilogue, What Epilogue?"

Harry/Hermione shippers were somewhat vindicated in an interview with Rowling in February 2014 in Wonderland Magazine in which she stated that she thought that realistically "in some ways Harry and Hermione are a better fit [in comparison to Ron and Hermione]" and that Hermione and Ron had "too much fundamental incompatibility." She stated that Hermione and Ron were written together "as a form of wish fulfillment" as way to reconcile a relationship she herself was once in. She went on to say that perhaps with marriage counseling Ron and Hermione would have been all right. She also went on to say in a talk at Exeter University that Harry's love for Ginny is true, thereby denying anything between Harry and Hermione. In spite of that, the ship debates still continue.

Xena: Warrior Princess Fandom

The 1995-2001 action/fantasy TV series Xena: Warrior Princess often saw "shipping wars" that turned especially intense due to spillover from real-life debates abouthomosexuality and gay rights. Shortly after the series' debut, fans started discussing the possibility of a relationship between Xena and her sidekick and best friend Gabrielle. Towards the end of the first season, the show's producers began to play to this perception by deliberately inserting usually humorous lesbian innuendo into some episodes. The show acquired a cult following in the lesbian community. However, Xena had a number of male love interests as well, and from the first season she had an adversarial but sexually charged dynamic with Ares, the God of War, who frequently tried to win her over as his "Warrior Queen." Gabrielle herself had once had a male husband, and his death deeply affected her.

According to journalist Cathy Young, the quarrel between online fans of the show about whether there should be a relationship between Xena and Gabrielle had a sociopolitical angle, in which some on the anti-relationship side were "undoubtedly driven by bona fide bigotry", while some on the pro-relationship side were lesbians who "approached the argument as a real-life gay rights struggle" in which "denying a sexual relationship between Xena and Gabrielle was tantamount to denying the reality of their own lives". She added:

" In a way, knowing that the staff paid attention to fan opinions may have made matters worse: There was an incentive for the rival groups to out-shout one another to make themselves heard. Many fans who had no appetite for these wars fled the online fandom. Storylines that were seen as betraying the subtext, particularly the Xena-Ares relationship in the fifth season, were met with intense hostility from a small but vocal group; at other times, non-subtext fans grumbled about what they saw as pandering to the pro-subtext fan base (such as several sixth-season episodes emphasizing Xena and Gabrielle's transcendent bond as soul mates)."

In 2000, during the airing of the fifth season, the intensity and sometimes nastiness of the "shipping wars" in the Xena fandom was chronicled (from a non-subtexter's point of view) by Australian artist Nancy Lorenz in an article titled "The Discrimination in the Xenaverse" in the online Xena fan magazine Whoosh!, and also in numerous letters in response.

The wars did not abate after the series came to an end in 2001. With no new material from the show itself, the debates were further fueled by various statements from the cast and crew. In January 2003, Lucy Lawless, the show's star, told Lesbian News magazine that after watching the series finale (in which Gabrielle revived Xena with a mouth-to-mouth water transfer filmed to look like a full kiss) she had come to believe that Xena and Gabrielle's relationship was "definitely gay." However, in the interviews and commentaries on the DVD sets released in 2003–2005, the actors, writers and producers continued to stress the ambiguity of the relationship, and in several interviews both Lawless and Renee O'Connor, who played Gabrielle, spoke of Ares as a principal love interest for Xena. In the interview for the Season 6 episode "Coming Home", O'Connor commented, "If there was ever going to be one man in Xena's life, it would be Ares." In March 2005, one-time Xena screenwriter Katherine Fugate, an outspoken supporter of the Xena/Gabrielle pairing, posted a statement on her web site appealing for tolerance in the fandom: " The show existed as it did, when it did. And it enabled many to be empowered on many levels, for many walks of life. So if one definition doesn't work for you, then discard it. If it does, hold it gently. But please, allow everyone the grace to take what they need from the show and make it theirs. Let them have what moved them – be it that Xena was in love with Gabrielle or Xena was in love with Ares. Please stop the arguing and name-calling and need to be right, because in the end, the show worked, it healed, it changed lives, it created new friendships, new loves and new thought, and it was bloody fantastic. And that's what matters. That it simply lived.

SEA LANE

A sea lane, sea road or shipping lane is a regularly used route for vessels on oceans and large lakes. In the Age of Sail they were not only determined by the distribution of land masses but also the prevailing winds, whose discovery was crucial for the success of long voyages. Sea lanes are very important for trade by sea.

HISTORY

The establishment of the North Atlantic sea lanes was inspired by the sinking of the US mail steamer SS Arctic by collision with the French steamer SS Vesta in October 1854 which resulted in the loss of over 300 lives. Lieutenant M. F. Maury of the US Navy first published a section titled "Steam Lanes Across the Atlantic" in his 1855 Sailing Directions proposing sea lanes along the 42 degreelatitude. A number of international conferences and committees were held in 1866, 1872, 1887, 1889, and 1891 all of which left the designation of sea lanes to the principal trans-Atlantic steamship companies at the time; Cunard, White Star, Inman, National Line, andGuion Lines. In 1913-1914 the International Convention for Safety of Life at Sea held in London again reaffirmed that the selection of routes across the Atlantic in both directions is left to the responsibility of the steamship companies.

Shipping lanes came to be by analysing the prevailing winds. The trade winds allowed ships to sail towards the west quickly, and that the westerlies allowed ships to travel to the east quickly. As such, the sea lanes are mostly chosen to take full advantage of these winds. Currents are also similarly followed as well, which also gives an advantage to the vessel.

Some routes, such as that from Cape Town to Rio de Janeiro (passing Tristan da Cunha), weren't able to take advantage of these natural factors. Main sea lanes may also attract pirates. Pax Britannica was the period from 1815–1914 during which the British Royal Navycontrolled most of the key maritime trade routes, and also suppressed piracy and the slave trade. During World War I, as German U-boats began hitting American and British shipping, the Allied trade vessels began to move out of the usual sea lanes to be escorted by naval ships.

ADVANTAGES

Although most ships no longer use sails (having switched them for engines), the wind still creates waves, and this can cause heeling. As such following the overall direction of the trade winds and westerlies is still very useful. However, any vessel that is not engaged in trading, or is smaller than a certain length, is best to avoid the lanes. This is not only because the slight chance of a collision with a large ship can easily cause a smaller ship to sink, but also because large vessels are much less maneuverable than smaller ships, and need much more depth. Smaller ships can thus easily take courses that are nearer to the shore. Unlike with road traffic, there is no exact "road" a ship must follow, so this can easily be done.

Fig. Behind the Cardinal Mark is a Sea Lane Opened on an Ice-Covered Sea.

Shipping lanes are the busiest parts of the sea, thus being a useful place for stranded boaters whose boats are sinking or people on a liferaft to boat to, and be rescued by a passing ship.

THREATS FROM SHIPPING LANES

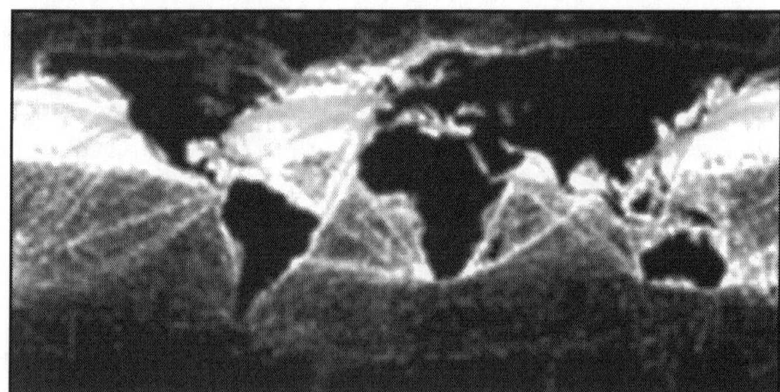

Fig. Left: This Map of Shipping Routes Illustrates the Present-Day Density of Commercial Shipping in the World's Oceans. Right: 16th Century and Also Current Day Trade Routes Prey to Pirating and Privateering.

Although the shipping lanes are useful, they do pose threats to some people:

- Divers should stay clear of shipping lanes when performing dives.
- Small boats also do best to avoid the lanes, in risk of conflicts with bigger ships.
- As the shipping lanes are very large, sections of the lane exist which can be shallow or have some kind of obstruction (*e.g.* sand bank). This threat is greatest when passing some narrows, such as between

islands in the Indian ocean (*e.g.* in Indonesia) as well as between islands in the Pacific (*e.g.* near the Marquesas islands, Tahiti)

- Some shipping lanes, such as the Straits of Malacca off Indonesia and Malaysia, along the waters offSomalia are frequented by pirates both in ancient times and modern times. Either operating independently or as privateers (for companies and countries). Passing ships run the risk of being attacked and held for ransom.

2

Global Shipping Industry

SHIPPING AND WORLD TRADE

Over 90 per cent of world trade is carried by the international shipping industry. Without shipping the import and export of goods on the scale necessary for the modern world would not be possible. Seaborne trade continues to expand, bringing benefits for consumers across the world through low and decreasing freight costs. Thanks to the growing efficiency of shipping as a mode of transport and increased economic liberalisation, the prospects for the industry's further growth continue to be strong. There are around 50,000 merchant ships trading internationally, transporting every kind of cargo. The world fleet is registered in over 150 nations, and manned by over a million seafarers of virtually every nationality.

VALUE OF VOLUME OF WORLD TRADE BY SEA

It is difficult to quantify the value of volume of world seaborne trade in monetary terms, as figures for trade estimates are traditionally in terms of tonnes or tonne-miles, and are therefore not comparable with monetary-based statistics for the value of the world economy. However, United Nations Conference on Trade and Development (UNCTAD) estimates that the operation of merchant ships contributes about US$380 billion in freight rates within the global economy, equivalent to about 5 per cent of total world trade. Shipping trade estimates are usually calculated in tonne-miles - a measurement of tonnes carried, multiplied by the distance travelled. In 2003, for example, the industry shipped around 6.1 thousand million tonnes over a distance of about 4 million miles, giving over 25 thousand billion tonne-miles of total trade.

Throughout the last century the shipping industry has seen a general trend of increases in total trade volume. Increasing industrialisation and the liberalisation of national economies have fuelled free trade and a growing demand for consumer products. Advances in technology have also made shipping an increasingly efficient and swift method of transportation. Over the last four decades total seaborne trade estimates have nearly quadrupled, from less than

6 thousand billion tonne-miles in 1965 to 25 thousand billion tonne-miles in 2003.

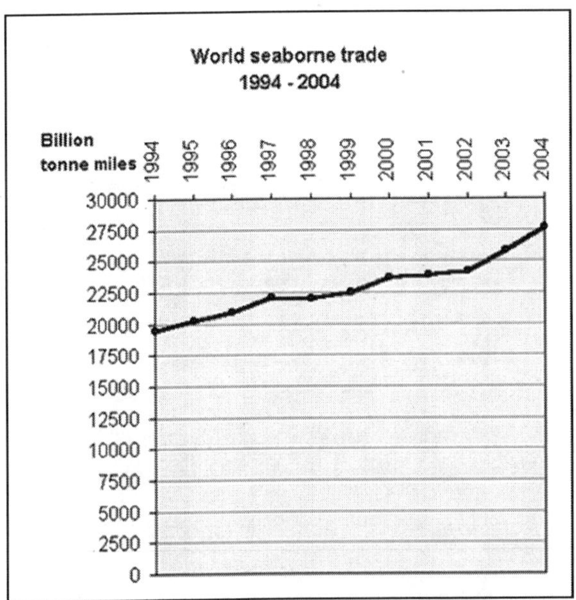

Fig. NB: Figure for 2004 is Estimated.

As with all industrial sectors, however, shipping is occasionally susceptible to economic downturns - a notable fall in trade occurred during the worldwide economic recession of the early 1980s. However although the growth in seaborne trade was tempered by the Asian financial crisis of the late 1990s there has generally been healthy growth in maritime trade since 1993.

THE LOW COST OF TRANSPORTING GOODS BY SEA

Between 1980 and 1999, the value of world trade grew at 12 per cent per year, whilst total freight costs during this period increased by only 7 per cent, demonstrating the falling unit costs of marine transportation. This transport cost element in the shelf price of consumer goods varies from product to product, but is ultimately marginal, for example, transport costs account for only 2 per cent of a television shelf price and only 1.2 per cent of a kilo of coffee.

THE LOW COST OF TRANSPORTING GOODS BY SEA

Between 1980 and 1999, the value of world trade grew at 12 per cent per year, whilst total freight costs during this period increased by only 7 per cent, demonstrating the falling unit costs of marine transportation. This transport cost element in the shelf price of consumer goods varies from product to product, but is ultimately marginal, for example, transport costs account for only 2 per cent of a television shelf price and only 1.2 per cent of a kilo of coffee.

The low costs of maritime transport

Due to continuous improvements in technology and efficiency maritime transport costs are very competitive.

- The typical cost to a consumer in the United States of transporting crude oil from the Middle East, in terms of the purchase price of gasoline at the pump, is about half a US cent per litre.
- The typical cost of transporting a tonne of iron ore from Australia to Europe by sea is about US $12.
- The typical cost of transporting a 20 foot container from Asia to Europe carrying over 20 tonnes of cargo is about the same as the economy airfare for a single passenger on the same journey.

Typical Ocean Freight Costs (Asia-US or Asia-Europe)

	Unit	Typical Shelf Price	Shipping Costs
TV Set	1 unit	$700.00	$10.00
DVD/CD Player	1 unit	$200.00	$1.50
Vacuum Cleaner	1 unit	$150.00	$1.00
Scotch Whisky	Bottle	$50.00	$0.15
Coffee	1 kg	$15.00	$0.15
Biscuits	Tin	$3.00	$0.05
Beer	Can	$1.00	$0.01

2. Shipping is the safest and most environmentally benign form of commercial transport. Perhaps uniquely amongst industries involving physical risk, commitment to safety has long pervaded virtually all deep sea shipping operations. Shipping was amongst the very first industries to adopt widely implemented international safety standards.

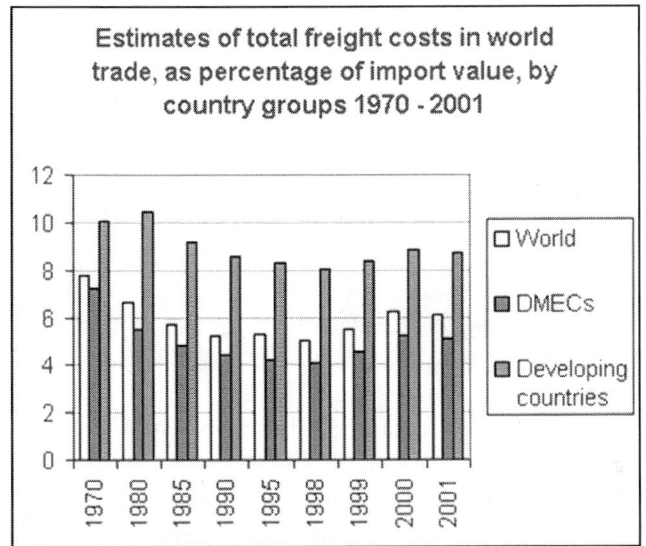

SAFETY AND REGULATION

HOW SHIPPING IS REGULATED INTERNATIONALLY

Merchant shipping is one of the most heavily regulated industries and was amongst the first to adopt widely implemented international safety standards. Regulations concerning shipping are developed at the global level. Because shipping is inherently international, it is vital that shipping is subject to uniform regulations on matters such as construction standards, navigational rules and standards of crew competence.

The alternative would be a plethora of conflicting national regulations resulting in commercial distortion and administrative confusion which would compromise the efficiency of world trade.

The shipping industry is principally regulated by the International Maritime Organization (IMO), which is the London based United Nations agency responsible for the safety of life at sea and the protection of the marine environment.

The International Labour Organisation (ILO) is also responsible for the development of labour standards applicable to seafarers worldwide. IMO has adopted a comprehensive framework of detailed technical regulations, in the form of international diplomatic conventions which govern the safety of ships and protection of the marine environment. National governments, which form the membership of IMO, are required to implement and enforce these international rules, and ensure that the ships which are registered under their national flags comply.

The level of ratification and enforcement of IMO Conventions is generally very high in comparison with international rules adopted for shore based industries. The principal responsibility for enforcing IMO regulations concerning ship safety and environmental protection rests with the flag states (*i.e.* the countries in which merchant ships are registered - which may be different to the country in which they are owned).

Flag states enforce IMO requirements through inspections of ships conducted by a network of international surveyors. Much of this work is delegated to bodies called classification societies. However, flag state enforcement is supplemented by what is known as Port State Control, whereby officials in any country which a ship may visit can inspect foreign flag ships to ensure that they comply with international requirements. Port State Control officers have the power to detain foreign ships in port if they do not conform to international requirements.

As a consequence, most IMO regulations are enforced on a more or less global basis. Shipping is the safest and most environmentally benign form of commercial transport.

Perhaps uniquely amongst industries involving physical risk, commitment to safety has long pervaded virtually all deep sea shipping operations. Shipping was amongst the very first industries to adopt widely implemented international safety standards.

Because of its inherently international nature, the safety of shipping is regulated by various United Nations agencies, in particular the International Maritime Organization (IMO) which has developed a comprehensive framework of global maritime safety regulations.

THE PRINCIPAL REGULATIONS GOVERNING MARITIME SAFETY

The following are the major international shipping conventions, adopted by the International Maritime Organization (and the International Labour Organization) concerning safety and pollution prevention. However, many other maritime instruments concerning more specific issues are also in force worldwide.

DEALING WITH THE SHIP

SOLAS (International Convention for the Safety of Life at Sea, 1974) lays down a comprehensive range of minimum standards for the safe construction of ships and the basic safety equipment (*e.g.* fire protection, navigation, lifesaving and radio) to be carried on board. SOLAS also requires regular ship surveys and the issue by flag states of certificates of compliance.

MARPOL (International Convention for the Prevention of Pollution from Ships, 1973/1978) contains requirements to prevent pollution that may be caused both accidentally and in the course of routine operations. MARPOL concerns the prevention of pollution from oil, bulk chemicals, dangerous goods, sewage, garbage and atmospheric pollution, and includes provisions such as those which require certain oil tankers to have double hulls. COLREG (Convention on the International Regulations for Preventing Collisions at Sea, 1972) lays down the basic "rules of the road", such as rights of way and actions to avoid collisions. LOADLINE (International Convention on Loadlines, 1966) sets the minimum permissible free board, according to the season of the year and the ship's trading pattern.

ISPS (The International Ship and Port Facility Security Code, 2002) includes mandatory requirements to ensure ships and port facilities are secure at all stages during a voyage.

DEALING WITH THE SHIPPING COMPANY

ISM (The International Safety Management Code, 1993) effectively requires shipping companies to have a licence to operate. Companies and their ships must undergo regular audits to ensure that a safety management system is in place, including adequate procedures and lines of communication between ships and their managers ashore.

DEALING WITH THE SEAFARER

STCW (International Convention on Standards of Training, Certification and Watchkeeping for Seafarers, 1978/1995) establishes uniform standards of competence for seafarers.

ILO 147 (The ILO Merchant Shipping (Minimum Standards) Convention, 1976) requires national administrations to have effective legislation on labour issues such as hours of work, medical fitness and seafarers' working conditions.

THE REDUCTION IN THE NUMBER OF SHIP LOSSES

Relatively few ships actually sink at sea. The vast majority of the following "losses" simply refer to ships which are damaged and "written off" by the hull insurers as being beyond economical repair - described by underwriters as "total constructive losses". The figures below cover the entire global industry and indicate the steady improvement in safety performance since the 1990s.

THE REDUCTION IN THE NUMBER OF ACCIDENTS

The following figures concern insurance claims for third party liability, such as incidents involving personal injury, cargo damage, pollution, or damage to property (*e.g.* other ships or port equipment).

The figures have been produced by the UK P and I Club, which insures around 20 per cent of the world's ships, and take account of changes in the number of ships entered in the Club. The decrease in the number of large claims (over US $100,000) is all the more significant given the increasing value of claims that are made.

ENVIRONMENTAL PERFORMANCE

THE REDUCTION IN THE QUANTITY OF OIL SPILLED BY SHIPS

Quantity of Oil Spilled, Tonnes

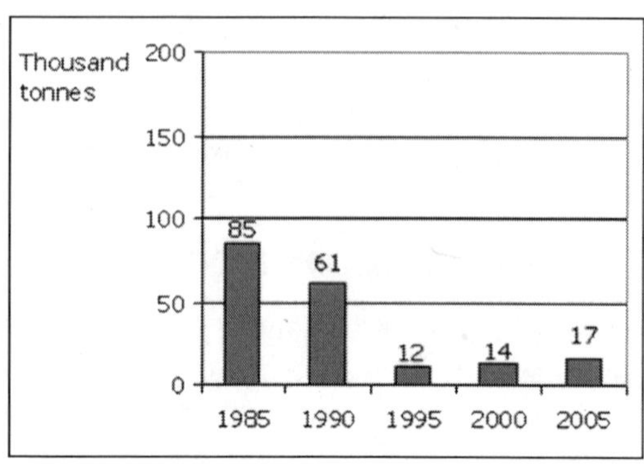

Lives Lost at Sea (1995 - 2002)

As in all transport sectors, lives are sadly lost as a result of accidents. However, the loss of life in shipping is in fact relatively modest, and the overall trend is one of reduction in the number of fatalities, which is all the more impressive in view of the growth in the number of ships in the world fleet. The figures below relate to lives lost on cargo ships and cover the entire international industry, which employs over one and a quarter million people, plus many more employed in coastal trades.

GLOBAL SHIPPING NETWORK

The Global shipping network is the worldwide network of maritime traffic. From a network science perspective ports represent nodes and routes represent lines. Transportation networks have a crucial role in today's economy, more precisely, maritime traffic is one of the most important drivers of global trade.

Fig. Container Ship: Loading.

HISTORY

Despite the estimates that 90 per cent of world trade is transported on water, the shipping industry is probably less in the public eye than other sectors. Due to bigger vessels and economies of scale – partly also because of the appearance of standardized containers - the cost of shipping is quite cheap: a transport of a DVD player costs only $1.5 to reach Europe. Today's most crowded sea route is between China and the US, which is also quite unbalanced, as the amount of goods travelling from China to the US are four times higher than the opposite direction. Also new routes can be opened – for example Russia's Northeast Passage is a quicker way to get to Europe from China. High-tech Ports are also having ever better services. (automated terminals etc.)

Until recently one could not really know much about how these ports and kilometer long ferries are related from a network science perspective. Luckily we can have a detailed picture about how maritime traffic works. Due to a Climatological Database a visualization can be seen on the 18-19th century ocean traffic. Not only the year-to-year changes – that mostly represent strong trade relations between countries like England and India – but seasonal changes can be also recognized.

THE NETWORK SCIENCE PERSPECTIVE

As with every network, maritime traffic can be also viewed through a network scientist's glass. Ports can be regarded as edges and the paths ferries travelling on are the lines. If this network is just as any other like railway or airport networks, one can have valid statements about its operation. The ocean's traffic system also has its routes, gateways, some of which functioning as a major hub or interconnection.

A paper by Kaluza et al. investigates cargo ship movements on real data. They use data on all major ports and the largest ships, that can be regarded as the majority of the shipping transport – it contains 93 per cent of the total world capacity of cargo ship transport. Here, "each trajectory can be interpreted as a small directed network where the nodes are ports linked together if the ship travelled directly between ports". The weights of the links between i and j ports are the potential space of the ships travelling between them.

Asymmetry

The global directed ship network's prominent characteristics is that it is asymmetric – as 59 per cent of the linked pairs have only one direction. The routes are short – there is no need for a lot of steps to get from one port to another, as the average path length is 2.5, with maximum of 8 and 52 per cent of the pairs can be connected by two steps. This is much more fewer than in the case of airport networks as both the average and the maximum are significantly higher: 4.4 and 15 respectively. (Guimera et al.)

Clusters

The shipping network is highly clustered, its clustering coefficient is 0.49, which can be interpreted that any given node's neighbours are also connected to each other.

The average number of links of a node is 76.5, which is much higher as opposed to the airport network, that is 19.4. These facts show that shipping networks are denser, which also gives a higher robustness to it. As many real-world networks it also has the property of having a lot of nodes with only a few links but some having extremely lot of links. Although it is not exactly a scale-free network, the distribution of link weights follows a power law. The distribution of the nodes strength (average link weights arriving and departing from port i) also follows a power law, which means that only a few ports manage immense amounts of cargo.

Betweenness Centrality

Betweenness centrality is another important concept. It is basically the sum of the directed paths in the network that pass through a particular node. Ports with high betweenness are quite important. Such nodes are the Panama and Suez canals or Shanghai and Antwerp.

Different Subnetworks

There are also differences between the main ship types: container ships, bulk dry carriers and oil tankers. These differences reflect to the fact that they follow distinctive traffic patterns. While container ships typically follow set schedules with fixed path for a regular service, dry carriers change their routes more often. Furthermore, container ships are much faster than the other categories - average days spent in the port is 1.9 in contrast to 5.6 of bulk dry carriers or 4.6 of oil tankers The proper kind of ports also affect the properties of the possible network.

GLOBAL SHIPPING INDUSTRY – FORECASTS TILL 2015

The global shipping industry is one of the biggest industries of today's times. During the coming years, it is expected to decline by 5-10 per cent due to oversupply and high bunker oil prices that will eventually lead to constraining of its performance. A sustained oversupply of vessels combined with high bunker oil prices will pressure margins in most shipping segments.

The tanker market has also been affected by the oversupply of vessels in the near term aided by lower OPEC production levels; though the outlook for the product tanker segment is more favorable since demand growth is likely to outpace supply during 2013, leading freight rates to rise by the end of this year. Box freight rates for the container segment have rebounded since March this year. However, strong improvement in earnings should not be expected for the full year in this segment. This reflects sustained high bunker oil costs and pressure on container rates stemming from recent increases in deployed tonnage of box ships. Although, Japanese conglomerates are likely to be affected to a lesser extent by negative market trends affecting other global shipping companies owing to their scale, diversification (including their liquefied natural gas, or LNG, fleets) and strong relationships with customers. AP Moller Maersk, Nippon Yusen, Kawasaki Kisen, Mitsui OSK Lines, China COSCO and Evergreen Marine are some top players in the industry. This product provides an analysis of the Global Shipping Industry.

The report covers the following:

- An analysis of the global shipping industry through an overall industry overview and an analysis of each segment. Each industry segment is analyzed by a market overview, industry statistics, and demand and supply statistics. The report will analyze 5 segments- Crude Tanker, Product Tanker, Chemical Tanker, Automobile Export Tanker, Dry Bulk Shipping segment, and the Containership Market.
- The author includes an analysis of the top 20 shipping markets in the world such as Australia, China/Hong Kong, Norway, Philippines, Russia, Singapore, UK, South Africa and the United States.
- Forecast till 2015 for the global shipping industry, global crude tanker industry, global product tanker industry, global chemical tanker industry, global dry bulk shipping industry and a forecast for the global containership industry is included.
- Analysis of 35 major shipping companies such as AP Moller Maersk, China COSCO, China Shipping Development, D/S Norden, Golar LNG, Kawasaki Kisen, Hyundai Merchant Marine, and others is included. Analysis of each player includes valuations and ratio analysis, investment risk analysis, company strategies, future risks, market value analysis, market share analysis, financial analysis, SWOT analysis, etc.

TEN LEGITIMATELY FASCINATING FACTS ABOUT THE SHIPPING INDUSTRY

Almost 90 percent of everything we buy arrives via ship, writes Rose George in her actually mind-blowing new book Ninety Percent of Everything, published tomorrow, which covers her months-long adventure with the shipping industry — the biggest business that you know nothing about.

"These ships and boxes belong to a business that feeds, clothes, warms, and supplies us. They have fueled if not created globalization. They are the reason behind your cheap T-shirt and reasonably priced television. But who looks behind a television now and sees the ship that brought it? Who cares about the men who steered your breakfast cereal through winter storms? How ironic that the more ships have grown in size and consequence, the less space they take up in our imagination."

With its wide scope, voice of intellectual curiosity, and inter-ocean adventure, the book is reminiscent of Donovan Hohn's popular Moby Duck, which followed the path of 28,000 bath toys lost at sea after a shipping container capsized.

Much as Hohn did in his book, George travels the world to show that shipping is actually pretty interesting. We sailed, as it were, through the book to bring you the Top 10 Most Fascinating Facts About the Shipping Industry:

SHIPPING IS THE "GREENEST" MASS TRANSPORT

Compared to the energy expended moving goods by plane or truck, shipping is far less damaging in terms of greenhouse gases released: "Sending a container from Shanghai to Le Havre (France) emits fewer greenhouse gases than the truck that takes the container on to Lyon." However, the shipping industry is so big that, if you added shipping to the list of the world's most polluting countries, it would come in sixth place. So it's not exactly environmentally beneficial. Plus, ships can't do this:

Ships are Incredibly Big

The largest container ship can carry 15,000 boxes, which would hold 746 million bananas. This would be about one banana for every person in Europe. (And a few animals, too.)

SHIPS COVER THE OCEANS

At least 20 million containers are currently traveling across the oceans. That's a lot of bananas!

SHIPPING IS A HUGE SOURCE OF REVENUE

Economically, the shipping industry is monstrous in its size. In the United Kingdom, shipping accounts for more of the GDP than restaurants, takeaway food, and civil engineering combined — about 2 percent of the GDP by itself, just behind construction.

PIRATES ARE DANGEROUS AND PREVALENT

The rate of attacks on seafarers by pirates (for example, off the coast of Somalia) was higher last year than violent assaults in South Africa, which has the highest level of crime in the world.

SHIPPING IS INCREDIBLY CHEAP.

It's less expensive to ship Scottish cod 10,000 miles away to China to be filleted and then sent back to Scotland than it is to pay Scottish filleters to do the job. Of course, this reflects mostly on the cheapness of Chinese labour, but it does also show shipping's low costs.

INSPECTION OF CONTAINERS IS RARE.

Remember the second season of The Wire, in which the dockworkers sketchily smuggled in drugs and prostitutes via shipping containers? Well, George's book shows why that would be so easy. Only 5 percent of the containers shipped to U.S. ports are physically inspected, and that number is even lower in Europe. This probably would help explain Jack Sparrow's common question.

THE OCEANS ARE VAST.

A container ship travels the equivalent of three-quarters of the way to the moon and back in one year during its regular travel across the oceans.

SHIPPING COMPANIES DON'T LIKE OUTSIDERS.

Shipping companies are so secretive and private that, for example, the official Greek shipowners' association refuses to reveal how many members it actually has. And, George points out, that's not considered weird in the industry.

SHIPWORKER DEMOGRAPHICS ARE EXTREMELY PREDICTABLE.

On average, the typical shipworker is a male Filipino; Filipinos make up one third of all shipworkers, and men constitute 98 percent of the workforce. As a British, white female, author Rose George was thus very much an outlier on her sea journeys. But these are just statistics, and George personalizes them in the book as, according to the jacket copy, "she joins seafaring chaplains, patrols the Indian Ocean with an antipiracy task force, and investigates the harm that fishing trawlers are inflicting on endangered whales." Meanwhile, the rest of us will sit in our shipped office chairs, wearing our shipped clothing, eating our shipped bananas, and working on our shipped computers. What a life.

3

Shipping Logistics

Essar Shipping is an integrated logistics solution provider with investments in logistics services, sea transportation and oilfield drilling services.. Essar's logistics business provides end-to-end logistics services – from ships to ports, lighterage services to plants, intra-plant logistics and dispatching finished products to the final customer. We own transshipment assets to provide lighterage support services, and onshore and offshore logistics services. We also manage a fleet of 5,000 trucks for the inland transportation of steel and petroleum products. The sea transportation business has a diversified fleet of 15 vessels including VLCCs, capes,mini-capes bulk, Supramaxes, and handy-sizes to provide crude oil and bulk commodity transportation services. We have more than 220 ship years serving leading Indian and global oil majors and commodity traders and a combined tonnage of over 1.84 million. We currently have an order book of 4 new building vessels.

Essar Shipping, through its subsidiaries Essar Oilfields Services Ltd (EOSL) and Essar Oilfield Services (India) Ltd. (EOSIL), provides quality onshore and offshore drilling services and related services to international clients. Own a fleet of 16 rigs, which includes one semi-submersible rig and 15 onshore rigs. Our integrated business model provides opportunities to cater to the complete supply chain management services to clients in oil and gas, steel, and power generation industries, and focuses on the intrinsic and captive demand for transportation services, logistics and cargo handling infrastructure. With interests in crude and dry bulk carriers, port-to-plant logistics and oilfield services, the company continues to provide end-to-end logistics solutions to its customers in a very cost-effective manner.

- Our contracted revenue is based on various spot, medium-term and long-term contracts with domestic and international clientele, catered by a diversified mix of assets.
- Essar Shipping Limited is the first Indian Shipping company to publish a Sustainability Report. The company continues to set benchmarks among the Indian Shipping companies with its third successive year of publishing Sustainability report.

LOGISTICS

Logistics is the management of the flow of things between the point of origin and the point of consumption in order to meet requirements of customers or corporations. The resources managed in logistics can include physical items, such as food, materials, animals, equipment and liquids, as well as abstract items, such as time and information. The logistics of physical items usually involves the integration of information flow, material handling, production, packaging, inventory, transportation, warehousing, and often security.

In military science, logistics is concerned with maintaining an army supply lines while disrupting those of the enemy, since an armed force without resources and transportation is defenseless. Military logistics was already practiced in the ancient world and as modern military have a significant need for logistics solutions, advanced implementations have been developed, especially for theUnited States Armed Forces. In military logistics, logistics officers manage how and when to move resources to the places they are needed.

Logistics management is the part of supply chain management that plans, implements, and controls the efficient, effectiveforward, and reverse flow and storage of goods, services, and related information between the point of origin and the point of consumption in order to meet customer's requirements. The complexity of logistics can be modeled, analyzed, visualized, and optimized by dedicated simulation software. The minimization of the use of resources is a common motivation in all logistics fields. A professional working in the field of logistics management is called a logistician.

Fig. Configuring and Managing Warehouses is a Central Concern for Bothbusiness Logistics and Military Logistics.

Logistics Specialist Inventories Supplies in a Storeroom Aboard the Aircraft Carrier USS George H.W. Bush, where Inventorying Means Making a Report on Stock Availability. Notice how Every Stock Keeping Unithas an Individual Code and a Code Corresponding to a Specific Subclass from a Given Drawer.

ORIGINS AND DEFINITION

The prevalent view is that the term logistics comes from the late 19th century: from French logistique (logermeans to lodge) and was first used by Baron de Jomini. Others attribute a Greek origin to the word: λογοιζ meaning reason or speech; λογιστικοζ, meaning accountant or responsible for counting.

The Oxford English Dictionary defines logistics as "the branch of military science relating to procuring, maintaining and transporting material, personnel and facilities". However, the New Oxford American Dictionary defines logistics as "the detailed coordination of a complex operation involving many people, facilities, or supplies," and the Oxford Dictionary on-line defines it as "the detailed organization and implementation of a complex operation". As such, logistics is commonly seen as a branch of engineeringthat creates "people systems" rather than "machine systems."

According to the Council of Supply Chain Management Professionals (previously the Council of Logistics Management) logistics is the process of planning, implementing and controlling procedures for the efficient and effective transportation and storage of goods including services and related information from the point of origin to the point of consumption for the purpose of conforming to customer requirements and includes inbound, outbound, internal and external movements. Academics and practitioners traditionally refer to the terms operations or production management when referring to physical transformations taking place in a single business location (factory, restaurant or even bank clerking) and reserve the term logistics for activities related to distribution, that is, moving products on the territory. Managing a distribution center is seen, therefore, as pertaining to the realm of logistics since, while in theory the products made by a factory are ready for consumption they still need to be moved along the distribution network according to some logic, and the distribution center aggregates and processes orders coming from different areas of the territory. That being said, from a modeling perspective, there are similarities between operations management and logistics, and companies sometimes use hybrid professionals, with for ex.

"Director of Operations" or "Logistics Officer" working on similar problems. Furthermore, the term supply chain management originally refers to, among other issues, having an integrated vision in of both production and logistics from point of origin to point of production. All these terms may suffer from semantic change as a side effect of advertising.

LOGISTICS ACTIVITIES AND FIELDS

A basic distinction in the nature of logistics activities is between inbound and outbound logistics. Inbound logistics is one of the primary processes of logistics, concentrating on purchasing and arranging the inbound movement of materials, parts, and/or finished inventory from suppliers to manufacturing or assembly plants, warehouses, or retail stores. Outbound logistics is the process related to the storage and movement of the final product and the related information flows from the end of the production line to the end user.

Given the services performed by logisticians, the main fields of logistics can be broken down as follows:

- Procurement logistics
- Distribution logistics
- After-sales logistics
- Disposal logistics
- Reverse logistics
- Green logistics
- Global logistics
- Domestics logistics
- Concierge Service
- RAM logistics
- Asset Control Logistics
- POS Material Logistics
- Emergency Logistics
- Production Logistics

Procurement logistics consists of activities such as market research, requirements planning, make-or-buy decisions, supplier management, ordering, and order controlling. The targets in procurement logistics might be contradictory: maximizing efficiency by concentrating on core competences, outsourcing while maintaining the autonomy of the company, or minimizing procurement costs while maximizing security within the supply process.

Distribution logistics has, as main tasks, the delivery of the finished products to the customer. It consists of order processing, warehousing, and transportation. Distribution logistics is necessary because the time, place, and quantity of production differs with the time, place, and quantity of consumption. Disposal logistics has as its main function to reduce logistics cost(s) and enhance service(s) related to the disposal of waste produced during the operation of a business.

Reverse logistics denotes all those operations related to the reuse of products and materials. The reverse logistics process includes the management and the sale of surpluses, as well as products being returned to vendors from buyers. Reverse logistics stands for all operations related to the reuse of products and materials. It is "the process of planning, implementing, and controlling the efficient, cost effective flow of raw materials, in-process inventory, finished goods and related information from the point of consumption to the point of origin for the purpose of recapturing value or proper disposal. More precisely, reverse logistics is the process of moving goods from their typical final destination for the purpose of capturing value, or proper disposal. The opposite of reverse logistics is forward logistics.

Green Logistics describes all attempts to measure and minimize the ecological impact of logistics activities. This includes all activities of the forward and reverse flows. This can be achieved through intermodal freight transport, path optimization, vehicle saturation and city logistics. RAM Logistics combines both business logistics and military logistics since it is concerned with highly complicated technological systems for which Reliability, Availability and Maintainability are essential, ex: weapon systems and military supercomputers. Asset Control Logistics: companies in the retail channels, both organized retailers and suppliers, often deploy assets required for the display, preservation, promotion of their products. Some examples are refrigerators, stands, display monitors, seasonal equipment, poster stands and frames.

Fig. A Forklift Truck Loads a Pallet of Humanitarian Aid to Pakistan on Board a C-17 Aircraft, Following Devastating Floods in the Country in 2010.

Emergency logistics (or Humanitarian Logistics) is a term used by the logistics, supply chain, and manufacturing industries to denote specific time-critical modes of transport used to move goods or objects rapidly in the event of an emergency. The reason for enlisting emergency logistics services could be a production delay or anticipated production delay, or an urgent need for specialized equipment to prevent events such as aircraft being grounded (also known as "aircraft on ground"—AOG), ships being delayed, or telecommunications failure. Humanitarian logistics involves governments, the military, aid agencies, donors, non-governmental organizations and emergency logistics services are typically sourced from a specialist provider.

The term production logistics describes logistic processes within a value adding system (ex: factory or a mine). Production logistics aims to ensure that each machine and workstation receives the right product in the right quantity and quality at the right time. The concern is with production, testing, transportation, storage and supply. Production logistics can operate in existing as well as new plants: since manufacturing in an existing plant is a constantly changing process, machines are exchanged and new ones added, which gives the opportunity to improve the production logistics system accordingly. Production logistics provides the means to achieve customer response and capital efficiency. Production logistics becomes more important with decreasing batch sizes. In many industries (*e.g.* mobile phones), the short-term goal is a batch size of one, allowing even a single customer's demand to be fulfilled efficiently. Track and tracing, which is an essential part of production logistics due to product safety and reliability issues, is also gaining importance, especially in the automotive and medical industries.

MILITARY LOGISTICS

Punjab Regiment uses mules for carrying cargo inBurma during WWII. Animals have been used for logistic purposes by different people throughout history, the Roman army in particular preferred mules over donkeys for their moving capacity.

In military science, maintaining one's supply lines while disrupting those of the enemy is a crucial—some would say the most crucial—element of military strategy, since an armed force without resources and transportation is defenseless. The historical leaders Hannibal, Alexander the Great, and the Duke of Wellington are considered to have been logistical geniuses: Alexander's expedition, the longest military campaign ever undertaken, benefited consiberably from his meticulous attention to the provisioning of his army, Hannibal is credited to have "taught logistics" to the Romans during the Punic Wars and the success of the Anglo-Portuguese army in the Peninsula War was the due to the effectiveness of Wellington's supply system, despite the numerical disadvantage. The defeat of the British in the American War of Independence and the defeat of the Axis in the African theater of World War II are attributed by some scholars to logistical failures.

Military have a significant need for logistics solutions and so have developed advanced implementations. Integrated Logistics Support (ILS) is a discipline used in military industries to ensure an easily supportable system with a robust customer service (logistic) concept at the lowest cost and in line with (often high) reliability, availability, maintainability, and other requirements, as defined for the project. In military logistics, logistics officers manage how and when to move resources to the places they are needed. Supply chain management in military logistics often deals with a number of variables in predicting cost, deterioration,consumption, and future demand. The United States Armed Forces' categorical supply classification was developed in such a way that categories of supply with similar consumption variables are grouped together for planning purposes. For instance, peacetime consumption of ammunition and fuel will be considerably lower than wartime consumption of these items, whereas other classes of supply such as subsistence and clothing have a relatively consistent consumption rate regardless of war or peace.

Some classes of supply have a linear demand relationship: as more troops are added, more supply items are needed; or as more equipment is used, more fuel and ammunition are consumed. Other classes of supply must consider a third variable besides usage and quantity: time. As equipment ages, more and more repair parts are needed over time, even when usage and quantity stays consistent. By recording and analyzing these trends over time and applying them to future scenarios, the US Armed Forces can accurately supply troops with the items necessary at the precise moment they are needed. History has shown that good logistical planning creates a lean and efficient fighting force. The lack thereof can lead to a clunky, slow, and ill-equipped force with too much or too little supply.

BUSINESS LOGISTICS

One definition of business logistics speaks of "having the right item in the right quantity at the right time at the right place for the right price in the right condition to the right customer". Business logistics incorporates all industry sectors and aims to manage the fruition of project life cycles, supply chains, and resultant efficiencies.

The term "business logistics" has evolved since the 1960s due to the increasing complexity of supplying businesses with materials and shipping out products in an increasingly globalized supply chain, leading to a call for professionals called "supply chain logisticians". In business, logistics may have either an internal focus (inbound logistics) or an external focus (outbound logistics), covering the flow and storage of materials from point of origin to point of consumption. The main functions of a qualified logistician include inventory management, purchasing, transportation, warehousing, consultation, and the organizing and planning of these activities. Logisticians combine a professional knowledge of each of these functions to coordinate resources in an organization.

Fig. A Forklift Stacking a Logistics Provider's Warehouse of Goods on Pallets.

There are two fundamentally different forms of logistics: one optimizes a steady flow of material through a network oftransport links and storage nodes, while the other coordinates a sequence of resources to carry out some project(ex:restructuring a warehouse).

Nodes of a Distribution Network

The nodes of a distribution network include:

- Factories where products are manufactured or assembled
- A depot or deposit is a standard type of warehouse thought for storing merchandise (high level of inventory).
- Distribution centers are for order processing and order fulfillment (lower level of inventory) and also for receiving returning items from clients.
- Transit points are built for cross docking activities, which consist in reassembling cargo units based on deliveries scheduled (only moving merchandise).
- Traditional retail stores of the Mom and Pop variety, modern supermarkets, hypermarkets, discount stores or also voluntary chains, consumer cooperative, groups of consumer with collective buying power. Note that subsidiaries will be mostly owned by another company and franchisers, although using other company brands, actually own the point of sale.

There may be some intermediaries operating for representative matters between nodes such as sales agents or brokers.

Logistic Families and Metrics

A logistic family is a set of products which share a common characteristic: weight and volumetric characteristics, physical storing needs (temperature, radiation,...), handling needs, order frequency, package size, etc.

The following metrics may be used by the company to organize its products in different families:

- Physical metrics used to evaluate inventory systems include stocking capacity, selectivity, superficial utilization, volumetric utilization, transport capacity, transport capacity utilization.
- Monetary metrics used include space holding costs (building, shelving and services) and handling costs (people, handling machinery, energy and maintenance).

Other metrics may present themselves in both physical or monetary form, such as the standard Inventory turnover.

Handling and Order Processing

Fig. Unit Loads for Transportation of Luggage at the Airport, in this Case the Unit Load has Protective Function.

Unit loads are combinations of individual items which are moved by handling systems, usually employing a pallet of normed dimensions. Handling systems include: trans-pallet handlers, counterweight handler, retractable mast handler, bilateral handlers, trilateral handlers,AGV and stacker handlers. Storage systems include: pile stocking, cell racks (either static or movable), cantilever racks and gravity racks. Order processing is a sequential process involving: processing withdrawal list, picking (selective removal of items from loading units), sorting (assembling items based on destination), package formation (weighting, labeling and packing), order consolidation (gathering packages into loading units for transportation, control and bill of lading).

Picking can be both manual or automated. Manual picking can be both man to goods, *i.e.* operator using a cart or conveyor belt, or goods to man, *i.e.* the operator benefiting from the presence of a mini-load ASRS, vertical or horizontal carousel or from an Automatic Vertical Storage System (AVSS). Automatic picking is done either with dispensers or depalletizing robots. Sorting can be done manually through carts or conveyor belts, or automatically through sorters.

Transportation

Cargo, *i.e.* merchandise being transported, can be moved through a variety of transportation means and is organized in different shipment categories. Unit loads are usually assembled into higher standardized units such as: ISO containers, swap bodies or semi-trailers. Especially for very long distances, product transportation will likely benefit from using different transportation means: multimodal transport, intermodal transport (no handling) and combined transport (minimal road transport). When moving cargo, typical constraints are maximum weight and volume. Operators involved in transportation include: all train, road vehicles, boats, airplanes companies, couriers, freight forwarders and multi-modal transport operators. Merchandise being transported internationally is usually subject to the Incoterms standards issued by the International Chamber of Commerce.

Configuration and Management

Fig. Push-Back Rack for Motorcycles, aLIFO Rack System for Storage.

Similarly to production systems, logistic systems need to be properly configured and managed. Actually a number of methodologies have been directly borrowed from operations management such as using Economic Order Quantity models for managing inventory in the nodes of the network. Distribution resource planning (DRP) is similar to MRP, except that it doesn't concern activities inside the nodes of the network but planning distribution when moving goods through the links of the network. Traditionally in logistics configuration may be at the level of the warehouse (node) or at level of the distribution system (network). Regarding a single warehouse, besides the issue of designing and building the warehouse, configuration means solving a number of interrelated technical-economic problems: dimensioning rack cells, choosing a palletizing method (manual or through robots), rack dimensioning and design, number of racks, number and typology of retrieval systems (*e.g.* stacker cranes). Some important constraints have to be satisfied: fork and load beams resistance to bending and proper placement of sprinklers. Although picking is more of a tactical planning decision than a configuration problem, it is important to take it into account when deciding the racks layout inside the warehouse and buying tools such as handlers and motorized carts since once those decisions are taken they will work as constraints when managing the warehouse, same reasoning for sorting when designing the conveyor system and/or installing automatic dispensers.

Configuration at the level of the distribution system concerns primarily the problem of location of the nodes in a geographic space and distribution of capacity among the nodes. The first may be referred to as facility location (with the special case of site selection) while the latter to as capacity allocation. The problem of outsourcing typically arises at this level: the nodes of a supply chain are very rarely owned by a single enterprise.

Distribution networks can be characterized by numbers of levels, namely the number of intermediary nodes between supplier and consumer:

- Direct store delivery, *i.e.* zero levels
- *One level network:* Central warehouse
- *Two level network:* Central and peripheral warehouses

This distinction is more useful for modeling purposes, but it relates also to a tactical decision regarding safety stocks: considering a two level network, if safety inventory is kept only in peripheral warehouses then it is called a dependent system (from suppliers), if safety inventory is distributed among central and peripheral warehouses it is called an independent system (from suppliers). Transportation from producer to the second level is called primary transportation, from the second level to consumer is called secondary transportation. Although configuring a distribution network from zero is possible, logisticians usually have to deal with restructuring existing networks due to presence of an array of factors: changing demand, product or process innovation, opportunities for outsourcing, change of government policy towards trade barriers, innovation in transportation means (bothvehicles or thoroughfares), introduction of regulations (notably those regarding pollution) and availability of ICT supporting systems (*e.g.* ERP or e-commerce).

Once a logistic system is configured, management, meaning tactical decisions, takes place, once again, at the level of the warehouse and of the distribution network. Decisions have to be made under a set of constraints: internal, such as using the available infrastructure, or external, such as complying with given product shelf lifes and expiration dates. At the warehouse level, the logistician must decide how to distribute merchandise over the racks. Three basic situations are traditionally considered: shared storage, dedicated storage (rack space reserved for specific merchandise) and class based storage (class meaning merchandise organized in different areas according to their access index).

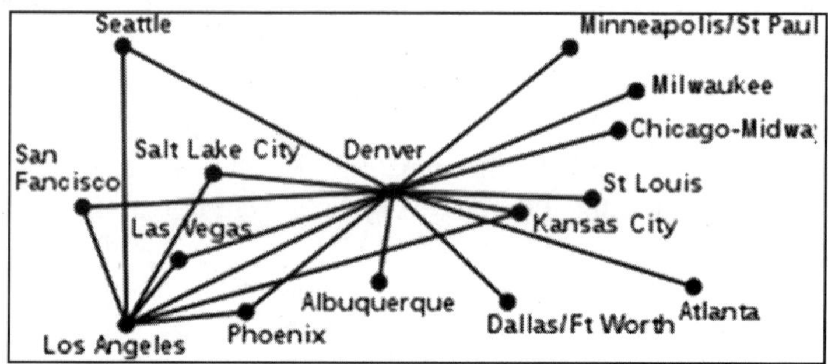

Airline logistic network. Note how Denver works ashub in the network. Picking efficiency varies greatly depending on the situation. For man to goods situation, a distinction is carried out between high level picking (vertical component significant) and low level picking (vertical component insignificant).

A number of tactical decisions regarding picking must be made:

- *Routing path:* Standard alternatives include transversal routing, return routing, midpoint routing and largest gap return routing
- *Replenishment method:* Standard alternatives include equal space supply for each product class and equal time supply for each product class.
- *Picking logic:* Order picking vs batch picking

At the level of the distribution network, tactical decisions involve mainly inventory control and delivery path optimization. Note that the logistician may be required to manage the reverse flow along with the forward flow.

Warehouse Management and Control

Although there is some overlap in functionality, warehouse management systems (WMS) can differ significantly from warehouse control systems (WCS). Simply put, a WMS plans a weekly activity forecast based on such factors as statistics and trends, whereas a WCS acts like a floor supervisor, working in real time to get the job done by the most effective means. For instance, a WMS can tell the system that it is going to need five of stock-keeping unit (SKU) A and five of SKU B hours in advance, but by the time it acts, other considerations may have come into play or there could be a logjam on a conveyor. A WCS can prevent that problem by working in real time and adapting to the situation by making a last-minute decision based on current activity and operational status. Working synergistically, WMS and WCS can resolve these issues and maximize efficiency for companies that rely on the effective operation of their warehouse or distribution center.

Logistics Outsourcing

Logistics outsourcing involves a relationship between a company and an LSP (logistic service provider), which, compared with basic logistics services, has more customized offerings, encompasses a broad number of service activities, is characterized by a long-term orientation, and thus has a strategic nature.

Outsourcing does not have to be complete externalization to a LSP, but can also be partial:

- A single contract for supplying a specific service on occasion
- Creation of a spin-off
- Creation of a joint venture

Third-party logistics (3PL) involves using external organizations to execute logistics activities that have traditionally been performed within an organization itself. According to this definition, third-party logistics includes any form of outsourcing of logistics activities previously performed in house. For example, if a company with its own warehousing facilities decides to employ external transportation, this would be an example of third-party logistics. Logistics is an emerging business area in many countries.

The concept of a fourth-party logistics (4PL) provider was first defined by Andersen Consulting (now Accenture) as an integrator that assembles the resources, planning capabilities, and technology of its own organization and other organizations to design, build, and run comprehensive supply chain solutions. Whereas a third-party logistics (3PL) service provider targets a single function, a 4PL targets management of the entire process. Some have described a 4PL as a general contractor that manages other 3PLs, truckers, forwarders, custom house agents, and others, essentially taking responsibility of a complete process for the customer.

Horizontal Alliances Between Logistics Service Providers

Horizontal business alliances often occur between logistics service providers, *i.e.*, the cooperation between two or more logistics companies that are potentially competing. In a horizontal alliance, these partners can benefit twofold. On one hand, they can "access tangible resources which are directly exploitable." In this example extending common transportation networks, their warehouse infrastructure and the ability to provide more complex service packages can be achieved by combining resources. On the other hand, partners can "access intangible resources, which are not directly exploitable." This typically includes know-how and information and, in turn, innovation.

LOGISTICS AUTOMATION

Logistics automation is the application of computer software and/or automated machinery to improve the efficiency of logistics operations. Typically this refers to operations within a warehouse or distribution center, with broader tasks undertaken by supply chain managementsystems and enterprise resource planning systems.

Industrial machinery can typically identify products through either Bar Code or RFID technologies. Information in traditional bar codes is stored as a sequence of black and white bars varying in width, which when read by laser is translated in a binary sequence, which according to fixed rules can be converted in a decimal number. Sometimes information in a bar code can be transmitted through radio frequency, more typically radio transmission is used in RFID tags. An RFID tag is card containing a memory chip and an antenna which transmits signals to a reader. RFID may be found on merchandise, animals, vehicles and people as well.

LOGISTICS: PROFESSION AND ORGANIZATIONS

A logistician is a professional logistics practitioner. Professional logisticians are often certified by professional associations. One can either work in a pure logistics company, such as a shipping line, airport, or freight forwarder, or within the logistics department of a company. However, as mentioned above, logistics is a broad field, encompassing procurement, production, distribution, and disposal activities. Hence, career perspectives are broad as well. A new trend in the industry are the 4PL, or fourth-party logistics, firms, consulting companies offering logistics services. Some universities and academic institutions train students as logisticians, offering undergraduate and postgraduate programmes. A university with a primary focus on logistics is Kühne Logistics University in Hamburg, Germany. It is non profit and supported by Kühne-Foundation of the logistics entrepreneur Klaus Michael Kühne.

The Chartered Institute of Logistics and Transport (CILT), established in the United Kingdom in 1919, received a Royal Charter in 1926. The Chartered Institute is one of theprofessional bodies or institutions for the logistics and transport sectors that offers professional qualifications or degrees in logistics management. CILT programmes can be studied at centers around UK, some of which also offer distance learning options. The institute also have overseas branches namely The Chartered Institute of Logistics and Transport Australia (CILTA) in Australia and Chartered Institute of Logistics and Transport in Hong Kong (CILTHK) in Hong Kong. The International Association of Public Health Logisticians (IAPHL) is a professional network that promotes the professional development of supply chain managers and others working in the field of public health logistics and commodity security, with particular focus on developing countries. The association supports logisticians worldwide by providing a community of practice, where members can network, exchange ideas, and improve their professional skills.

THE DIFFERENCE BETWEEN SHIPPING AND LOGISTICS

UPS has, for the last few months, sought to position themselves as a logistics company rather than a shipping company. Though logistics is considered as one of the four types of intelligence in the Myers-Briggs personality test, along with strategic, tactical, and diplomatic intelligence, and the special domain of the traditionalist and materially minded SJ personality types, the term itself is an unfamiliar one. Why UPS would choose such an unfamiliar word to brand its company is a worthwhile question to bring up a more important underlying issue.

First, though, we must understand what logistics is. Specifically, logistics is supply management, the ability to monitor, control, organize, and direct supplies. Logistics has always been among the more important military arts (this is probably why I'm familiar with it), responsible for keeping soldiers well-fed, well-armed, and well-supplied and thus able to fight. George Washington is considered the nonpareil logistical general within the American military experience, keeping the American Revolution alive by keeping his army whole, despite the rudimentary state of supply within the early American Republic (and that is putting it generously). Logistics may have been decisive in the Civil War, despite its obscurity as a field. The fact that logistics involves the prompt transfer of supplies from where they are stored to where they are needed is itself involved deeply with shipping, it is clearly an area of core competence for UPS, so it makes intellectual sense to use the word (so long as one is willing to explain what one means).

The larger question, though, is why UPS would choose to market itself using such an unfamiliar term? Since UPS is known as a shipping company, it must have some greater strategy in positioning itself as a logistics company rather than merely a shipping company? Let us speculate some of the likeliest reasons and their implications on the larger business culture of the United States.

The difference between shipping and logistics is largely in semantics and perception, but it is an important perceptual difference in the larger cultural divide of businesses. It is essentially a question of status and class (and such questions deeply interest me). Shipping is largely "blue collar" service work. It is a low-skill, low-status profession where one simply takes packages from one person or company and delivers it to another. It is a menial task delegated to servants or an unpleasant duty that is outsourced to others. Logistics, on the other hand, is a "white collar" profession, an aspect of management, a high-status task requiring considerable expertise (specifically in supply chain management) and thus a profession with honour, glory, and widely recognized worth. It is, in a sense, the "bigger picture" that shipping is a small and not very prestigious part of.

And that is the genius of the UPS labeling of itself as a logistics firm rather than a shipping firm. Since logistics is the bigger picture, it can expand its business to related core competencies in the "logistics" family that serve as higher profit and higher status positions, increasing the reputation of its company and its employees, and leveraging its considerable and hard-earned expertise in supply chain management to lucrative consulting opportunities to businesses.

By labeling itself under a term obscure enough that no one else has taken it and that is descriptive enough to describe its core competence in a broad, brief, and compelling way, UPS has cornered the domain of "logistics" as its own domain in its entire span as a company, allowing it to preserve its standing in shipping and expand into more lucrative and higher status consulting opportunities for businesses, while increasing the status of the company and its employees. In the process, UPS is also serving (at least indirectly) to educate the business world to the often-neglected importance and value of logistics as a field while positioning itself as a leader in that field. Time will tell if the effort of UPS to corner the market and increase its status and profitability and range of core competencies is successful, but it is a bold initiative that deserves high praise however it turns out.

In early 1990, American President Companies started double-stack container rail service from Woodhaven, Michigan to Ford Motor Company's auto assembly plant in Hermosillo, Mexico. APC coordinates all the information, transportation, and inventory handling necessary to pick up parts and components from vendors and sequence-load them into containers for delivery on a just-in-time basis to Hermosillo. The movement includes coordination over four railroads and with Mexican customs officials for delay-free clearance. At the plant, Ford has built a state-of-the-art stack train terminal to smooth the flow of sequenced parts into assembly operations. APC provides cranes and management to break down the containers. The partners collaborate to return containers to the United States carrying components produced in the Maquiladora region and specialized part racks.

- A warehouse service venture of Lever Brothers and Distribution Centers, Inc. is bearing fruit. DCI has built, staffed, and operates a high-tech dedicated distribution warehouse for the toiletries maker in Columbus, Ohio. The companies share the benefits and risks: if warehouse utilization falls below a certain point, Lever helps cover the overhead; in return, DCI shares the productivity benefits when utilization approaches full-capacity economies of scale. A similar arrangement exists between Lever Brothers and Dry Storage Corporation in Atlanta.

- Schneider National furnished initial computerized scheduling and electronic data interchange for 90 Minnesota Mining and Manufacturing Company shipping locations that were revamping their transportation operations in the late 1980s. The service included coordination of freight transit and associated documentation for all motor carriers 3M was using. 3M got the benefits of the latest information technology, and Schneider gained and still enjoys the position of nationwide core carrier for 3M.

These examples illustrate logistics alliances that are becoming commonplace business arrangements. Virtually unheard of a decade ago, such agreements are now spreading as a way of lowering distribution and storage operating costs. For many manufacturers and vendors, these ventures offer opportunities to dramatically improve the quality of customer service. The principals in a typical agreement are a provider of customized logistics services and a producer of goods that jointly engineer and launch a system to speed goods to customers. But there are other forms too, like arrangements between two service providers and between two product marketers. (The insert, "Anatomy of Alliances," discusses several formats.)

ANATOMY OF ALLIANCES

Three characteristics distinguish logistics partnerships from run-of-the-mill cooperative business arrangements. First is a far more extensive link that makes the venture almost an extended organization with its own role, rules, values, and objectives. In the traditional purchasing situation, outsourcing is a make versus buy decision guided mostly by cost considerations. The logistics alliance is a special business compact in which the parties seek to benefit from the synergy of working together. The second characteristic is concentration on a relationship continuum instead of a series of single transactions. A high degree of dependency develops, which stimulates further cooperation. Trust builds as the parties focus on customer satisfaction and loyalty.

Of the forms these ventures take, the most common involves a product marketer and a service provider like a warehousing company or a rail carrier. For example, look at the joint operation of Sears Business Systems and Itel Distribution Systems in Alsip, Illinois. Sears runs a reconfiguration room in Itel's warehouse for modifying equipment to customers' specifications. Itel supplies full-service logistics tying into Sears's information network. Itel assembles basic orders, positioning equipment requiring modification in the reconfiguration room. Itel then assembles the complete order and performs the tasks necessary for timely delivery to the customer.

Some alliances combine the resources of service providers seeking to bolster their competitive positions. The Santa Fe Railway and J.B. Hunt Transport Services recently established intermodal freight transport whereby the former provides line-haul service and the latter, pickup and delivery. To stabilize the service—scheduled to run daily between Chicago and Los Angeles—the partners snared freight business from UPS and Ralston Purina. Some ventures between service companies may involve joint provision of service to a product marketer.

A common format for an alliance is a vertical alignment between two or more product marketers, usually marked by transfer of inventory ownership. (Some of these include a service supplier.) A simple instance is a distribution link between Procter and Gamble and Wal-Mart. A more complicated version is a projected consortium of four companies in the women's ready-to-wear apparel business: Du Pont, which makes the fibre; Milliken, which converts the fibre into fabric; Leslie Fay, which produces women's garments; and Dillard Department Stores, which sells them. The arrangement makes the use of resources more efficient in the face of volatile fashion demand. The arrangement is geared to speed inventory replenishment and to reduce the time elapsing from fibre to retail rack.

Yet another type is horizontal alignment of product marketers selling to the same customer base. (It may include a service company as coordinator.) In the hospital supply business, such an alliance offers frequent joint delivery of member-company products—all facilitated by electronic data interchange. Formed in 1987 by Abbott Laboratories and the 3M Company, the group has expanded to include Standard Register (business forms), IBM (computer network services), Kimberly-Clark (nonwoven disposable products), and C.R. Bard (urological products). Abbott and 3M made their move initially to compete more effectively against rivals Baxter Health care and Johnson and Johnson Hospital Supply.

Outsourcing of transportation or warehousing requirements to a specialist is, of course, an everyday matter. What is unusual about the relationships described here is the innovative manner in which the parties commingle their operations to obtain mutual benefits. A prime example is Drug Transport, Inc., which has carved out a niche in less-than-truckload distribution in the pharmaceutical and office supply fields. To permit wholesalers to offer daily delivery to retail customers at specified times, the Atlanta-based carrier has established an array of services and pricing.

The rates are based on guaranteed delivery, at a fixed charge, to the retailer of whatever product quantity is required. The charge is based on average shipment weight at a rate negotiated in advance of each 30-day planning period; it remains the same throughout the period regardless of the quantity of freight shipped. The result is a dependable daily service at a fixed cost that the wholesalers and retailers know in advance. For Drug Transport, the arrangement means guaranteed revenue and stable operations for route planning and equipment scheduling.

Another feature of these arrangements is the cooperation they engender that replaces the sometimes adversarial stance separating buyers and sellers. Many of these relationships endure for five or more years, and many operate with informal understandings rather than formal contracts. The level of involvement of specialists ranges from the routine services they perform as a matter of course to complete responsibility for the logistics requirements of a customer or a customer's unit. Informal partnerships are common in the transport sector. For instance, CenTra, Inc.'s Central Transport Division provides time-phased delivery of components and parts to General Motors's BOC Group plants in Lansing, Michigan. No specialized equipment is needed, and the arrangement is subject to annual review. At the other end of the spectrum is the long-term contract between NYK Line (Nippon Yusen Kaisha) and Pioneer Electronic, whereby NYK is handling all logistics aspects, from importing to customer distribution of mixed shipments of products, from a network of over one million square feet of warehouse space in the Los Angeles area.

Often these compacts call for the service provider to perform highly customized activity. Not long ago, Southern Bonded Warehouse agreed to combine U.S.-made bubble gum and Portuguese-made soccer balls into a point-of-sale promotion package. The Georgia company had to (1) take three pounds of gum from a bulk container, weigh it, and put it in a heat-sealed, tamperproof package; (2) inflate and inspect the soccer ball; (3) place the gum bag in the ball box; (4) place the ball on top of the box and stretch-wrap the package; and (5) put a certain number of units in a master carton and label and seal it. In these alliances, the service provider usually assumes a certain amount of risk through an agreement calling for a penalty, such as an automatic reduction in revenues, when performance is poorer than specified. On the other hand, the agreements often include rewards for superior performance, such as a greater than expected percentage of on-time delivery. As indicated, the risk also may include a capital investment on the provider's part.

Sometimes, however, the synergy obtained involves less risk for one of the partners. Owens-Corning Fibreglas, to boost productivity and gain competitive advantage, has taken on some tasks that traditionally are the carriers' burden. Once a trucker delivers ready-to-use trailers to an Owens-Corning plant, its on-site responsibility ends. The manufacturer positions the trailers at docks and does the loading according to destination. Timing shipments for off-peak traffic periods helps to cut cost and boost driver productivity. The over-the-road movement direct from Owens-Corning plants to customer construction sites avoids costly pickup and origin terminal routing cost. Gaining lower operating costs and predictable equipment location, the carriers can reduce their freight rates. They share the savings with Owens-Corning. For the manufacturer, however, the great benefit is the competitive advantage it gains by supplying dependable job-site delivery within very tight time windows. The benefits of these alliances are tangible enough and often big enough to attract quite a few players—many of them strangers to the logistics service industry. A very fast-growing segment of the field is the fulfillment or full-support company that specializes in turnkey services, from order processing to customer order delivery. By the mid-1990s, such value-added logistics business is expected to surpass $20 billion in volume. A few of these integrated providers pursuing full-service work are Roadway Logistics, Trammell Crow Distribution Corporation, KLS Logistics, CSL Logistics (part of CSX), USCO, Itel Distribution Systems, and Caterpillar Logistics Services.

FORCES OF IMPETUS

What accounts for this surge of enterprise in an activity that has often been a corporate stepchild? Among the multiplicity of forces creating a favorable environment for logistics alliances, four dominate.

1. The political-legal terrain of the 1980s stimulated the development of integrated service practices. Deregulation of transportation and communications, coupled with relaxed antitrust enforcement—intended to give productivity a charge—generated an atmosphere conducive to innovation. Washington is looking benignly at business alliances as long as they do not inhibit the prevailing level of competition in end-user markets. The National Cooperative Research Act of 1984, permitting some cooperation among competitors, is being construed to apply to logistics coalitions.
2. The explosion in information technology has made computerization cheap, and computers hold logistics alliances together. Schneider National, for example, has put satellite communications in all its over-the-road trucks so it can keep real-time track of vehicle location and on-board shipment data from headquarters in Wisconsin. Other late technological advances, like cellular phones, laser-based bar codes, and radio frequency transmissions, are in standard use at diverse haulers like Roadway, UPS, the Union Pacific Railroad, and Sea-Land.
3. Today's emphasis on leaner organization makes managers more likely to turn to external specialists to solve problems or perform tasks outside the organization's sphere of expertise. The objective of competing more effectively—through greater asset utilization, higher leverage, and faster responsiveness—is a prime stimulant towards logistics collaboration.
4. An escalating competitive environment forces the players to do all they can to become lowest cost competitors. Efficiency in logistics is particularly important for companies that are doing business abroad. Distribution costs, as a percentage of revenue, are greater for

international companies than for their domestic counterparts. Complexity, long order lead times, unusual product-service requirements, and differing legal and cultural factors in foreign countries combine to create a much more challenging operating environment. Consequently, headquarters is willing to use qualified external support.

STRATEGIC VISION

For companies successful with logistics partnerships, a common factor overriding all others is a recognition that this business activity is an important part of marketing strategy. Product, promotion, and price are the traditional competitive ingredients, while time and place competencies have taken a back seat. That relative neglect is changing. Those companies forming alliances are seeking to exploit their logistical competencies—not weaknesses. During the course of conducting research into the practices of more than 1,000 manufacturers, retailers, and wholesalers, it was clearly shown that some companies stand head and shoulders above their competitors in logistics performance, and they use this superiority to gain and keep customer loyalty. Superiority over the competition means placing a premium on being easy to do business with. All top managers "feel" they know what customers want. But fewer than one out of five companies establish rigid customer service standards, regularly measure performance to standards, or systematically digest feedback to improve operations.

Logistically speaking, being easy to do business with means that suppliers meet commitments and shipments arrive when and where promised. When problems crop up, progressive companies develop work-arounds that smoothly take care of the difficulty. Most noteworthy is the way that top performers use electronically conveyed information to gain competitive advantage. They specialize in eliminating surprises and in providing same-call responses to customer inquiries. Strategic vision, however, calls for more than readiness to serve the customer; it calls for a willingness to offer extra, value-adding services. The object, of course, is to become a preferred supplier of key customers. Companies committed to strategic use of logistics usually outperform the competition in speed and consistency of order cycle. They normally have standards they intend customers to rely on and expect employees to adhere to. For Federal Express, the standard is delivery of all premium-service packages within 24 hours.

Often difficult to apply, reasonable but effective standards are also not always easy to set. A product marketer may feel comfortable promising the trade a 95 per cent case-fill rate, supported by a five- to seven-day delivery that it expects to achieve 98 per cent of the time. This goal, even if met, means that at least 5 per cent of customers will always be disappointed in what they receive and at least 2 per cent in when they receive it. Such statistically based performance, while once acceptable, does not fit a business strategy based on just-in-time or quick-response inventory replenishment.

A shrewd marketer will strive not only to consistently deliver complete orders to customers at the time and location requested but also to expand the scope and upgrade the level of service to keep a customer's loyalty. At Atlanta-based Genuine Parts, the logistics staff is authorized to procure a critical out-of-stock part from a competitor rather than fail to deliver a key customer's order. Leading companies recognize that while perfection in service may be unattainable, a culture based on an acceptable rate of failure will fail. By developing a high level of standard performance, they reduce the number of less-than-standard situations that have to be resolved. Moreover, high-quality logistics service compliance is almost invariably less expensive than a procedure based on an expected percentage of failure that demands frequent correction.

The drive to secure and hold customers reaches its peak in the leveraging of resources in the form of strategic alliances. Procter and Gamble, with its outstanding product supply network, can divert a customer's shipment from a warehouse directly to a store on short notice. Drug wholesalers Bergen Brunswig, McKesson, and Alco Health Services offer their customers complete electronic inventory replenishment and merchandising control. Wal-Mart Stores has alliances with important suppliers of merchandise through which they manage their inventory levels and resupply in Wal-Mart warehouses. In these alliances, specialization through a dedicated resource base generates economies of scale. For example, Dauphin Distribution Services Company, a warehouse specialist, can furnish consolidated inbound delivery for Shaw's Supermarkets. In a single truck, Shaw's outlet gets a mix of products from a combination of suppliers. Similarly, Continental Freezers of Illinois provides inbound staging and frozen food assortment service for Jewel Food Stores supermarkets. Normal distribution arrangements are more expensive and much less efficient.

The spread of risk is another attraction of these ventures; meshed operations between a product marketer and a service provider offer what amounts to risk insurance. Not only is the chance of error much less because each party is focusing on its specialty but also the partners share the consequences of failure if the compact includes performance guarantees. In the Hermosillo plant situation, Ford, American President Companies, and the four railroads share the risk. The synergy stimulated by the joint effort can create a coalition of great strength. One reason for the synergy is the focus generated by a reduction in suppliers by the product marketer and a limit on the service provider's number of customers (normal by-products of an alliance). Once focused, the two organizations often begin to seek growth opportunities for each other—to their mutual benefit. The fact that each views the logistics process from a different vantage point inspires creativity.

WHAT THEY BRING TO THE PARTY?

Because the core business of an enterprise is the focal point or target of the logistics partnership, the players must be economically and managerially strong. The typical alliance is a long-term arrangement that is expected to survive the fluctuations characteristic of most businesses. To support an alliance, the service provider and marketer must have the staying power to weather the downs as well as exploit the ups. To justify using customized logistics services, the marketer needs an opportunity with a key customer or in a niche market for a rich return in market share improvement or competitive superiority. For Wal-Mart, the criterion is the volume of potential business at stake. Moreover, the potential supplier's technological sophistication must be advanced enough to permit direct electronic connection with Wal-Mart's satellite communications network. Otherwise, sharing the assortment of information required to make the alliance work is impractical. As I have noted, information sharing is the glue that holds these ventures together. Synchronization of activities and progress towards shared goals require open disclosure, from operating details to strategic planning. Technology has kept pace to provide such capability. Some service providers have full-disclosure information systems in place.

Systems are available that permit real-time tracking of shipments at case-level or stockkeeping-unit detail throughout the distribution process. In some instances, as at Skyway Freight and Systems, a traffic manager wanting to know the projected arrival time can get a computer screen view of the in-transit status of a shipment. Estimated time of arrival (ETA) projections supply the information for evaluating the cost versus benefit of expediting a shipment to meet a required delivery time. Such in-transit control is a feature of a double-stack container service, operated by the Union Pacific Railroad and American President Companies, that links Pacific Rim garment manufacturers with the interior of North America. The service offers containerized delivery of goods on hangers that are size-and colour-sequenced to particular retailers' specifications before loading in Asia.

To perform effectively, each partner must operate on two levels. One level is performance of a specified role in a well-understood operating domain. The logistics process may take place across an enormous geographical playing field in what amounts to a 24-hour, 7-day-a-week, 52-week-a-year engagement. There is no room for ambiguity regarding who is responsible for doing what. Effectiveness depends on near error-free task completion and meshing of tasks.

The meshing of tasks is the second level of operation. Each party must see its assignment in terms of its contribution to the alliance and the way it adds value for customers. Otherwise, it may develop role myopia. The service provider and the marketer have to understand each other's culture. The provider must appreciate the value system that drives the marketer's decision-making process. The marketer must grasp how the provider approaches the marketer's business. (Cultural absorption admittedly gets tricky when a service provider is simultaneously engaged in multiple alliances.) A grasp of the whole distribution channel is necessary but sometimes difficult, especially for service providers. Moving damaged goods or product recalls back to the source is a headache for retailers and wholesalers. On their part, manufacturers do not want damaged goods for which they have already given credit to reappear on sale somewhere. The carrier, if it is not considering the entire channel, might treat its partners' serious concerns too lightly.

Robin Transport's understanding of GM's parts delivery needs and of the total distribution channel led the Lansing, Michigan company to an innovation that benefited all parties. Robin designed trailers with fabric walls that made the trailers capable of being unloaded from the sides as well as from the rear. The trailers could load and unload in places where the standard trailer could not go, and they could be unloaded from three sides at once, near points of assembly. Robin loads the trailers in sequence for ease of components handling and delivers at certain specified times when GM is ready to take the shipments. To justify its investment in special handling equipment in the trailers and the dedication of part of its over-the-road fleet, Robin sought and got status as a preferred carrier at a premium rate. GM set up its production assembly to benefit from the different mode of materials handling. The manufacturer benefited from Robin's understanding of the distribution channel by realizing productivity improvement through inventory reduction, JIT delivery, and more efficient materials handling.

The hallmark of these ventures is cooperation. An effective way to signal willingness to work together is to establish ground rules at the outset. These rules should include a procedure for conflict resolution so that any friction that arises is smoothed over before it harms the arrangement. Negotiation of roles before operations start, with clear ground rules for the parties, helps perpetuate alliance longevity. Even so, partnerships often evolve or are modified for good reasons, especially changing business conditions. Signal Freight's operation that supports the Sears-Whirlpool alliance has shifted significantly over the years to accommodate the customers. Sears's recent decision to stock a variety of national-brand appliances (its "Brand Central" promotion) has meant one more adjustment for this Leaseway Transportation Division.

A provision allowing for changed circumstances, negotiated before startup, is especially important for the service provider, since in a typical logistics alliance the marketing organization holds the power. Carriers and other service providers have usually been at the mercy of product marketers because transportation can always be purchased on a trip-by-trip basis and warehouse agreements can be limited to 30-day commitments. Provision for an exit from the agreement is a sensitive matter, but in fairness to the service provider it should be negotiated. (Where special-purpose equipment or facilities are involved, it is the practice to incorporate buy-sell agreements in the alliance documents.)

Exel Logistics, a subsidiary of the U.K.-based conglomerate NFC, has rules regarding this issue. It requires that all contracts signed by Exel affiliates include a framework outlining the dissolution procedure and an agenda of exit negotiation items. Although several of these contracts have operating horizons of a decade or more, Exel management is convinced that such a framework is essential to establish a sound platform for the alliance up front and that, in fact, spelling everything out strengthens the relationship.

WHY ALLIANCES FAIL?

While simulation of alternatives is sometimes possible, many operations represent a leap of faith; the parties are obliged to forge ahead, full of hope. When Procter and Gamble decided to consolidate its West Coast distribution facilities into one giant 400,000-plus square-foot facility in Sacramento, the company obviously could not test the idea.

Without the benefit of complete information, P and G and its warehouse partner hammered out agreements concerning goals, expected benefits, and contingent responsibilities. The warehouse installation proceeded without major problems. Such a plunge into the unknown complicates the all-important business of establishing relationships and developing a clear vision of mutual expectations. In such situations, the managers involved often are simply incapable of overcoming the limits of their different cultures. Given people's natural resistance to change, it is reasonable to expect clashes of culture and styles when employees of two or more companies commence working together towards common objectives. Often they are working side by side more or less permanently.

Developing the trust that makes the alliance work requires an open door and an open mind. This attitude is not easy for managers schooled in an adversarial tradition. For example, the belief that carriers and warehouse-based service companies promote the alliance concept as a subterfuge for selling the same old service is widespread among shipper executives. (One category of service providers actually tries to exploit this suspicion.

The entry strategy of Global Logistics Venture, a joint venture of AMR and CSX, calls for provision of information technology to coordinate the purchase of services from a number of specialists, in contrast to actual provision of the services.) In the traditional kind of negotiation of a service agreement, the tone is adversarial and the parties rely on a host of competitive checks and balances to ensure buyers that they are getting a good deal. In an alliance, trust has to substitute for many of the perceived benefits of competitive bidding. The partners' reluctance to share ideas can abort an agreement, once entered into, if they also have to share information they consider to be confidential. Then how do you build trust in situations where no track record exists? One way to resolve this dilemma is through a procedure used by Union Pacific Logistics for building trust progressively during the evaluation and negotiation of an alliance. The instrument is a facilitator acceptable to all the parties and connected with none of them.

This person tries to put the negotiations on an objective basis by acting as the neutral focal point during the bargaining. As the alliance matures, trust level and operational success become inseparable. Failure to develop trust during the early stages spells trouble. One supplier of multiple logistics services recently ended negotiations with a consortium of shippers because the supplier decided that the group was not truly seeking a total system solution for their joint requirements. Early on, the supplier became convinced that the consortium was really trying to leverage its purchasing power to get a low price from the supplier, and so trust never developed.

As in this case, the reality is that one of the parties usually has more at stake than the others. There is often an imbalance of power as well. The result: uneven commitment to the welfare of the arrangement. Sometimes an alliance is forged at high levels of the companies involved, but little attention is paid to getting the lower echelons, which will be charged to make it work, to sign on. The middle managers who play a key role in the operation may see the prospects as jeopardizing their careers, particularly if their areas of expertise become the focus of outsourcing. Moreover, if they remain unacquainted with the goals of the programme, they may perceive the objective as simply to cut costs. Why then, they say, throw out the old, proven techniques? Why do we need all these people from the other company around?

But business cannot be operations as usual under the umbrella of a logistics alliance. At one retailer, a warehouse traditionally granted delivery appointments no earlier than 24 hours in advance, and then on a first-come, first-unloaded basis. The practice frustrated a fully integrated, quick-response inventory replenishment system arranged with a carrier. Dedicated equipment loaded with time-sensitive merchandise was left undelivered at the warehouse. In traditional operations, it is unnecessary to separate ownership from control. But in an alliance, the separation has to be part of daily practice because ownership spreads across the joint process and at all the levels concerned. Control is recognized in a framework of interorganizational operating principles expressing what the alliance is supposed to do and how it will get done. Included are measures to be taken by each party when things go wrong, as they inevitably will.

The operating framework will falter if it omits mutually accepted yardsticks for gauging performance and progress. Conflict will arise if all the parties do not fully understand the score. The appropriate accounting for total costs and asset-driven activity is not easy to establish when two or more organizations are involved. From a service supplier's viewpoint, the key to accurate measurement may be an understanding of the client's critical business success factors. For example, price margins based on average cost have little, if any, usefulness in specialized service situations. In an alliance, selling margins may be much lower but utilization of assets much higher. Bergen Brunswig recently reported a sharp improvement in pretax income despite big gross margin reductions. This improvement comes from a disciplined approach to distribution and an improved return on net assets produced by alliances with druggists.

For a product marketer, the major benefit of an alliance could be as basic as improved reliability. The partners must see to it that measurement of this factor gets translated into numbers that can be put on paper and compared with some prior period. The reliability improvement may start with the fact that the same truck drivers are visiting key customers continually and thus forming relationships with them. Eventually this intangible gets translated into something more tangible and thus measurable.

MAKING A PARTNERSHIP WORK

Logistics alliances are making U.S. industry more efficient and thus more competitive. Logistics costs in 1990 are expected to exceed $525 billion, or about 10.5 per cent of GNP. In 1981, the proportion was 15.4 per cent. In terms of comparative assets to GNP, the distribution system is operating this year on $100 billion less average inventory than it did in 1981. Some of these improvements can be attributed to logistics partnerships. While cost reductions are, of course, very desirable, they are not an end in themselves. The main rationale for orchestrating an alliance is to increase competitive advantage. As one executive put it, "For us, the reason for this venture is market impact. Cost reduction is important but secondary."

To make a partnership work, experience provides these guidelines:

- View the arrangement as the implementation of a strategic plan. Encourage the participants involved to consider their roles in terms of a value-added process.
- Seek an arrangement that achieves scale-economy benefits while spreading risk.
- Recognizing that the benefits can be gained only through a long-term relationship in which the parties are interdependent, make sure that the information necessary to function well is shared between them.
- Build trust between the organizations by setting unambiguous goals, establishing clear roles, laying down firm rules, and measuring performance rigourously.
- Start the venture on a realistic course by acknowledging that eventually the alliance may have to be terminated.

LOGISTICS PLANNING PROCESS

Proper logistics planning entails considering logistical aspects throughout the various stages of the procurement process. It contributes to efficient procurement processes, and reduces the risk of incurring problems that may lead to additional costs and delay. Logistics planning starts at the needs assessment phase of procurement by considering the desired result of the requisitioner and the end-user and from there working backwards to determine what will lead to a successful completion of the activity. Ideally this process should begin even before the requisition is placed, through close cooperation and efficient communication between the operational unit requesting the purchase and procurement officers.

The aspects of logistics planning that should be considered during the various stages of the procurement process (planning, requirement definition, sourcing, and evaluation) are detailed below:

- Understanding the operational context of the required product, and, if possible, assist in developing specifications suitable to local conditions.
- Evaluating the procurement activity and the time and financial resources available in order to determine urgency of the requirement. Urgency may determine location of the purchase and thereby also the mode of transport.
- Determining the type of sourcing.
- Goods may be purchased locally/regionally or internationally, or through established LTAs. However, in some organizations, goods may also already be available in a warehouse, as surplus stock from another project, or in pipeline already purchased for another purpose, but available for diversion in order to cover a more urgent need. Goods may even be borrowed from a sister organization, or be available as a donation in kind.
- Goods may also have been pre-positioned as part of an emergency stockpile policy, either globally, regionally or on a local level. These options should be considered when determining whether to purchase, and how and where to purchase, the required product, in order to meet end-user's needs in a timely and cost efficient manner.
- Determining which markets are best positioned to respond to the end-user's delivery requirements by evaluating total delivered costs as well as lead times, in addition to conformity with technical criteria, for example, tractors from one region are not necessarily the most suitable for another region, even though they may be very competitive and reasonably priced.
- There is usually a trade off between the purchase price of a product and their transport costs and delivery lead-time. The relative

importance of these factors will determine where the goods are purchased and how they are transported. It should be noted that geographic distance does not necessarily determine the cost and delivery time. Trade lanes and feeder vessels will have an impact.

- Accepting a more expensive offer in order to conform to the requested delivery date should be carefully assessed and discussed with the requisitioner and end-user in order to ensure the most effective use of funds. When the delivery date is the primary factor in awarding a contract, it should be clearly stated in the solicitation document. In such a case, any offer not in compliance with the requested delivery schedule must be rejected.
- Reviewing the delivery and transport requirements, as well as the budget, and ensuring that they are complete and realistic.
- The cost of transportation is a significant component in the cost of goods procured and delivered to the designated site. Procurement officers should therefore ensure proper logistics planning in making every effort to keep the transportation costs down. However, in logistics planning, the cheapest alternative may not always be the one that offers the lowest overall cost.
- A low-cost, but poor delivery strategy may result in delays, damaged or stolen goods, excessive port charges, etc. All factors should therefore be assessed when choosing the appropriate logistical solution.
- Determining and comparing total lead time, including logistics activities. Different logistics corridors incur different costs, but also have an impact on total lead times. One route may, for example, be cheaper but experiences many difficulties and delays in clearing transit goods. An alternate route may cut transport time. In some source countries, for example, export processing may take longer, or ports may experience much congestion. Total supply chain lead times should be taken into account.
- Determining the most cost effective means of contracting transport, *i.e.* from the supplier included in the purchase order, or contracted to independent freight forwarder. Some organizations also allow transportation with their own resources (*e.g.* transportation of goods in project vehicles by project personnel).
- Tendering for freight services, if determined under aspect number 6 listed above, and checking availability and competitiveness of an LTA for freight services. For large consignments where more favourable rates can possibly be obtained, spot tenders are advisable.
- Insuring a consignment in accordance with the policy of the organization.

- Ensuring that shipping documents received from the supplier and freight forwarder are complete and accurate and that the consignee has received their set.
- Ensuring that necessary arrangements are in place to clear cargo on arrival. Depending upon the procedures in the country, the consignee could be responsible for custom clearance of the goods, however, customs clearance is part of the procurement procedure, and thus the responsibility of procurement officers.
- Arrange for acceptance of goods on arrival by the receiving unit and ensure that claims are initiated within the time frame stipulated in the cargo insurance to secure the interests of the organization in the case of missing or damaged cargo.
- Obtaining acknowledgement from consignee that the shipment has been received in good order.
- Throughout this process, the requisitioner and/or end-user should be kept informed of expected and actual delivery dates in order for them to account for it in their local planning.

LOGISTICS REQUIREMENTS FOR GOODS

The following logistical requirements should be considered for the shipment of goods:

- Packing and containerization
- Packing and shipping instructions
- Labelling and shipping marks
- Modes of transportation
- Forwarding agents
- Incoterms
- Insurance during transportation
- Shipping documents
- Receipt of consignment.

PACKING

The nature of the goods together with the mode of shipment and the climatic conditions during transit and at the destination, determine the required packaging. The durability, size and weight of the packages should be considered in relation to the planned means of transportation. It should be ensured that the equipment, warehouse facilities, operators and labourers involved in the shipment of the goods have the capacity to handle the goods in the chosen packaging. For instance, some port facilities can only handle 20ft containers so 40ft containers should not be used. Further, axle weight road restrictions should be considered for certain road shipments and maximum vessel draught allowed for shallow ports, etc.

Climatic conditions both at the end destination, but also in transit, should be considered to ensure the packaging can withstand heat, cold, rain, humidity, mould, dust, salt water spray, etc., if required. Certain types of goods require a constant temperature and air shipment, cold chain equipment and temperature monitoring. To be on the safe side, always assume that shipments will be handled roughly and loaded and offloaded numerous times before reaching the final destination.

Containerization

Unless the goods are shipped in 20 foot/40 foot containers, the organization should specify that it should be shipped below deck in order to avoid damages during transport (*e.g.* risks of rust, humidity, etc.). Containerization could be considered for extra protection and to handle the shipment more effectively, however, this may increase cost. If containers are used, it is recommended to try to make full use of space and ship only full containers in order to save costs, as the rate for shipment usually does not depend on weight. The use of LCL (less than container load) containers that consolidates consignments from different clients, will expose the shipment to the risks of abuse and delays if one or several consignments should experience difficulties in clearing customs. Further, small consignments risk hanging around for weeks in order to make up a full container load. It is therefore recommended, where possible, to plan loads that fill the container. It should be noted that containerization will not reduce the need for appropriate packing, as part of the journey usually takes place outside of the container. Containers have the following approximate size, volume and payload (note sizes can vary slightly depending on the manufacturer).

Dimensions	20 ft container	40 ft container
Inner length	5.90 m	12.02 m
Inner width	2.33 m	2.33 m
Inner height	2.21 m	2.21 m
Door width	2.30 m	2.30 m
Door height	2.14 m	2.21 m
Payload (approx.)	18-19.5 metric tons	28 metric tons

There are different types of containers, which can be used depending on the size and type of products to be shipped as described in the table below:

Container type	Features
Dry	Most common type of container.
Open top	No hard top.
Flat racks	No top and no sides.
Refrigerated	For the transport of perishable items.
Super	Higher than standard dry type containers.

Packing and Shipping Instructions

Standard packing and shipping instructions are documents specifying how the goods are to be packed and shipped, and who to notify upon shipment. They list all the documents required for customs clearance and for payment purposes. Packing and shipping instructions should form part of all purchase orders. The packing and shipping instructions are linked to the Incoterms used. Procurement officers should refer to the standard documents available in the organization.

Labelling and Shipping Marks

To facilitate the identification of goods and handling whilst in transit, suppliers should be instructed to provide clear and complete labelling and shipping marks on all packages.

The labelling and shipping marks should include:

- Consignee
- Destination
- Port of unloading
- Project identification
- Order number
- Case number.

Contents of the packages should not be included to discourage theft and pilferage.

Modes of Transport

Four basic modes of freight transportation are used, either individually or in combination: sea, rail, road, and air. Procurement officers should consider both economy and efficiency when choosing the mode of transport. In general, rail, road and air transport costs are comparatively higher than freight by sea, thus in general sea transport is recommended. Maritime freight typically counts for 15-20 percent of the costs of the goods, and airfreight may represent up to 100 percent.

International shipments by sea average three to five weeks (but can be considerably longer), while air shipments usually take less then a week. The balance of operational parameters such as time and financial resources should determine the mode of transportation.

Procurement officers should prioritize transport preferences in accordance with the following criteria:

1. The cheapest means of transport that meets delivery requirements.
2. Scheduling through the fewest number of trans-shipment points.
3. Shipping via preferred trans-shipment points and customs.
4. Using dedicated freight forwarders wherever possible.
5. Applying a 1:4 ratio rule for air shipment (ship by air if less than 25 percent of cost of goods).

6. Shipping by air if weight is less than 200 kg.
7. Shipping by air when a cold chain is required.
8. Shipping by land or sea if dangerous goods are involved.

Finally, procurement officers should make a prioritized list of all technically feasible solutions.

If a priority solution falls within the pre-defined budgetary framework, the plan should be executed. If the best solutions fall outside the framework or if no solution is feasible, procurement officers should present the existing options to the requesting operational unit and ask for a decision.

FORWARDING AGENTS

Forwarding agents, also known as freight forwarders or freight brokers, are contracted by the UN organization or the supplier to carry out the formalities and operations of consignment. The forwarding agent can also be employed by the organization to receive goods where UN staff members may not be physically present in order to engage in the prompt clearance and collection of goods vulnerable to loss or pilferage. The use of an appropriate freight forwarder reduces the risk of the procurement operation, since part of the risk is transferred from the organization to the selected forwarding agent. Further, the choice of an appropriate forwarder in itself reduces risk due to the forwarder's experience and specialized knowledge. Procurement officers should ensure that the respective forwarding agent has all necessary documents for the release of goods in transit.

INCOTERMS

Incoterms (The International Commerce Terms) are standard terms defining the obligations of both the buyer and seller relating to the shipment of goods. They are used world wide in both international and local trading. Incoterms have been established by the International Chamber of Commerce (ICC).

The clear definition of trade terms reduces the risk of misunderstanding and, as the ICC offers an arbitration service, their interpretation is widely accepted. Incoterms 2000 should govern shipment terms of all contracts and reference to an appropriate Incoterm should be made in all contracts requiring shipment. The Incoterm should always refer to a named place (city, country, etc.). Procurement officers need to be familiar with Incoterms in order to understand the division of responsibilities and risks between the buyer and the seller. Further information can be sought through the ICC web site at www.iccwbo.org.

Use of Incoterms

The table below lists the Incoterms most commonly used by UN organizations, and in which situations they should be used:

Term	For...
FCA (Free Carrier)	International procurement where the supplier of the goods does not arrange transportation.
CPT (Carriage Paid To)	International procurement where the supplier arranges transportation.
DDU (Delivery Duty Unpaid)	Local procurement use. International procurement where the UN organization elects the supplier to bear all risks and costs associated with the transport of goods to the country of destination. However, considering the very good all-risk insurance coverage offered under the insurance programme negotiated globally by various UN organizations, it is highly recommended to purchase CPT for all international procurement and have the goods insured under the global insurance programme of the organization. Note: DDU for international procurement is justified in very few countries where the insurance programme does not provide full coverage (e.g. it excludes war risk).

Note: All the terms referred to above should be followed by the name of the destination point (for example CPT Baku, Azerbaijan).

INSURANCE DURING TRANSPORTATION

During transportation and storage, all cargo is vulnerable to a range of risks, such as damage, pilferage and theft, breakage, non-receipt of part of or an entire consignment. Cargo insurance provides protection against potential financial losses resulting from such risks. It is important to ensure protection for goods subject to risks, including war, strikes, riots and civil commotion. Further, the duration of insurance coverage should be sufficient for the period of transportation, from warehouse to warehouse, including storage at the destination site. Goods are insured for the cost, insurance and freight value plus an agreed percentage to reflect the indirect cost of replacing goods.

In view of the above, most UN organizations have negotiated a global cargo insurance contract that all offices are encouraged to use. The insurance is usually an all-risk insurance with world wide coverage with the exception of war risk. War risk can be covered by an extra premium (sea and air transport). War risk on land is often a different coverage and might have to be contracted separately. Procurement officers should consult whoever is responsible within an organization for more information on the coverage, if in doubt. In the event of a claim, or event likely to give rise to a claim, notice should be given as early as possible, following the internal procedures of the organization. Note that insurance policies might have short deadlines for submission of claims.

SHIPPING DOCUMENTS

Complete and appropriate shipping documents are of critical importance for the timely delivery of goods. The supplier needs documents to move the order from its premises, and to receive payment from the buyer. The freight forwarder requires documents to contract carriage, the consignee requires documents to claim the goods at arrival, and the consignee or notify party requires documents to handle customs clearance. Each stage of the shipment generates documents that may even be required once the equipment is in the country, for instance to register a vehicle or radio equipment. The exact contents of a set of shipping documents depend on the type of goods being shipped, the means of transport, who is shipping the goods (freight forwarder, supplier, etc.), and any special requirements of the receiving country.

While the particular documents required vary from case to case, every shipment should have documented evidence of:

- Contents of the shipment
- Weight and volume of contents
- Origin of goods (if required)
- Price of the goods
- Evidence of transport of the goods.

The following shipping documents are common to all shipments:

Shipping document	Purpose
Bill of Lading (B/L) (for sea shipment) Waybill (other modes of transport)	• The contract of carriage between the shipper and the carrier, indicating how goods are being shipped and when they will arrive. • Evidences that the carrier has received the goods for shipment, and is conclusive evidence that the goods were shipped as stated. • Documents ownership to the goods specified (a document of title). It is recommended to specify that the B/L be marked 'clean on board and freight prepaid' (especially when using the CPT Incoterm).
Commercial Invoices and Pro Forma Invoices	• Describes the goods and indicates their value. • Proves the value of the goods.
Packing lists	Describes the content, total number of packing units, markings, weight and volume of each unit.
Certificates of Origin	• Indicates the country of origin or manufacture of the goods and are always issued by a local Chamber of Commerce. • Required for importation and also used for statistical purposes.
Gift Certificate	• Replaces the commercial invoice and certificate of origin in the case of goods from warehouse or in-kind donations. • Proves the value of the goods.
Additional documents required when using a freight forwarder	
Forwarder's Certificate of Receipt	Proof that the supplier has handed over goods to the freight forwarder.
Freight Invoice	Indicates shipping details and charges.
Additional documents	
Certificates certifying quality	• May be required to certify quality. • Usually provided by the supplier.

Responsibility

The supplier or the freight forwarder (depending on who is organising the transport) is responsible for consolidating the shipping documents received, and should be instructed to courier one original set of documents to the consignee and the remaining two sets to the procuring entity. Documents should be checked to ensure that all information is correct and consistent in all the documents. Further, procurement officers should ensure that the documents have been received by the consignee.

Terms Used in Shipping Documents

The following terms are frequently used in shipping documents:

CONSIGNEE

The consignee is the receiver of the goods, usually, but not necessarily, an office of a UN organization. The consignee may be, but is not necessarily, identical to the delivery address. The consignee should always receive a copy of the shipping documents. The consignee may take care of customs clearance and other government formalities upon the request of the individual responsible for the procurement activity in question, however this may also be handled by a notify party. Consignee details, such as address, country, name, phone/fax, e-mail, and contact person should be included in the purchase order and in the labelling of the packages.

NOTIFY PARTY

A notify party may be engaged by procurement officers (or the consignee) in order to arrange customs clearance of goods and other government formalities. In such case, shipping documents are also to be forwarded to the notify party.

DELIVERY ADDRESS/FINAL DESTINATION

The delivery address or final destination is the address of the end-user where the goods are to be physically delivered.

RECEIPT OF CONSIGNMENTS

When a consignment is delivered to the consignee, it is common practice for the carrier to request a receipt. At the same time, the consignee should perform a cursory inspection of packages against all shipping documents. If, in apparent good order, it is recommended that an endorsement be given (*e.g.* "received in good external condition – contents unchecked"). If, however, signs of tampering are visible, the receipt should state necessary reservations (*e.g.* "cases broken", "contents lacking", "cartons opened with signs of pilferage"). Where possible, packages should be weighed to determine differences between declared and actual weights, documenting any discrepancies on the delivery notes.

RESTRICTIONS ON THE EXPORT OR IMPORT OF GOODS

Exporting countries may restrict the shipment of certain classes of goods to certain countries or ban their export altogether. Equipment that has a dual civilian/military use or high-end computer and telecommunications technology are commonly considered. The procurement officer should be aware of these restrictions so that lead time required for authorisation can be calculated and the sourcing strategy modified if necessary. Importing countries may also impose restrictions. Telecommunications equipment and pharmaceuticals typically require prior authorisation from the concerned ministry who will issue a licence. Other equipment, such as used vehicles older than a certain age, may be banned outright. Some countries ban goods of certain origins for political reasons. Obtaining permits is generally a protracted exercise. The receiving office must confirm that it is in hand before the supplier is authorized to ship the goods. The likely consequence of shipping without the permit is that the receiver will be required to pay the cost of storage in the port and applicable liner charges until the authorisation is issued. There is also the considerable risk that the cargo will deteriorate or go missing during this period. There are also UN restrictions for countries.

4

Development Liner Service Network and Container Shipping

Container liner shipping has a relatively short history. In 1956 Malcolm McLean launched the first containership Ideal X. Ten years later the first transatlantic container service between the US East Coast and North Europe marked the real start of long distance scheduled container liner services. The first specialized cellular containerships were delivered in 1968. In the 1970s the containerization process expanded rapidly due to the adoption of standard container sizes and the awareness of industry players about the advantages and cost savings containerization brought (Rodrigue and Notteboom, 2009; Levinson, 2006). Although container shipping occupies a relatively minor share of the whole maritime fleet (about 12 per cent), it is the fastest growing sector and currently concentrates more than half of world trade value, regularly expanding to other commodities (*e.g.* neo bulks).

The world container traffic, the absolute number of containers being carried by sea, increased from 28.7 million TEU in 1990 to 152 million TEU in 2008 or an average annual increase of 9.5 per cent. Worldwide container port throughput increased from 36 million TEU in 1980 and 88 million TEU in 1990 to about 535 million TEU in 2008. A comparison between world container traffic and world container port throughput reveals a container on average was handled (loaded or discharged) 3.5 times between the first port of loading and the last port of discharge in 2008.

This figure amounted to 3 in 1990. The rise in the average number of port handlings per box is the result of more complex configurations in liner service networks as will be explained later in this chapter. Furthermore, the centre of gravity of these liner service networks has shifted to Asia. The dominance of Asia is reflected in world container port rankings. In 2009 fourteen of the twenty busiest container ports came from Asia, mainly from China. In the mid 1980s there were only six Asian ports in the top 20, mainly Japanese load centres. The emerging worldwide container shipping networks helped to reshape global supply chain practices and supported the globalization in production and consumption. New supply chain practices in turn increased the requirements on container shipping service networks in terms of frequency, schedule reliability/integrity, global coverage of services and rate setting.

This chapter analyses liner service networks as configured by container shipping lines. In a first section we discuss the drivers of and decision variables in liner service design as well as the different liner service types. A global snapshot of the worldwide liner shipping network based on vessel movement data. The changing geographic distribution of main inter-port links is explored in the light of recent reconfigurations of liner shipping networks. Third, we zoom in on the position of seaports in liner shipping networks referring to concepts of centrality, hierarchy, and selection factors. The chapter concludes by elaborating on the interactions and interdependencies between seaport development and liner shipping network development notably under current economic changes.

CONFIGURATION AND DESIGN OF LINER SHIPPING SERVICES

THE CONFIGURATION OF LINER SHIPPING SERVICES AND NETWORKS

Liner shipping networks are developed to meet the growing demand in global supply chains in terms of frequency, direct accessibility and transit times. Expansion of traffic has to be covered either by increasing the number of strings operated, or by vessel upsizing, or both. As such, increased cargo availability has triggered changes in vessel size, liner service schedules and in the structure of liner shipping.

When designing their networks, shipping lines implicitly have to make a trade-off between the requirements of the customers and operational cost considerations. A higher demand for service segmentation adds to the growing complexity of the networks. Shippers demand direct services between their preferred ports of loading and discharge. The demand side thus exerts a strong pressure on the service schedules, port rotations and feeder linkages. Shipping lines, however, have to design their liner services and networks in order to optimize ship utilization and benefit the most from scale economies in vessel size.

Their objective is to optimize their shipping networks by rationalizing coverage of ports, shipping routes and transit time (Zohil and Prijon, 1999; Lirn et al., 2004). Shipping lines may direct flows along paths that are optimal for the system, with the lowest cost for the entire network being achieved by indirect routing via hubs and the amalgamation of flows. However, the more efficient the network from the carrier's point of view, the less convenient that network could be for shippers' needs (Notteboom, 2006).

Bundling is one of the key drivers of container service network dynamics. The bundling of container cargo can take place at two levels: (1) bundling within an individual liner service and (2) bundling by combining/linking two or more liner services.

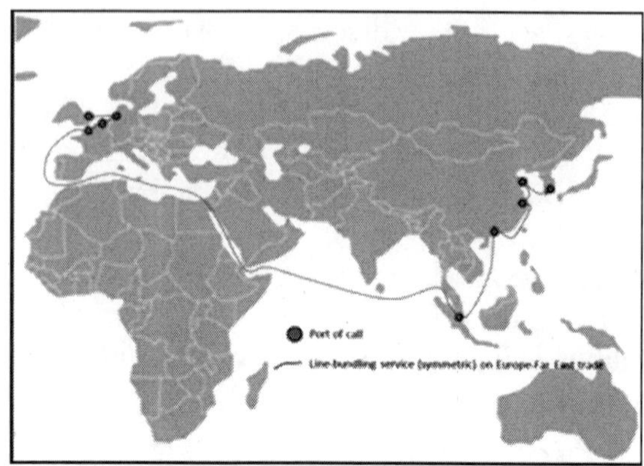

Fig. Bundling within an Individual Liner Service.

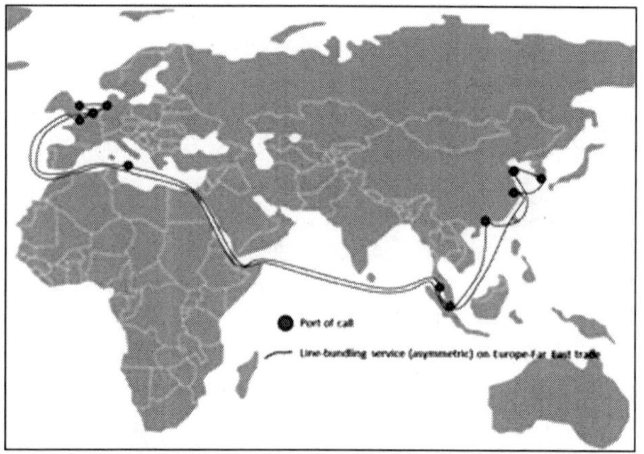

Fig. Line Bundling Service (Symmetric and Asymmetric).

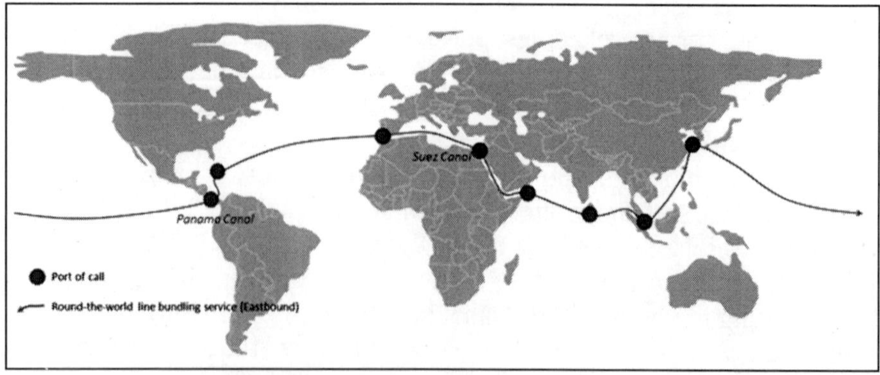

Fig. Round-the-World Service.

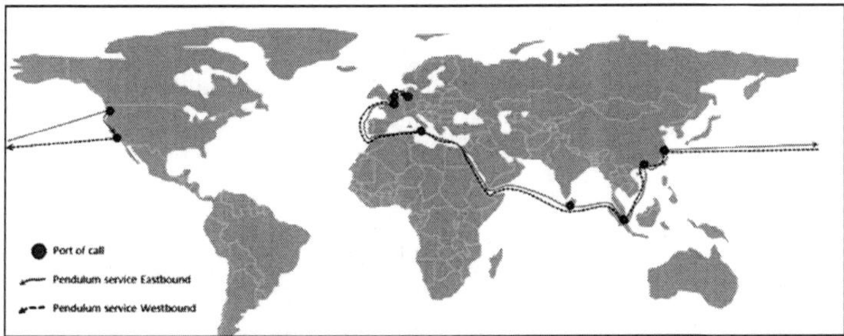

Fig. Pendulum Service.

The objective of bundling within an individual liner service is to collect container cargo by calling at various ports along the route instead of focusing on an end-to-end service. Such a line bundling service is conceived as a set of x roundtrips of y vessels each with a similar calling pattern in terms of the order of port calls and time intervals (*i.e.* frequency) between two consecutive port calls. By the overlay of these x roundtrips, shipping lines can offer a desired calling frequency in each of the ports of call of the loop (Notteboom, 2006). Line bundling operations can be symmetric (*i.e.* same ports of call for both sailing directions) or asymmetric (*i.e.* different ports of call on the way back). Most liner services are line bundling itineraries connecting between two and five ports of call scheduled in each of the main markets.

The Europe–Far East trade provides a good example. Most mainline operators and alliances running services from the Far East to North Europe stick to line bundling itineraries with direct calls scheduled in each of the main markets. Notwithstanding diversity in calling patterns on the observed routes, carriers select up to five regional ports of call per loop. Shipping lines have significantly increased average vessel sizes deployed on the route from around 4500 TEU in 2000 to over 8000 TEU in early 2011. These scale increases in vessel size have put a downward pressure on the average number of European port calls per loop on the Far East–North Europe trade: 4.9 ports of call in 1989, 3.84 in 1998, 3.77 in October 2000, 3.68 in February 2006, and 3.35 in December 2009. Two extreme forms of line bundling are round-the-world services and pendulum services.

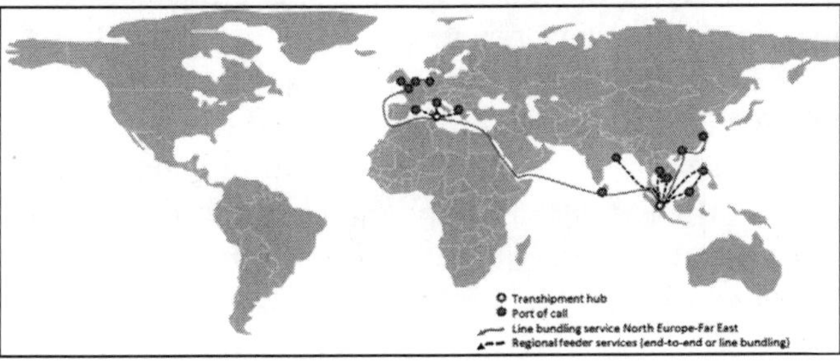

Fig. Bundling Container Cargo by Combining/Linking Two or More Liner Services. Hub/Feeder (Hub-and-Spoke) Network.

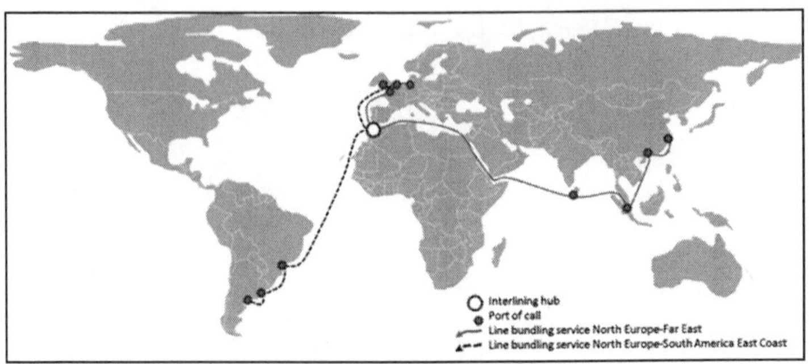

Fig. Interlining.

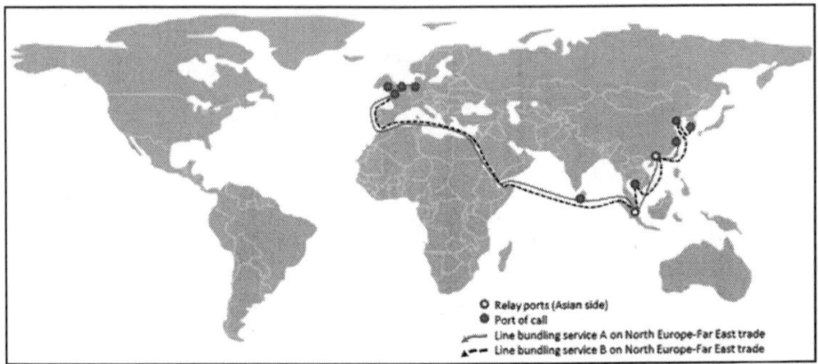

Fig. Relay.

The second possibility is to bundle container cargo by combining/linking two or more liner services. The three main bundling options in this category include a hub-and-spoke network (hub/feeder), interlining and relay. The establishment of global networks has given rise to hub port development at the crossing points of trade lanes. Intermediate hubs emerged since the mid-1990s within many global port systems: Freeport (Bahamas), Salalah (Oman), Tanjung Pelepas (Malaysia), Gioia Tauro, Algeciras, Taranto, Cagliari, Damietta and Malta in the Mediterranean, to name but a few. The role of intermediate hubs in maritime hub-and-spoke systems has been discussed extensively in recent literature.

The hubs have a range of common characteristics in terms of nautical accessibility, proximity to main shipping lanes and ownership, in whole or in part, by carriers or multinational terminal operators. Most of these intermediate hubs are located along the global beltway or equatorial round-the-world route (*i.e.* the Caribbean, Southeast and East Asia, the Middle East and the Mediterranean). These nodes multiply shipping options and improve connectivity within the network through their pivotal role in regional hub-and-spoke networks and in cargo relay and interlining operations between the carriers' east-west services and other inter- and intra-regional services. Container ports in Northern Europe, North America and mainland China mainly act as gateways to the respective hinterlands.

Two developments undermine the position of pure transhipment/interlining hubs (Rodrigue and Notteboom, 2010). First of all, the insertion of hubs often represents a temporary phase in connecting a region to global shipping networks. Hub-and-spoke networks would allow considerable economics of scale of equipment, but the cost efficiency of larger ships might be not sufficient to offset the extra feeder costs and container lift charges involved. Once traffic volumes for the gateway ports are sufficient, hubs are bypassed and become redundant. Secondly, transhipment cargo can easily be moved to new hub terminals that emerge along the long distance shipping lanes. The combination of these factors makes that seaports which are able to combine a transhipment function with gateway cargo obtain a less vulnerable and thus more sustainable position in shipping networks.

In channelling gateway and transhipment flows through their shipping networks, container carriers aim for control over key terminals in the network. Decisions on the desired port hierarchy are guided by strategic, commercial and operational considerations. Shipping lines rarely opt for the same port hierarchy in the sense that a terminal can be a regional hub for one shipping line and a secondary feeder port for another operator. For example, Antwerp in Belgium and Valencia in Spain are some of the main European hubs for Mediterranean Shipping Company (MSC) while they receive only few vessels from Maersk Line.

Zeebrugge and Algeciras are among the primary European ports of call in the service network of Maersk Line while these container ports are rather insignificant in the network of MSC.

The liner service configurations are often combined to form complex multi-layer networks. The advantages of complex bundling are higher load factors and/or the use of larger vessels in terms of TEU capacity and/or higher frequencies and/or more destinations served. Container service operators have to make a trade-off between frequency and volume on the trunk lines: smaller vessels allow meeting the shippers' demand for high frequencies and lower transit times, while larger units will allow operators to benefit from economies of vessel scale. The main disadvantages of complex bundling networks are the need for extra container handling at intermediate terminals and longer transport times and distances. Both elements incur additional costs and as such could counterbalance the cost advantages linked to higher load factors or the use of larger unit capacities.

Some have suggested that the most efficient east/west pattern is the equatorial round-the-world, following the beltway of the world (*e.g.* Ashar, 2002 and De Monie, 1997). This service pattern focuses on a hub-and-spoke system of ports that allows shipping lines to provide a global grid of east/west, north/south and regional services. The large ships on the east/west routes will call mainly at transhipment hubs where containers will be shifted to multi-layered feeder subsystems serving north/south, diagonal and regional routes. Some boxes in such a system would undergo as many as four transhipments before reaching the final port of discharge. The global grid would allow shipping lines to cope with the changes of trade flows as it combines all different routes in a network.

Existing liner shipping networks feature a great diversity in types of liner services and a great complexity in the way end-to-end services, line bundling services and transhipment/relay/interlining operations are connected to form extensive shipping networks. Maersk Line, MSC and CMA-CGM operate truly global liner service networks, with a strong presence also on secondary routes. Especially Maersk Line has created a balanced global coverage of liner services.

The networks of CMA-CGM and MSC differ from the general scheme of traffic circulation through a network of specific hubs (many of these hubs are not among the world's biggest container ports) and a more selective serving of secondary markets such as Africa (strong presence by MSC), the Caribbean and the East Mediterranean. Notwithstanding the demand pull for global services, a large number of individual carriers remains regionally based. Asian carriers such as APL, Hanjin, NYK, China Shipping and HMM mainly focus on intra-Asian trade, transpacific trade and the Europe – Far East route, partly because of their huge dependence on export flows generated by the respective Asian home bases.

MOL and Evergreen are among the few exceptions frequenting secondary routes such as Africa and South America. Profound differences exist in service network design among shipping lines. Some carriers have clearly opted for a true global coverage, others are somewhat stuck in a triad-based service network forcing them to develop a strong focus on cost bases. Alliance structures (cf. Grand Alliance, New World Alliance, and CYKH) provide its members easy access to more loops or services with relatively low-cost implications and allow them to share terminals.

THE PROCESS OF DESIGNING A LINER SERVICE

The liner service design process. Before an operator can start with the actual design of a regular container service, he will have to analyse the targeted trade route(s). The analysis should include elements related to the supply, demand and market profile of the trade route. Key considerations on the supply side include vessel capacity deployment and ulitzation, vessel size distribution, the configuration of existing liner services, the existing market structure and the port call patterns of existing operators. At the demand side, container lines focus on the characteristics of the market to be served, the geographical cargo distribution, seasonality and cargo imbalances. The interaction between demand and supply on the trade route considered results in specific freight rate fluctuations and the overall earning potential on the trade.

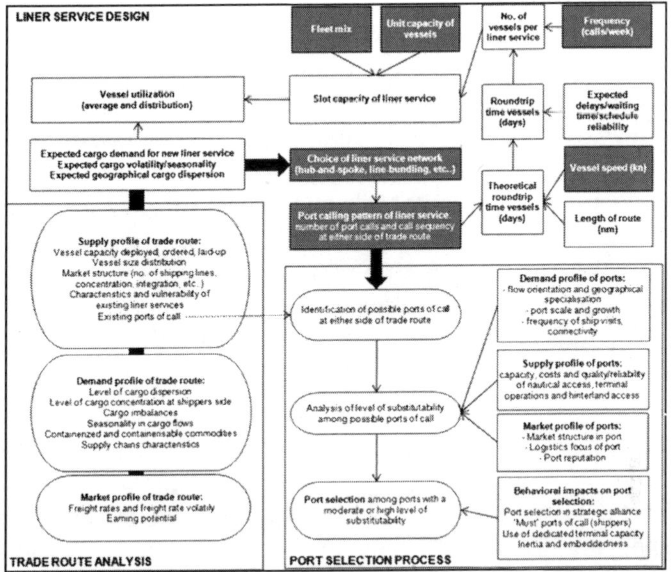

Fig. The Process of Liner Service Design.

Note: Dark gray/shaded areas are decision variables in liner service design

The ultimate goal of the market analysis is not only to estimate the potential cargo demand for a new liner service, but also to estimate the volatility, geographical dispersion and seasonality of such demand. These factors will eventually affect the earning potential of the new service. Once the market potential for a new service has been determined, the service planners need to take decisions on several inter-related core design variables. These design variables are indicated in dark gray/shaded boxes and mainly concern (1) the liner service type, (2) the number and order of port calls in combination with the actual port selection process, (3) vessel speed, (4) frequency and (5) vessel size and fleet mix.

The array of liner service types and bundling options available to shipping lines was discussed in the previous section.

Limiting the number of port calls shortens round voyage time and increases the number of round trips per year, thereby minimizing the number of vessels required for that specific liner service. However, fewer ports of call mean poorer access to more cargo catchment areas. Adding port calls can generate additional revenue if the additional costs from added calls are offset by revenue growth. The actual port selection is a complex issue. Traffic flows through ports are a physical outcome of route and port selection by the relevant actors in the chain. The most relevant service-related and cost factors explaining port selection by the main players of the transport chain (*e.g.* shippers, ocean carriers, and forwarders) are identified in the scientific literature on port choice, Murphy and Daley (1994), Malchow and Kanafani (2001), Tiwari et al.

(2003), Nir et al. (2003), Chou et al. (2003), Song and Yeo (2004), Guy and Urli (2006) and Wiegmans et al. (2008). Port choice has increasingly become a function of the overall network cost and performance. The approach of Notteboom (2009) to group port selection factors together in the demand profile of the port, the supply profile of the port, and the market profile of the port. Human behavioural aspects might impede carriers from achieving an optimal network configuration. Incorrect or incomplete information results in bounded rationality in carriers' network design, leading to sub-optimal decisions. Shippers sometimes impose bounded rational behaviour on shipping lines, *e.g.* in case the shipper asks to call at a specific port. Wiegmans et al. (2008) argue that port selection by shipping lines can also be heavily influenced by the balance of power among the shipping lines of the same strategic alliance, or the carrier's objective to make efficient use of its dedicated terminal capacity in specific ports.

The choice of vessel speed is mainly affected by the technical specifications of the vessel deployed (*i.e.* the design speed), the bunker price, environmental considerations (*e.g.* reduction of CO_2 through slow steaming) and the capacity situation in the market.

The number and order of port calls, the total two-way sailing distance and the vessel speed are the main determinants of the total vessel roundtrip time. The theoretical/optimal roundtrip time will seldomly be achieved in practice due to delays along the route and in ports giving rise to schedule reliability problems. Low schedule integrities can have many causes ranging from weather conditions, delays in the access to ports (pilotage, towage, locks, tides) to port terminal congestion or even security considerations (Notteboom, 2006). A shipping line can insert time buffers in the liner service to cope with the chance of delays. Time buffers reduce schedule unreliability, but increase the vessel roundtrip time.

When it comes to the service frequency, carriers typically aim for a weekly service. The service frequency and the total vessel roundtrip time determine the number of vessels required for the liner service. Carriers have to secure enough vessels to guarantee the desired frequency.

Given the number of vessels needed and the anticipated cargo volume for the liner service, the shipping line can then make a decision on the optimal vessel size and fleet mix. As economies of vessel size are more significant on longer distances, the biggest vessels are typically deployed on long and cargo-rich routes.

Decisions on all of the above key design variables will lead to a specific slot capacity offered by the new liner service. The resulting slot capacity should be in line with the actual demand as to maximize average vessel utilization (given expected traffic imbalances, cargo dispersion patterns and cargo seasonality and volatility).

SHIPPING ROUTES, NETWORK PATTERNS, AND PORT CENTRALITY

The aforementioned services altogether form a global maritime network within which local, regional and global links among ports become interconnected through the establishment of hub, interlining and relay ports.

THE DISTRIBUTION OF CONTAINER FLOWS

The weight and growth of major trade routes measured in TEUs provides evidence about the imbalanced structure of the global liner shipping network based on the offer of services. Their distribution confirms the predominance of the Europe-Asia link both in terms of weight and growth, closely followed by Asia-USA but with lower growth, while other links lag far behind in terms of the capacity deployed.

This confirms the study by Frémont and Soppé (2005) of the global container shipping network through the mapping of the top shipping lines' service offers among world regions. They explain the dominance of Asia by the role of the Newly Industrialised Countries (NICs) that provide consumers goods to industrialized countries, thus intensifying trans-Pacific flows at the expense of transatlantic flows. They also calculated that in 2002, such relations among the main economic poles of the "Triade" concentrated about 67 per cent of total service capacity, 22 per cent only remaining for North-South relations with these poles, and South-South relations being negligible in size.

Table. World's Major Trade Routes in 2007.

Main route	Transpacific		Europe-Asia		Transatlantic	
	Asia-USA	USA-Asia	Asia-Europe	Europe-Asia	USA-Europe	Europe-USA
Cargo flows (million TEUs)	15.4	4.9	17.7	10.0	2.7	4.5
Growth 2006-2007 (per cent)	2.8	3.0	15.5	9.0	7.3	1.6

A more precise method for measuring the weight of links is to trace the worldwide circulation of container vessels. Each time a vessel calls at one port, its capacity (in deadweight tonnage, DWT) is added to the port and to the inter-port link. The yearly total is thus an expression of the frequency and capacity of the links formed on various levels (*i.e.* ports, regions, continents) in an origin-destination matrix. One important aspect of the methodology is to have considered all ports of the same vessel voyage being interconnected, should they be or not adjacent calls in the sequence. This allows for a better view of the distribution of links and traffics.

The polarizing role of Asia appears even more explicitly, since most regions have their largest flow link directed to it at both years (Middle East, Oceania, North Europe, North America), or only in 2006 (Africa, South Europe, Latin America). In fact the latter regions have shifted their main traffic flow from North Europe, North America and South Europe respectively (in 1996) to Asia (in 2006), thereby illustrating the continuous influence of Asia on world trade patterns.

Links can also be differentiated by their traffic growth rate in a descending order, confirming the faster growth of South-linkages versus North-North and North-South linkages (albeit in smaller volumes than main routes):

- *Very fast growth (over 500 per cent):* Latin America-Oceania, Latin America-Middle East, and Middle East-Africa;
- *Fast growth (over 250 per cent):* Latin America-South Europe, Latin America-Africa, Latin America-South and East Asia, South Europe-South and East Asia, South and East Asia-Middle East;
- *Significant growth (over 100 per cent):* South Europe-Middle East, South Europe-Oceania, North Europe-all regions, South and East Asia-Oceania, South and East Asia-North Europe, North America-all regions;
- *Moderate growth (100 per cent or less):* Africa-Oceania, Oceania-Middle East, Africa-South Europe, North America-South and East Asia, South and East Asia-North Europe, North America-North Europe.

Table. Distribution of Interregional Flows in 1996 and 2006 (Million DWT).

Region	Oceania		South Europe		Latin America		Africa		North Europe		South & East Asia		North America	
Year	1996	2006	1996	2006	1996	2006	1996	2006	1996	2006	1996	2006	1996	2006
Middle East	3	6	53	180	3	20	9	55	70	166	212	759	24	75
Oceania			8	24	4	27	8	16	16	46	116	336	18	62
South Europe					69	341	149	286	269	582	248	973	95	296
Latin America							23	102	177	418	111	570	282	737
Africa									142	154	78	269	11	38
North Europe											793	1439	316	461
South & East Asia													905	1707

N.B. calculated based on direct and indirect calls between regions

The importance of intra-regional traffic is estimated based on the sequences of calls that are internal or external to LMIU regions. Such distinction provides a rough estimate on the extent to which different regions have different shipping dynamics. The intensity of intra-regional traffic in total traffic can be explained by various factors such as coastal morphology, the presence of hub ports, and the level of trade integration within the region. For instance, the low share of Africa and the Middle East in 1996 clearly reflects the lack of internal cohesion and integration, but the figure has changed dramatically in 2006, due to greater interdependency among regional ports.

Shipping networks are thus a good revelatory of trade and regionalization dynamics (Lemarchand and Joly, 2009). Regions with high internal connectivity through the extensive use of hub-and-feeder systems often have a high share of intra-regional traffic, such as Asia and North Europe, but also Latin America, which includes the Caribbean port system, whereas for North America, it is more the increase of multiple calls along East and West coasts, notably with the shift of major container traffic and intermodal facilities to the Southeast (*e.g.* Hampton Roads, Jacksonville, Miami).

Table. Share of Intraregional Traffic in Total Regional Traffic (Per cent DWT).

Region	1996	2006
South & east asia	69.8	70.6
Oceania	49.8	53.9
Latin america	59.1	57.1
North europe	48.4	52.2
World average	46.7	48.6
Africa	34.7	46.5
South europe	47.1	43.2
Middle east	32.4	33.3
North america	32.2	32.1

TOPOLOGY AND THE ROLE OF DISTANCE

Although maritime transport does not use an infrastructure of tracks like in road or rail transport, Ducruet and Notteboom (2011) calculated that the overall length of the network using orthodromic distance doubled between 1996 and 2006, from five to ten million kilometres. The length of the longest inter-port link has remained constant (10,000 km) but the average length has slightly increased from 1,000 to 1,200 km, as well as the traffic density from 331 to 407 TEU per kilometre. Such evidences validate the fact that shipping networks have constantly expanded geographically during this period.

In addition to these results, Ducruet and Notteboom (2011) also underline the influence of distance on traffic concentration. They show that most traffic occurs across relatively short distances: about 80 per cent of total worldwide traffic concentrates over direct links of 500 km or less, while links of 100 km or less support more than half. Besides the influence of coastal morphology and the necessity following successive calls in relative proximity, such figures can be explained by some local service configurations, as in the case of adjacent seaports serving shared hinterlands (*e.g.* Le Havre-Hamburg range) or acting as dual hubs (*e.g.* Busan and Gwangyang), which often receive multiple calls for the same vessels or liner services.

The noticeable increase of the longest links can be explained by stronger trans-Pacific ties and also by rapid technological progress in the shipping industry, allowing longer sailing distances between two ports: links of over 5,000 km concentrate 7 per cent and 10 per cent of worldwide traffic in 1996 and 2006 respectively. Overall, it could be calculated that the top 100 direct inter-port links in terms of traffic volume represent no less than 52 per cent and 39 per cent of worldwide container traffic in 1996 and 2006, respectively, thus confirming a trend of de-concentration due to the multiplication of links.

The spatial distribution of these top links also shows the dominance of intra-regional relations, with the exception of trans-Pacific links. The interregional inter-port (direct) links based on the definition of large world regions by the United Nations (*i.e.* Europe, Americas, Asia, Oceania, and Africa). We clearly observe a reduction and simplification of transatlantic and trans-Mediterranean links together with the appearance of new links in the top 100 such as Europe-Brazil links and Asia-Mexico links.

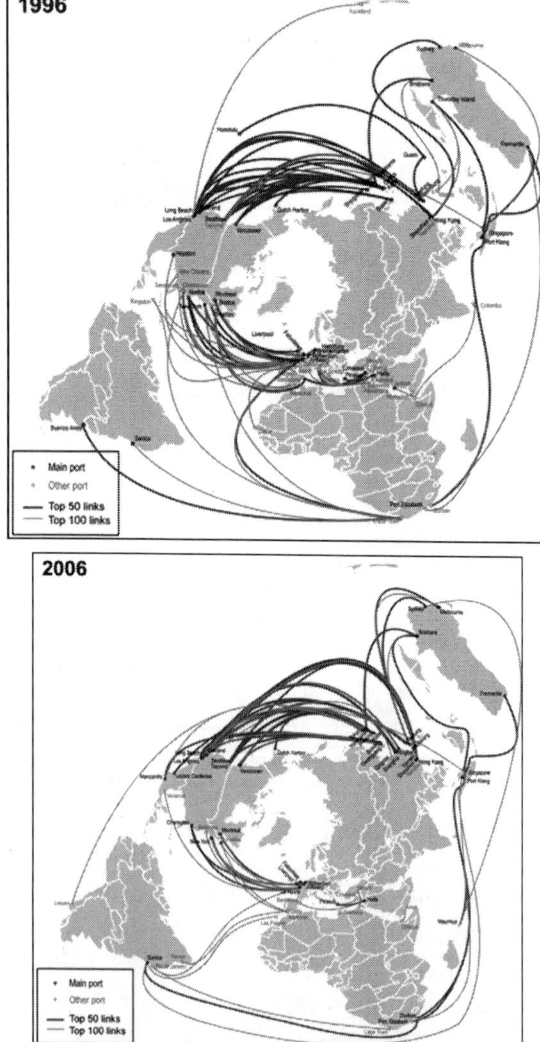

Fig. Top 100 Interregional Traffic Links in 1996 and 2006.

There is, however, also some continuity, since Le Havre - New York is the heaviest direct link connecting Europe with the world in both years, and Trans-Pacific links remain at centre stage, but with a shift of main links from Japanese to Chinese ports.

The extent to which the strategies of shipping lines are reflected in the topological structure of the network can also be verified by applying some measures from graph theory and complex networks. On a world level, Hu and Zhu (2009) were the first to confirm that container shipping networks belong to the category of so-called "scale-free" and "small-world" networks, *i.e.* where a limited number of nodes have the majority of links, the latter's frequency being distributed along a power-law, and with high cluster densities among smaller nodes outside hubs. Although Kaluza et al. (2010) contradict Deng et al. (2009) about the extent to which the global maritime network is more or less "efficient" (*i.e.* low average number of stops between two nodes) than other transport networks such as airlines, Ducruet and Notteboom (2010) underlined an increase in efficiency between 1996 and 2006, which is attributed to the expansion of the network as well as to the emergence of new hub ports.

Another important trend topologically speaking is the decreasing hierarchical structure of the network, as observed by Ducruet and Notteboom (2010) on a world level and by Ducruet et al. (2010a, 2010b) in Northeast Asia and the Atlantic regions. Such trend results from the combination of various factors such as regional integration processes (multiplication of intraregional links, opening of new direct call and multi-port services), diseconomies of scale in large gateway and hub ports, and competition between existing and emerging hub ports.

THE CENTRALITY OF CONTAINER PORTS

The impact of liner shipping network's operation on container ports is often analysed in terms of throughput, the most widely available indicator of port performance in official statistics. The classic port hierarchy with regard to the number of containers (TEUs) handled by top ports since the 1970s, regardless of the function of ports in the network. However, the network perspective allows for calculating the connectivity of ports, which is critically lacking in the related literature (De Langen et al., 2007). Two main measures of centrality in networks can be obtained based on the configuration of inter-port links in a binary port-to-port matrix (*i.e.* presence or absence of links between two given ports).

First, betweenness centrality counts the number of positions of a node on possible shortest paths among all nodes in the entire network (Ducruet and Rodrigue, 2011). It is a measure of accessibility or reachability. Second, degree centrality is the number of adjacent neighbours, which simply counts the number of ports connected to a given port. These are two very classic measures in network analysis across all fields of investigation from physics to sociology

(Wasserman and Faust, 1994), which can provide answers to theoretical configurations notably provided by Fleming and Hayuth (1994) on the centrality and intermediacy of transportation hubs. When it comes to ports, these measures can reveal other dimensions than sole throughput, with which they can be highly correlated.

Table. Top 20 Container Ports 1970-2009 (000s TEUs).

Rank	1970		1980		1990		2000		2009	
1	Oakland	336	New York	1947	Singapore	5224	Hong Kong	18098	Singapore	25866
2	Rotterdam	242	Rotterdam	1901	Hong Kong	5101	Singapore	17040	Shanghai	25002
3	Seattle	224	Hong Kong	1465	Rotterdam	3667	Busan	7540	Hong Kong	20983
4	Antwerp	215	Kaohsiung	979	Kaohsiung	3495	Kaohsiung	7426	Shenzhen	18250
5	Beifast	210	Singapore	917	Kobe	2596	Rotterdam	6280	Busan	11955
6	Bremen/Br.	195	Hamburg	783	Los Angeles	2587	Shanghai	5613	Guangzhou	11190
7	Los Angeles	165	Oakland	782	Busan	2348	Los Angeles	4879	Dubai	11124
8	Melbourne	158	Seattle	782	Hamburg	1969	Long Beach	4601	Ningbo	10503
9	Tilbury	155	Kobe	727	New York	1872	Hamburg	4248	Qingdao	10260
10	Larne	147	Antwerp	724	Keelung	1828	Antwerp	4082	Rotterdam	9743
11	Virginia	143	Yokohama	722	Yokohama	1648	Shenzhen	3994	Tianjin	8700
12	Liverpool	140	Bremen/Br.	703	Long Beach	1598	Port Klang	3207	Kaohsiung	8581
13	Harwich	140	Baltimore	663	Tokyo	1555	Dubai	3059	Port Klang	7310
14	Gothenburg	128	Keelung	660	Antwerp	1549	New York	3050	Antwerp	7310
15	Philadelphia	120	Busan	633	Felixstowe	1418	Tokyo	2899	Hamburg	7010
16	Sydney Harbour	118	Tokyo	632	San Juan	1381	Felixstowe	2853	Los Angeles	6749
17	Le Havre	108	Los Angeles	621	Bremen/Br.	1198	Bremen/Br.	2752	Tanjung Pelepas	6000
18	Anchorage	101	Jeddah	563	Seattle	1171	Gioia Tauro	2653	Long Beach	5068
19	Felixstowe	93	Long Beach	554	Oakland	1124	Melbourne	2550	Xiamen	4680
20	Kobe	90	Melbourne	513	Manila	1039	Durban	2497	Laem Chabang	4622
21	Hamburg	72	Le Havre	507	Bremerhaven	1030	Tanjung Priok	2476	New York	4562
22	Zeebrugge	70	Bordeaux	453	Bangkok	1018	Yokohama	2317	Dalian	4552
23	Montreal	68	Honolulu	441	Tacoma	938	Manila	2292	Bremen/Br.	4536
24	Hull	59	San Juan	428	Dubai	916	Kobe	2266	Jawaharlal Nehru	4061
25	Tokyo	54	Sydney Harbour	383	Nagoya	898	Yantian	2148	Tanjung Priok	3800
Total 25 ports		3552		19482		49168		120820		242417
World total		4423		34806		84642		235569		432018
Share 25 ports (per cent)		80		56		58		51		56

A first look at the top 25 central ports in the worldwide network provides some evidence about the usefulness of the measures and how they characterize the position of ports in the network. Unlike airline networks where anomalous centralities depict the peculiar position of very central airports (betweenness) with few direct connections (degree) (Guimera et al., 2005), liner shipping shows a good fit between betweenness and degree (Deng et al., 2009). Thus, very central ports in the entire liner shipping network are also those multiplying their connections towards other ports. This would mean that hub ports have many connections while being very central, unlike relay hubs in airline networks (*e.g.* Anchorage). Some exceptions, however, are visible in the results about ports, in light of the overall drop in the linear correlation among betweenness and degree from 0.84 in 1996 to 0.72 in 2006. This change suggests a more complex relationship between the two variables. Indeed in 2006, the peculiar position of some ports having less degree than betweenness appears with Surabaya and Miami. Those ports thus tend to have a role as regional hubs, with fewer connections to local ports that are not well connected to the rest of the network, and have no option but to go through Surabaya and Miami, such as several Indonesian and Caribbean ports. Surabaya and Miami thus benefit from their bridge position towards such smaller ports to raise their centrality in the global network. Such trend is also visible in the work of Ducruet et al. (2009) showing how Busan has increased its centrality within Northeast Asia but has simultaneously seen its centrality lowering in the worldwide network.

Table. Centrality of Top 25 Ports in 1996 and 2006.

1996			2006		
Port	**Betweenness Centrality**	**Degree Centrality**	**Port**	**Betweenness Centrality**	**Degree Centrality**
Singapore	150,240	165	Singapore	174,516	226
Rotterdam	97,875	140	Rotterdam	146,454	167
Hamburg	90,978	124	Hamburg	127,733	150
Hong Kong	61,839	126	Hong Kong	117,675	203
Antwerp	50,513	112	Busan	96,257	190
Busan	39,943	105	Shanghai	92,838	193
Le Havre	34,593	90	Bremerhaven	56,219	105
Houston	32,841	71	Antwerp	53,766	137
New York	32,536	70	Port Klang	52,191	148
Yokohama	31,090	83	Gioia Tauro	47,971	120
Los Angeles	30,726	66	Marsaxlokk	45,183	120
Felixstowe	27,606	88	Surabaya	39,030	50
Kaohsiung	27,551	82	Kingston(JAM)	37,495	104
Piraeus	24,827	71	Algeciras	36,846	130
Melbourne	22,516	44	Valencia	33,688	120
Philadelphia	21,867	44	Miami	32,963	83
Bremerhaven	21,661	56	Barcelona	32,462	118
Algeciras	20,373	72	Le Havre	31,623	98
Port Klang	19,782	58	Kaohsiung	31,419	125
Bilbao	19,549	60	New York	30,607	93
Valencia	17,380	78	Jebel Ali	28,785	97
Port Everglades	16,176	67	Felixstowe	28,216	92
Colombo	16,043	62	Durban	27,708	82
Izmir	14,854	55	Santos	26,306	92
Shanghai	14,719	59	Shenzhen	25,582	107

The extent to which network position relates with the hierarchy of container throughput is a crucial question. Interestingly, the correlation with betweenness and with degree has increased between 1996 and 2006, showing a better fit with container throughput. In terms of variance, betweenness centrality explains 40 per cent and 47 per cent of total throughput, while degree centrality explains 57 per cent and 66 per cent at respective years. This would suggest that network indicators are very good tools for understanding overall port performance, although they do not include land-based dimensions of hinterland connectivity, coverage, and other aspects of performance such as technical standards and the availability, quality, size, and cost of terminal handling facilities and services.

Overall, betweenness is less related with throughput than is degree, with regard to correlation levels and to the slope of the power-law line. Degree centrality scales superlinearly with throughput, which means that the number of connections is highly concentrated at large throughput ports. At the top of the hierarchy, large gateway ports such as Shenzhen and Yokohama may have less betweenness centrality than transhipment hubs, while ports combining both functions (cf. section 2.1) may rank high in the three indicators. Further analyses may better explain the role of network position on throughput performance as empirically tested by Ducruet et al. (2011). Overall, the position of ports in shipping networks seems to explain a large part of their overall activity.

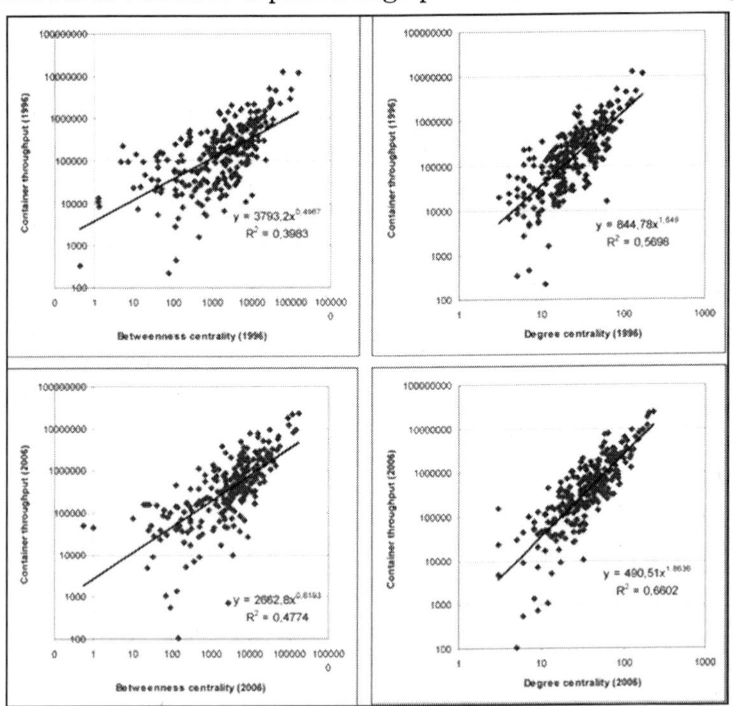

Fig. Centrality in Liner Shipping Networks and Container Throughput.

CONCLUSIONS

The extensive worldwide container shipping networks are key to globalization and global supply chains. The requirements on container shipping service networks have tightened in terms of frequency, schedule reliability/ integrity, global coverage of services and rate setting. The evolutionary path of liner shipping networks and port operations is characterised by drastic changes as well as permanencies.

Shipping lines have embraced a wide range of bundling concepts and liner service configurations to drive container service network dynamics. As global trade expands in economical and geographic terms, despite difficult conjunctures such as the global financial crisis, new ports and new shipping networks are regularly created to cope with demand. Shipping lines logically adapt to such trends as well as influence them, sometimes by refining their services through rationalization or by creating new service configurations through a combination of line bundling itineraries and transhipment/relay/interlining operations at pivotal ports of the network.

This chapter provided evidence about the increasing complexity and number of cargo movements that occurs in parallel with increased concentration and polarisation, depending on the measures and methodologies applied for revealing such trends. It discussed some fundamental aspects, such as the economic and geographic dimension of the variety of services offered by the industry, as well as the strong and growing interdependency between maritime centrality and port throughput for container ports, although in this simple equation, hinterland connectivity and port efficiency are not included. Looking at the distribution of main trading routes as well as disaggregated interregional and inter-port shipping links, the latter being compared with kilometric distance, we observed that the overall network is growing in size and length notably thanks to a catching-up of South-South linkages versus North-North and North-South linkages. However, most worldwide traffic still concentrates over very short distances, that is more specific to maritime transport than to air transport due to adjacent calls between ports.

In light of our results, further research on container shipping networks should go deeper in the analysis of the causal relationship between throughput and centrality for container ports, while better identifying specific cases and outliers. Another avenue of future research would be to test the impact of the global financial crisis on the overall structure of regional and global liner shipping networks, as well as on the position of individual container ports, which would complement the classic view of shipping based on aggregated cargo flows among major trade routes. The global database on vessel movements is being expanded to other years and other types of vessels so as to better appreciate the linkages between port hierarchy, global/regional trade patterns, and the evolution of network structure. Last but not least, the analysis of the situation of ports and cities within combined maritime and land-based networks would prove helpful for the study of logistics chains, the hinterland-foreland continuum, intermodal transport systems, and port competitiveness.

CONTAINER SHIP

Container ships are cargo ships that carry all of their load in truck-size intermodal containers, in a technique calledcontainerization. They are a common means of commercial intermodal freight transport and now carry most seagoing non-bulk cargo. Container ship capacity is measured in twenty-foot equivalent units (TEU). Typical loads are a mix of 20-foot and 40-foot (2-TEU) ISO-standard containers, with the latter predominant.

Today, about 90 per cent of non-bulk cargo worldwide is transported by container, and modern container ships can carry up to 16,020 TEU. Container ships now rival crude oil tankers and bulk carriers as the largest commercial vessels on the ocean.

HISTORY

Fig. Container Ships Avoid the Complexstevedoring of Break-Bulk Shipping.

There are two main types of dry cargo: bulk cargo and break bulk cargo. Bulk cargoes, like grain or coal, are transported unpackaged in the hull of the ship, generally in large volume.

Break-bulk cargoes, on the other hand, are transported in packages, and are generally manufactured goods. Before the advent of containerization in the 1950s, break-bulk items were loaded, lashed, unlashed and unloaded from the ship one piece at a time.

However, by grouping cargo into containers, 1,000 to 3,000 cubic feet (28 to 85 m3) of cargo, or up to about 64,000 pounds (29,000 kg), is moved at once and each container is secured to the ship once in a standardized way.Containerization has increased the efficiency of moving traditional break-bulk cargoes significantly, reducing shipping time by 84 per cent and costs by 35 per cent. In 2001, more than 90 per cent of world trade in non-bulk goods was transported in ISO containers. In 2009, almost one quarter of the world's dry cargo was shipped by container, an estimated 125 million TEU or 1.19 billion metric tons worth of cargo.

The first ships designed to carrying standardized load units were use in the late 18th century in England . In 1766 James Brindleydesigned the box boat "Starvationer" with 10 wooden containers, to transport coal from Worsley Delph to Manchester by Bridgewater Canal. Before the Second World War first container ships were used to carrying baggages of the luxury passenger train from London to Paris, Golden Arrow/Fleche d'Or, in 1926 by Southern Railway. These containers were loaded in London or Paris and carried to ports, Dover or Calais, on flat cars in the UK and "CIWL Pullman Golden Arrow Fourgon of CIWL" in France.

The earliest container ships after Second Word War were converted tankers, built up from surplus T2 tankers after World War II. In 1951, the first purpose-built container vessels began operating in Denmark, and between Seattle and Alaska.

The first commercially successful container ship was the Ideal X, a T2 tanker, owned by Malcom McLean, which carried 58 metal containers between Newark, New Jersey and Houston, Texas on its first voyage. In 1955, McLean built his company, McLean Trucking into one of United States' biggest freighter fleets. In 1955, he purchased the small Pan Atlantic Steamship Company from Waterman Steamship and adapted its ships to carry cargo in large uniform metal containers. On April 26, 1956, the first of these rebuilt container vessels, the Ideal X, left the Port Newark in New Jersey and a new revolution in modern shipping resulted.

Fig. The Earliest Container Ships were Converted T2 Tankers in the 1940s After World War II.

Container vessels eliminate the individual hatches, holds and dividers of the traditional general cargo vessels. The hull of a typical container ship is a huge warehouse divided into cells by vertical guide rails. These cells are designed to hold cargo in pre-packed units – containers. Shipping containers are usually made of steel, but other materials like aluminum, fibreglass or plywood are also used. They are designed to be entirely transferred to and from smaller coastal carriers, trains, trucks and/or semi-trailers (and so are carried by different modes of transport during one voyage, thus giving the name intermodal transport) There are several types of containers and they are categorized according to their size and functions.

Today, about 90 per cent of non-bulk cargo worldwide is transported by container, and modern container ships can carry up to 16,020 twenty-foot equivalent units (TEU) (CMA CGM Marco Polo). As a class, container ships now rival crude oil tankers and bulk carriers as the largest commercial vessels on the ocean.

Although containerization caused a revolution in the world of shipping, its introduction did not have an easy passage. Ports, railway (railroad in the US) companies, and shippers were concerned about the huge costs of developing the ports and railway infrastructure needed to handle container ships, and for the movement of containers on land by rail and road. Trade unions were concerned about massive job loss among port and dock workers at ports, as containers were sure to eliminate several manual jobs of cargo handling at ports. It took ten years of legal battles before container ships would be pressed into international service.

In 1966, a container liner service from the USA to the Dutch city of Rotterdam commenced.

Containerization changed not only the face of shipping, but it also revolutionized world trade as well. A container ship can be loaded and unloaded in a few hours compared to days in a traditional cargo vessel. This, besides cutting labour costs, has reduced shipping times between ports to a great extent; for example, it takes a few weeks instead of months for a consignment to be delivered from India to Europe and vice versa. It has also resulted in less breakage due to less handling; also, there is less danger of cargo shifting during a voyage. As containers are sealed and only opened at the destination, pilferage and theft levels have been greatly reduced.

Fig. Container Ship Tan Cang 15 in the Saigon River in Ho Chi Minh City, Vietnam.

Fig. A Delmas Container Ship Unloading at the Zanzibar Port in Tanzania.

Containerization has lowered shipping expense and decreased shipping time, and this has in turn helped the growth of international trade. Cargo that once arrived in cartons, crates, bales, barrels or bags now comes in factory sealed containers, with no indication to the human eye of their contents, except for a product code that machines can scan and computers trace. This system of tracking has been so exact that a two-week voyage can be timed for arrival with an accuracy of under fifteen minutes.

It has resulted in such revolutions ason time guaranteed delivery and just in time manufacturing. Raw materials arrive from factories in sealed containers less than an hour before they are required in manufacture, resulting in reduced inventory expense.

The aforementioned reduction in ship operating costs accrue to companies owning or operating container ships. But for others connected with trade, such as ports, railways, road transporters and trade (exporters and importers), the operating costs have risen exponentially. Several elements of costs that were borne in the past by ship operators are now borne by trade, as standard terms of carriage of goods by sea have now been drastically revised by container-shipping lines. Despite saving in operating costs, shipping freight have not fallen significantly because freight is globally fixed sector-wise by shipping cartels. In short, containers have helped to optimize the operation of ships, while the additional burden of ancillary costs that has been transferred from ships onto other (*i.e.* onshore) entities is normally ignored in public perception.

Exporters load merchandise in boxes that are provided by the shipping companies. They are then delivered to the docks by road, rail or a combination of both for loading on to container ships. Prior to containerization, huge gangs of men would spend hours fitting various items of cargo into different holds. Today, cranes, installed either on the pier or on the ship, are used to place containers on board the ship. When the hull has been fully loaded, additional containers are stacked on the deck. Today's largest container ships measure almost 400 metres (1,300 ft) in length. They carry loads equal to the cargo-carrying capacity of sixteen to seventeen pre-WWII freighter ships.

ARCHITECTURE

Fig. Container Ship Under Construction.

Fig. USNS Regulus (T-AKR-292) Began its Career as Sea-Land's SL-7 Class Container Ship SS Sea-Land Commerce.

There are several key points in the design of modern container ships. The hull, similar to bulk carriers and general cargo ships, is built around a strong keel. Into this frame is set one or more below-deck cargo holds, numerous tanks, and the engine room. The holds are topped by hatch covers, onto which more containers can be stacked. Many container ships have cargo cranes installed on them, and some have specialized systems for securing containers on board. The hull of a modern cargo ship is a complex arrangement of steel plates and strengthening beams. The hull is built around the keel.Resembling ribs, and fastened at right-angles to the keel are the ship's frames. The ship's main deck, the metal platework that covers the top of the hull framework, is supported by beams that are attached to the tops of the frames and run the full breadth of the ship.The beams not only support the deck, but along with the deck, frames, and transverse bulkheads, strengthen and reinforce the shell.Another feature of recent hulls is a set of double-bottom tanks, which provide a second watertight shell that runs most of the length of a ship. The double-bottoms generally hold liquids such as fuel oil, ballast water or fresh water. A ship's engine room houses its main engines and auxiliary machinery such as the fresh water and sewage systems, electrical generators, fire pumps, and air conditioners. In most new ships, the engine room is located in the aft portion of the ship.

Size Categories

Container ships are distinguished into 7 major size categories: small feeder, feeder, feedermax, panamax, post-panamax, new panamax and ultra-large. As of December 2012, there are 161 container ships in the VLCS class (Very Large Container Ships, more than 10,000 TEU), and 51 ports in the world can accommodate them.

The size of a panamax vessel is limited by the Panama canal's lock chambers, which can accommodate ships with a beam of up to 32.31 m, a length overall of up to 294.13 m, and a draft of up to 12.04 m. The "post panamax" category has historically been used to describe ships with a moulded breadth over 32.31 m, however the Panama Canal expansion project is causing some changes in terminology. The "new panamax" category is based on the maximum vessel-size that will be able to transit a new third set of locks.The new locks are being built to accommodate a container ship with a length overall of 366 metres (1,201 ft), a maximum width of 49 metres (161 ft), and tropical fresh-water draft of 15.2 metres (50 ft). Such a vessel would be wide enough to carry 19 rows of containers, have a total capacity of approximately 12,000 TEU and be comparable in size to a capesize bulk carrier or a suezmaxtanker.

Container ships under 3,000 TEU are generally called feeders. Feeders are small ships that typically operate between smaller container ports. Some feeders collect their cargo from small ports, drop it off at large ports for transshipment on larger ships, and distribute containers from the large port to smaller regional ports. This size of vessel is the most likely to carry cargo cranes on board.

Container Ship Size Categories

Name	Capacity (TEU)	Length	Beam	Draft	Example
Ultra Large Container Vessel (ULCV)	14,501 and higher	1,200 ft (366 m) and longer	160.7 ft (49 m) and wider	49.9 ft (15.2 m) and deeper	With a length of 400 m, a width of 59 m, draft of 14.5 m, and a capacity of 18,270 Tps of the Maersk Triple E class are able to transit the Suez canal. (Fig. MV Mærsk Mc-Kinney Møller.) 
New panamax	10,000 –14,500	1,200 ft (366 m)	160.7 ft (49 m)	49.9 ft (15.2 m)	With a beam of 43m, ships of the COSCO Guangzhou class are much too big to fit through the Panama Canal's old locks, but could easily fit through the new expansion. (Fig. The 9,500 TEU MV COSCO Guangzhou pierside in Hamburg.) 
Post panamax	5,101 –10,000				
Panamax	3,001 –	965 ft (2	106 ft (3	39.5 ft (1	Ships of the Bay-class
5,100	94.13 m)	2.31 m)	2.04 m)		are at the upper limit of the Panamax class, with an overall length of 292.15 m, beam of 32.2m, and maximum depth of 13.3 m. (Fig. The 4,224 TEU MV Pr ovidence Baypassing through the Panama Canal.) 
Feedermax	2,001–3,000				Container ships under 3,000 TEU are typically called feeders. In some areas of the world,they might be outfitted with cargo cranes. (Fig. The 384 TEU MV Trans Atlantic at anchor.) 
Feeder	1,001–2,000				
Small feeder	Up to 1,000				

Cargo Cranes

A major characteristic of a container ship is whether it has cranes installed for handling its cargo. Those that have cargo cranes are called geared and those that don't are called ungeared or gearless. The earliest purpose-built container ships in the 1970s were all gearless. Since then, the percentage of geared newbuilds has fluctuated widely, but has been decreasing overall, with only 7.5 per cent of the container ship capacity in 2009 being equipped with cranes. While geared container ships are more flexible in that they can visit ports that are not equipped with pierside container cranes, they suffer from several drawbacks. To begin with, geared ships will cost more to purchase than a gearless ship. Geared ships also incur greater recurring expenses, such as maintenance and fuel costs. The United Nations Council on Trade and Development characterizes geared ships as a "niche market only appropriate for those ports where low cargo volumes do not justify investment in port cranes or where the public sector does not have the financial resources for such investment." Instead of the rotary cranes, some geared ships have gantry cranes installed. These cranes, specialized for container work, are able to roll forward and aft on rails. In addition to the additional capital expense and maintenance costs, these cranes generally load and discharge containers much more slowly than their shoreside counterparts.

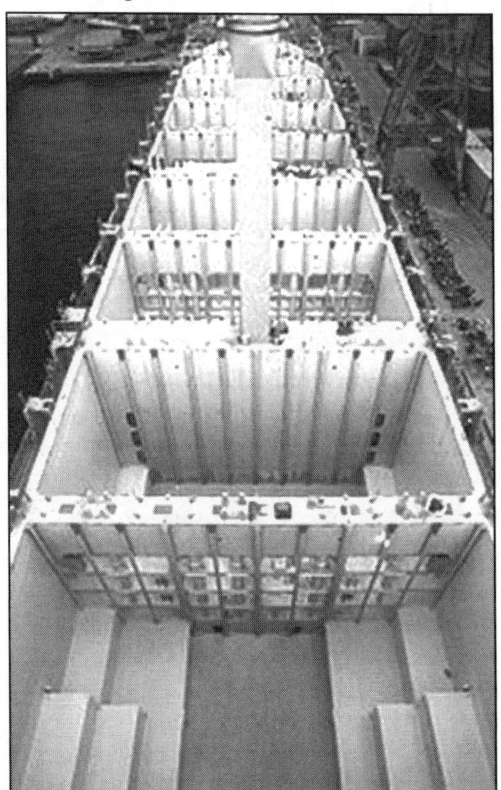

Fig. A View Into the Holds of a Container Ship. Of Note are the Vertical Cell Guides that Organize Containers Sthwartships.

The introduction and improvement of shoreside cranes have been a key to the success of the container ship. The first crane that was specifically designed for container work was built in California's Port of Alameda in 1959. By the 1980s, shoreside gantry cranes were capable of moving containers on a 3-minute-cycle, or up to 400 tons per hour. In March 2010, at Port Klang in Malaysia, a new world record was set when 734 container moves were made in a single hour. The record was achieved using 9 cranes to simultaneously load and unload the MV CSCL Pusan, a ship with a capacity of 9,600 TEU. Vessels in the 1,500–2,499 TEU range are the most likely size class to have cranes, with more than 60 per cent of this category being geared ships. Slightly less than a third of the very smallest ships (from 100–499 TEU) are geared, and almost no ships with a capacity of over 4,000 TEU are geared.

Cargo Holds

Efficiency has always been key in the design of container ships. While containers may be carried on conventional break-bulk ships, cargo holds for dedicated container ships are specially constructed to speed loading and unloading, and to efficiently keep containers secure while at sea. A key aspect of container ship specialization is the design of the hatches, the openings from the main deck to the cargo holds.

The hatch openings stretch the entire breadth of the cargo holds, and are surrounded by a raised steel structure known as the hatch coaming. On top of the hatch coamings are the hatch covers. Until the 1950s, hatches were typically secured with wooden boards and tarpaulins held down with battens. Today, some hatch covers can be solid metal plates that are lifted on and off the ship by cranes, while others are articulated mechanisms that are opened and closed using powerful hydraulic rams.

Another key component of dedicated container-ship design is the use of cell guides. Cell guides are strong vertical structures constructed of metal installed into a ship's cargo holds. These structures guide containers into well-defined rows during the loading process and provide some support for containers against the ship's rolling at sea. So fundamental to container ship design are cell guides that organizations such as the United Nations Conference on Trade and Development use their presence to distinguish dedicated container ships from general break-bulk cargo ships.

A system of three dimensions is used in cargo plans to describe the position of a container aboard the ship. The first coordinate is therow, which starts at the front of the ship and increases aft. The second coordinate is tier, with the first tier at the bottom of the cargo holds, the second tier on top of that, and so forth. The third coordinate is the slot. Slots on the starboard side are given odd numbers and those on the port side are given even numbers. The slots nearest the centerline are given low numbers, and the numbers increase for slots further from the centerline.

Container ships only take 20 foot, 40 foot, and 45 foot containers. 45 footers only fit above deck. 40 foot containers are the primary container size, making up about 90 per cent of all container shipping and since container shipping moves 90 per cent of the world's freight, over 80 per cent of the world's freight moves via 40 foot containers.

Lashing Systems

Fig. Twist-locks and lashing rods (pictured) are widely used to secure containers aboard ships.

Numerous systems are used to secure containers aboard ships, depending on factors such as the type of ship, the type of container, and the location of the container. Stowage inside the holds of fully cellular (FC) ships is simplest, typically using simple metal forms called container guides, locating cones, and anti-rack spacers to lock the containers together. Above-decks, without the extra support of the cell guides, more complicated equipment is used.

Three types of systems are currently in wide use: lashing systems, locking systems, and buttress systems. Lashing systems secure containers to the ship using devices made from wire rope, rigid rods, or chains and devices to tension the lashings, such as turnbuckles. The effectiveness of lashings is increased by securing containers to each other, either by simple metal forms (such as stacking cones) or more complicated devices such as twist-lock stackers. A typicaltwist-lock is inserted into the casting hole of one container and rotated to hold it in place, then another container is lowered on top of it.The two containers are locked together by twisting the device's handle. A typical twist-lock is constructed of forged steel and ductile iron and has a shear strength of 48 metric tons. The buttress system, used on some large container ships, uses a system of large towers attached to the ship at both ends of each cargo hold. As the ship is loaded, a rigid, removable stacking frame is added, structurally securing each tier of containers together.

Bridge

Containerships have typically had a single bridge and accommodation unit towards the rear, but to reconcile demand for larger container capacity with SOLAS visibility requirements, several new designs have been developed. As of 2015, some large containerships are being developed with the bridge further forward, separate from the exhaust stack. Some smaller containerships working in European ports and rivers have liftable wheelhouses, which can be lowered to pass under low bridges. HHI has developed theSkybench movable bridge to allow more capacity on large containerships.

FLEET CHARACTERISTICS

As of 2010, container ships made up 13.3 per cent of the world's fleet in terms of deadweight tonnage. The world's total of container ship deadweight tonnage has increased from 11 million DWT in 1980 to 169.0 million DWT in 2010. The combined deadweight tonnage of container ships and general cargo ships, which also often carry containers, represents 21.8 per cent of the world's fleet. As of 2009, the average age of container ships worldwide was 10.6 years, making them the youngest general vessel type, followed by bulk carriers at 16.6 years, oil tankers at 17 years, general cargo ships at 24.6 years, and others at 25.3 years. Most of the world's carrying capacity in fully cellular container ships is in the liner service, where ships trade on scheduled routes. As of January 2010, the top 20 liner companies controlled 67.5 per cent of the world's fully cellular container capacity, with 2,673 vessels of an average capacity of 3,774 TEU. The remaining fully 6,862 fully cellular ships have an average capacity of 709 TEU each. The vast majority of the capacity of fully cellular container ships used in the liner trade is owned by German shipowners, with approximately 75 per cent owned by Hamburg brokers. It is a common practice for the large container lines to supplement their own ships with chartered-in ships, for example in 2009, 48.9 per cent of the tonnage of the top 20 liner companies was chartered-in in this manner.

Flag States

International law requires that every merchant ship be registered in a country, called its flag state. A ship's flag state exercises regulatory control over the vessel and is required to inspect it regularly, certify the ship's equipment and crew, and issue safety and pollution prevention documents. As of 2006, the United States Bureau of Transportation Statistics count 2,837 container ships of 10,000 long tons deadweight(DWT) or greater worldwide. Panama was the world's largest flag state for container ships, with 541 of the vessels in its registry. Seven other flag states had more than 100 registered container ships: Liberia (415), Germany (248), Singapore (177), Cyprus (139), the Marshall Islands (118) and the United Kingdom (104). The Panamanian, Liberian, and Marshallese flags are open registries and considered by theInternational Transport Workers' Federation to be flags of convenience. By way of comparison, traditional maritime nations such as the United States and Japan only had 75 and 11 registered container ships, respectively.

Vessel Purchases

In 2009, 11,669,000 gross tons of newly built container ships were delivered. Over 85 per cent of this new capacity was built in the Republic of Korea, China, and Japan, with Korea accounting for over 57 per cent of the world's total alone. New container ships accounted for 15 per cent of the total new tonnage that year, behind bulk carriers at 28.9 per cent and oil tankers at 22.6 per cent.

Scrapping

Most ships are removed from the fleet through a process known as scrapping. Scrapping is rare for ships under 18 years old and common for those over 40 years in age. Ship-owners and buyers negotiate scrap prices based on factors such as the ship's empty weight (called light ton displacement or LTD) and prices in the scrap metal market. Scrapping rates are volatile, the price per light ton displacement has swung from a high of $650 per LTD in mid-2008 to $200 per LTD in early 2009, before building to $400 per LTD in March 2010. As of 2009, over 96 per cent of the world's scrapping activity takes place in China, India, Bangladesh, and Pakistan.

The global economic downturn of 2008–2009 resulted in more ships than usual being sold for scrap. In 2009, 364,300 TEU worth of container ship capacity was scrapped, up from 99,900 TEU in 2008. Container ships accounted for 22.6 per cent of the total gross tonnage of ships scrapped that year. Despite the surge, the capacity removed from the fleet only accounted for 3 per cent of the world's containership capacity. The average age of container ships scrapped in 2009 was 27.0 years.

Largest Ships

Table. Twelve Largest Container Ship Classes, Listed by TEU Capacity.

Built	Name	Class size	Maximum TEU	Sources
2013	Mærsk Mc-Kinney Møller	20	18,270	
2012	CMA CGM Marco Polo	8	16,020	
2006	Emma Mærsk	8	15,200–15,550	
2009	MSC Danit	7	14,000	
2009	MSC Beatrice	7	14,000	
2010	MSC Fabiola	7	12,600	
2008	CMA CGM Thalassa	2	10,960	
2005	Gudrun Mærsk	6	10,150	
2002	Clementine Maersk	7	9,600	
2006	COSCO Guangzhou	5	9,500	
2006	CMA CGM Medea	4	9,415	
2003	Axel Mærsk	6	9,310	

Economies of scale have dictated an upward trend in sizes of container ships in order to reduce expense. However, there are certain limitations to the size of container ships. Primarily, these are the availability of sufficiently large main engines and the availability of a sufficient number of ports and terminals prepared and equipped to handle ultra-large container ships. Furthermore, the permissible maximum ship dimensions in some of the world's main waterways could present an upper limit in terms of vessel growth. This primarily concerns the Suez Canal and the Singapore Strait.

In 2008 the South Korean shipbuilder STX announced plans to construct a container ship capable of carrying 22,000 TEU, and with a proposed length of 450 metres and a beam of 60 metres. If constructed, the container ship would become the largest seagoing vessel in the world.

Since even very large container ships are vessels with relatively low draft compared to large tankers and bulk carriers, there is still considerable room for vessel growth. Compared to today's largest container ships, Maersk Line's 15,200 TEUEmma Mærsk-type series, a 20,000 TEU container ship would only be moderately larger in terms of exterior dimensions. According to a 2011 estimate, an ultra-large container ship of 20,250 TEU would measure 440m × 59m, compared to 397.71 × 56.40m for the Emma Mærsk class. It would have an estimated deadweight of circa 220,000 tons. While such a vessel might be near the upper limit for a Suez Canal passage, the so-called Malaccamax concept (for Straits of Malacca) does not apply for container ships, since the Malacca and Singapore Straits' draft limit of about 21 metres is still above that of any conceivable container ship design. In 2011, Maersk announced plans to build a new "Triple E" family of containerships with a capacity of 18,000TEU, with an emphasis on lower fuel consumption.

Fig. CSCL Globe is One of the Largest Container Ships in the World.

In the present market situation, main engines will not be as much of a limiting factor for vessel growth either. The steadily rising expense of fuel oil has prompted most container lines to adapt a slower, more economical voyage speed of about 21 knots, compared to earlier top speeds of 25 or more knots. Subsequently, new-built container ships can be fitted with a smaller main engine.

Engine types fitted to today's ships of 14,000 TEU are thus sufficiently large to propel future vessels of 20,000 TEU or more. Maersk Line, the world's largest container shipping line, nevertheless opted for twin engines (two smaller engines working two separate propellers), when ordering a series of ten 18,000 TEU vessels from Daewoo Shipbuilding in February 2011. The ships will be delivered between 2013 and 2014.

Freight Market

The act of hiring a ship to carry cargo is called chartering. Outside special bulk cargo markets, ships are hired by three types of charter agreements: the voyage charter, the time charter, and the bareboat charter. In a voyage charter, the charterer rents the vessel from the loading port to the discharge port. In a time charter, the vessel is hired for a set period of time, to perform voyages as the charterer directs. In a bareboat charter, the charterer acts as the ship's operator and manager, taking on responsibilities such as providing the crew and maintaining the vessel. The completed chartering contract is known as a charter party.

The United Nations Conference on Trade and Development, or UNCTAD, in its 2010 Review of Maritime Trade tracks two aspects of container shipping prices. The first is a chartering price, specifically the price to time-charter a 1 TEU slot for a 14 metric ton cargo on a container ship. The other is the freight rate, or comprehensive daily cost to deliver one-TEU worth of cargo on a given route. As a result of the late-2000s recession, both indicators showed sharp drops during 2008–2009, and have shown signs of stabilization since 2010.

UNCTAD uses the Hamburg Shipbrokers' Association (formally the Vereinigung Hamburger Schiffsmakler und Schiffsagenten e. V. or VHSS for short) as its main industry source for container ship freight prices. The VHSS maintains a few indices of container ship charter prices. The oldest, which dates back to 1998, is called the Hamburg Index. This index considers time-charters on fully cellular containerships controlled by Hamburg brokers. It is limited to charters of 3 months or more, and presented as the average daily cost in U.S. dollars for a one-TEU slot with a weight of 14 metric tons. The Hamburg Index data is divided into ten categories based primarily on vessel carrying capacity. Two additional categories exist for small vessels of under 500 TEU that carry their own cargo cranes. In 2007, VHSS started another index, the New ConTex which tracks similar data obtained from an international group of shipbrokers.

The Hamburg Index shows some clear trends in recent chartering markets. First, rates were generally increasing from 2000 to 2005. From 2005 to 2008, rates slowly decreased, and in mid-2008 began a "dramatic decline" of approximately 75 per cent, which lasted until rates stabilized in April 2009. Rates have ranged from \$2.70 to \$35.40 in this period, with prices generally lower on larger ships. The most resilient sized vessel in this time period were those from 200–300 TEU, a fact that the United Nations Council on Trade and Development attributes to lack of competition in this sector. Overall, in 2010, these rates rebounded somewhat, but remained at approximately half of their 2008 values. As of 2011, the index shows signs of recovery for container shipping, and combined with increases in global capacity, indicates a positive outlook for the sector in the near future.

Recent liner freight rates (in 1000 US$/TEU)									
From	To	2008				2009			
		Q1	Q2	Q3	Q4	Q1	Q2	Q3	Q4
Asia	U.S.	1.8	1.8	1.9	1.9	1.7	1.4	1.2	1.3
U.S.	Asia	0.8	1.0	1.2	1.2	0.9	0.8	0.8	0.9
Europe	Asia	1.0	1.1	1.1	1.1	0.9	0.7	0.8	0.9
Asia	Europe	2.0	1.9	1.8	1.6	1.0	0.9	1.0	1.4
U.S.	Europe	1.3	1.4	1.6	1.7	1.5	1.4	1.4	1.5
Europe	U.S.	1.6	1.6	1.6	1.6	1.3	1.2	1.1	1.3

UNCTAD also tracks container freight rates. Freight rates are expressed as the total price in U.S. dollars for a shipper to transport one TEU worth of cargo along a given route. Data is given for the three main container liner routes: U.S.-Asia, U.S.-Europe, and Europe-Asia. Prices are typically different between the two legs of a voyage, for example the Asia-U.S. rates have been significantly higher than the return U.S.-Asia rates in recent years. Generally, from the fourth quarter of 2008 through the third quarter of 2009, both the volume of container cargo and freight rates have dropped sharply. In 2009, the freight rates on the U.S.–Europe route were sturdiest, while the Asia-U.S. route fell the most.

Liner companies responded to their overcapacity in several ways. For example, in early 2009, some container lines dropped their freight rates to zero on the Asia-Europe route, charging shippers only a surcharge to cover operating costs. They decreased their overcapacity by lowering the ships' speed (a strategy called "slow steaming") and by laying up ships. Slow steaming increased the length of the Europe-Asia routes to a record high of over 40 days. Another strategy used by some companies was to manipulate the market by publishing notices of rate increases in the press, and when "a notice had been issued by one carrier, other carriers followed suit." The Trans-Siberian Railroad (TSR) has recently become a more viable alternative to container ships on the Asia-Europe route. This railroad can typically deliver containers in 1/3 to 1/2 of the time of a sea voyage, and in late 2009 announced a 20 per cent reduction in its container shipping rates. With its 2009 rate schedule, the TSR will transport a forty-foot container to Poland from Yokohama for $2,820, or from Pusan for $2,154.

Shipping Industry Alliances

In an effort to control costs and maximize capacity utilization on ever larger ships, vessel sharing agreements, co-operative agreements and slot-exchanges and have become a growing feature of the maritime container shipping industry.

As of March 2015, 16 of the world's largest container shipping lines had consolidated their routes and services accounting for 95 percent of container cargo volumes moving in the dominant east-west trade routes. Carriers remain operationally independent, forbidden by antitrust regulators in multiple jurisdictions from colluding on freight rates or capacity.

Container ship industry alliances, as of March 2015	
Alliance name	**Alliance participating companies**
2M	Maersk Line, MSC
Ocean Three	CMA CGM, CSCL, UASC
CKYHE Alliance	COSCO, K Line, Yang Ming, Hanjin, Evergreen
G6	APL, MOL, Hyundai, OOCL, NYK Line, Hapag-Lloyd

CONTAINER PORTS

Fig. Big Chinese Container Vessel in the Port of Rotterdam.

Container traffic through a port is often tracked in terms of twenty foot equivalent units or TEU of throughput. As of 2009, the Port of Singapore was the world's busiest container port, with 25,866,000 TEU handled. That year, six of the busiest ten container ports were in the People's Republic of China, with Shanghai in 2nd place, Port of Hong Kong in 3rd, Shenzhen 4th, Guangzhou 6th, Ningbo 8th, andQingdao 9th. Rounding out the top ten ports were Busan in South Korea at number 5, Dubai in the United Arab Emirates at number 7, and Rotterdam in the Netherlands in the 10th position with 9,743,290 TEU served. In total, the busiest twenty container ports handled 220,905,805 TEU in 2009, almost half of the world's total estimated container traffic that year of 465,597,537 TEU.

SAFETY ISSUES

In March 2007, a London-based container ship capsized in Antwerp, Belgium while loading. Maneuvers in coastal waters and ports managed in the wheel house may be dangerous, as evidenced by a container ship hitting the San Francisco – Oakland Bay Bridge on November 7, 2007.

Fig. Three Pier-Side Gantry Cranes Tower Over a Container Ship.

It has been estimated that container ships lose between 2,000 and 10,000 containers at sea each year, costing $370 million per year. Most go overboard on the open sea during storms but there are some examples of whole ships being lost with their cargo.When containers are dropped, they immediately become an environmental threat – termed "marine debris". Once in the ocean, they fill with water and sink if the contents cannot hold air. Rough waters smash the container, sinking it quickly. The threat of piracy can cost a container shipping company as much as $100 million per year due to longer routes and higher speed, particularly near East Africa.

LINER SHIPPING

Vessels that sail on a fixed schedule between fixed ports are often termed "liners". Ships could be carrying on board General cargo, Containers, Passengers etc. This kind of shipping is very different from another broad distinction called "tramps". In liner shipping, vessels sail on a given schedule - whether full or not.

HISTORY

Transportation by sea in the early days was done by sailing ships, which depended on wind and weather. Reliability came in as steam engines started to propel ships and scheduled services started by early 18th century. There was an increasing need for shipping following increased colonization in the 1800's. Finished goods moved from Europe to the colonies and raw material, tea and spices moved back from the Colonies.

Operators on the same trade lane with same ports of call started to co operate to share the huge fixed costs. In a way, thus originated the conference system (Calcutta conference in 1875), which was formed to share costs and prevent price wars. Switching costs were high for shippers using services and carriers of one conference to change to other shipping lines (Loyalty Discounts)

CURRENT DAY

Containerisation brought about a big change in the way trade was done. It has all the benefits of standardization with the additional benefits of pilferage prevention, productivity improvements etc. Of all the cargo that is carried by liner shipping, a large chunk in terms value and volume is containersed. Containers carry a wide variety of cargo from branded shoes, Garments on Hangers to French wine and frozen meat. Cargo volumes has been growing steadily over the last 55 years and the Global container trade is estimated to be at 125 Million TEU (2009 - ESCAP). Ships on which these containers are carried vary widely in size. Sizes range from a few TEU's on Barges or Feeders to Ultra Large container ships which carry greater than 10,000 TEU on board.(Read - Container Ship)

Trade lanes exist between the production centers and the consumption belts and today the biggest trade lanes are the 3 main East-West trades.

- Asia Europe
- Trans Pacific
- Trans Atlantic

Intra Asia trades and North-South trades are growing at a robust rate and increasing in prominence.

CARGO LINER

Fig. RMS St Helena in James Bay, Island of St. Helena.

A cargo liner is a type of merchant ship which carries general cargo and often passengers. They became common just after the middle of the 19th century, and eventually gave way to container ships and other more specialized carriers in the latter half of the 20th century.

CHARACTERISTICS

A cargo liner has been defined as:

A vessel which operated a regular scheduled service on a fixed route between designated ports and carries many consignments of different commodities. Cargo liners transported general freight, from raw materials to manufactures to merchandise. Many had cargo holds adapted to particular services, with refrigerator space for frozen meats or chilled fruit, tanks for liquid cargos such as plant oils, and lockers for valuables. Cargo liners typically carried passengers as well, usually in a single class.They differed from ocean liners which focussed on the passenger trade, and from tramp steamers which did not operate on regular schedules. Cargo liners sailed from port to port along routes and on schedules published in advance.

HISTORY

The cargo liner developed in the mid-19th century with the advancement of technology allowing bigger steamships to be built. As cargo liners were generally faster than cargo ships, they were used for the transport of perishable and high-value goods, as well as providing a passenger service. At first, they were used in Europe and between Europe and America. Longer routes, such as that to Australia, remained in the hands of sailing ships, due to the inefficiency of the steamship of the time.

The use and increased reliability of the compound steam engine gave greater fuel efficiency and opened these routes up to steamships. Alfred Holt pioneered the use of these engines in his steamships. By the last third of the Nineteenth Century it was possible for a steamship to carry enough coal to travel 6,000 miles (9,700 km) before needing to refuel. The opening of the Suez Canal in 1869 and the Panama Canal in 1914 also made the use of cargo liners more profitable, and made possible regular scheduled overseas services. Cargo liners soon comprised "the great portion of the British merchant fleet", the largest in the world. With a focus on high-value freight, most cargo liners carried a limited number of passengers, most commonly 12, as British regulations required a doctor for ships with over 12 passengers.

CARGO SHIP

Fig. The Colombo Express, one of the Largest Container Ships in the World (when She was Built in 2005), Owned and Operated by Hapag-Lloyd of Germany.

A cargo ship or freighter is any sort of ship or vessel that carries cargo, goods, and materials from one port to another. Thousands of cargo carriers ply the world's seas and oceans each year, handling the bulk of international trade. Cargo ships are usually specially designed for the task, often being equipped with cranes and other mechanisms to load and unload, and come in all sizes. Today, they are almost always built by welded steel, and with some exceptions generally have a life expectancy of 25 to 30 years before being scrapped.

TYPES

Fig. Loading of a General Cargo Vessel in 1959.

Cargo ships/freighters can be divided into five groups, according to the type of cargo they carry.

These groups are:

1. General cargo vessels
2. Tankers
3. Dry bulk carriers
4. Multi-purpose vessels
5. Reefer ships

General cargo vessels carry packaged items like chemicals, foods, furniture, machinery, motor- and military vehicles, footwear, garments, etc.

Tankers carry petroleum products or other liquid cargo.

Dry bulk carriers carry coal, grain, ore and other similar products in loose form. Multi-purpose vessels, as the name suggests, carry different classes of cargo – *e.g.* liquid and general cargo – at the same time. A Reefer (or Refrigerated) ship is specifically designed and used for shipping perishable commodities which require temperature-controlled, mostly fruits, meat, fish,vegetables, dairy products and other foodstuffs.

Specialized types of cargo vessels include container ships and bulk carriers (technically tankers of all sizes are cargo ships, although they are routinely thought of as a separate category). Cargo ships fall into two further categories that reflect the services they offer to industry: liner and tramp services. Those on a fixed published schedule and fixed tariff rates are cargo liners. Tramp ships do not have fixed schedules. Users charter them to haul loads. Generally, the smaller shipping companies and private individuals operate tramp ships. Cargo liners run on fixed schedules published by the shipping companies. Each trip a liner takes is called a voyage. Liners mostly carry general cargo. However, some cargo liners may carry passengers also. A cargo liner that carries 12 or more passengers is called a combination or passenger-cum-cargo line.

HISTORY

The earliest records of waterborne activity mention the carriage of items for trade; the evidence of history and archaeology shows the practice to be widespread by the beginning of the 1st millennium BC, and as early as the 14th and 15th centuries BC small Mediterranean cargo ships like those of the 50 foot long (15 - 16 metre) Uluburun ship were carrying 20 tons of exotic cargo; 11 tons of raw copper, jars, glass, ivory, gold, spices, and treasures from Canaan, Greece, Egypt, and Africa. The desire to operate trade routes over longer distances, and throughout more seasons of the year, motivated improvements in ship design during the Middle Ages.

Before the middle of the 19th century, the incidence of piracy resulted in most cargo ships being armed, sometimes quite heavily, as in the case of the Manila galleons and East Indiamen. They were also sometimes escorted by warships.

PIRACY

Piracy is still quite common in some waters, particularly in the Malacca Straits, a narrow channel between Indonesia and Singapore / Malaysia, and cargo ships are still commonly targeted. In 2004, the governments of those three nations agreed to provide better protection for the ships passing through the Straits. The waters off Somalia andNigeria are also prone to piracy, while smaller vessels are also in danger along parts of the South American, Southeast Asian coasts and near the Caribbean Sea.

DEFINITIONS

Fig. A Delmas Container Ship Unloading at the Zanzibar Port in Tanzania.

The words cargo and freight have become interchangeable in casual usage. Technically, "cargo" refers to the goods carried aboard the ship for hire, while "freight" refers to the compensation the ship or charterer receives for carrying the cargo.

Generally, the modern ocean shipping business is divided into two classes:

1. *Liner business:* Typically (but not exclusively) container vessels (wherein "general cargo" is carried in 20 or 40-foot containers), operating as "common carriers", calling a regularly published schedule of ports. A common carrier refers to a regulated service where any member of the public may book cargo for shipment, according to long-established and internationally agreed rules.
2. *Tramp-tanker business:* Generally this is private business arranged between the shipper and receiver and facilitated by the vessel owners or operators, who offer their vessels for hire to carry bulk (dry or liquid) or break bulk (cargoes with individually handled pieces) to any suitable port(s) in the world, according to a specifically drawn contract, called a charter party.

Larger cargo ships are generally operated by shipping lines: companies that specialize in the handling of cargo in general. Smaller vessels, such as coasters, are often owned by their operators.

VESSEL PREFIXES

A category designation appears before the vessel's name. A few examples of prefixes for naval ships are "USS" (United States Ship), "HMS" (Her/His Majesty's Ship), "HMCS" (Her/His majesty's Canadian Ship) and "HTMS" (His Thai Majesty's Ship), while a few examples for prefixes for merchant ships are "RMS" (Royal Mail Ship, usually a passenger liner), "MV" (Motor Vessel, powered by diesel), "MT" (Motor Tanker, powered vessel carrying liquids only) "FV" Fishing Vessel and "SS" (Screw Streamer, driven by propellers or screws, often understood to stand for Steamship). "TS", sometimes found in first position before a merchant ship's prefix, denotes that it is a Turbine Steamer.

FAMOUS CARGO SHIPS

Famous cargo ships include the Liberty ships of World War II, partly based on a British design. Liberty ship sections were prefabricated in locations across the USA and then assembled by shipbuilders in an average of six weeks, with the record being just over four days. These ships allowed the Allies to replace sunken cargo vessels at a rate greater than the Kriegsmarine's U-boats could sink them, and contributed significantly to the war effort, the delivery of supplies, and eventual victory over the Axis powers. Lake freighters built for the Great Lakes in North America differ in design from sea water going ships because of the difference in wave size and frequency in the lakes. A number of these boats are so large that they cannot leave the lakes because they do not fit into the locks on the Saint Lawrence Seaway. Cargo ships are categorized partly by capacity, partly by weight, and partly by dimensions (often with reference to the various canals and canal locks they fit through).

Common categories include:

- Dry Cargo
- Small Handy size, carriers of 20,000 long tons deadweight (DWT)-28,000 DWT
- Handy size, carriers of 28,000-40,000 DWT
- Seawaymax, the largest size that can traverse the St Lawrence Seaway
- Handymax, carriers of 40,000-50,000 DWT
- Panamax, the largest size that can traverse the Panama Canal (generally: vessels with a width smaller than 32.2 m) Limited to 52,000 DWT loaded, 80,000 DWT empty.
- New Panamax, Upgraded Panama locks with 55m beam, 18M depth, 120,000 DWT
- Capesize, vessels larger than Panamax and Post-Panamax, and must traverse the Cape of Good Hope and Cape Horn to travel between oceans
- Chinamax, carriers of 380,000-400,000 DWT with main dimensions limited by port infrastructure in China
- Wet Cargo
- Aframax, oil tankers between 75,000 and 115,000 DWT. This is the largest size defined by the average freight rate assessment (AFRA) scheme.
- Suezmax, the largest size that can traverse the Suez Canal
- VLCC (Very Large Crude Carrier), supertankers between 150,000 and 320,000 DWT.
- Malaccamax, the largest size that can traverse the Strait of Malacca
- ULCC (Ultra Large Crude Carrier), enormous supertankers between 320,000 and 550,000 DWT

POLLUTION

Due to its low cost, most large cargo vessels are powered by bunker fuel also known as Heavy Fuel Oil which contains higher sulphur levels than diesel. This level of pollution is accelerating: with bunker fuel consumption at 278 million tonnes per year in 2001, it is projected to be at 500 million tonnes per year in 2020. International standards to dramatically reduce sulphur content in marine fuels and nitrogen oxide emissions have been put in place. Among some of the solutions offered is changing over the fuel intake to clean diesel or marine gas oil, while in restricted waters and Cold Ironing the ship while it is in port.

The process of removing sulphur from the fuel impacts the viscosity and lubricity of the marine gas oil though, which could cause damage in the engine fuel pump. The fuel viscosity can be raised by cooling the fuel down. If the various requirements are enforced, the International Maritime Organization's marine fuel requirement will mean a 90 per cent reduction in sulphur oxide emissions; whilst the European Union is planning stricter controls on emissions.

HOW LINER SHIPPING WORKS

Upto the begining of 1960s, cargo carried by liner shipping was known as "general cargo" and the vessels used to carry those general cargo, were small general dry cargo ships(twin-decker and multi-decker ship). The cargo was stowed in small pre-packed consignments involving labour intensive and time consuming method for loading and unloading. Due to this negative factor, ships stay in port became longer and even more longer during congestion. All these factors contributed to increase cost of transport and other related cost and thereby hindered international trade.

The situation started to change radically during late 1960s onwards with the introduction of "containerization" in the trade between United States and Europe. Subsequently this revolutionary changes in the mode of transportation was adopted speedily by rest of the world. General cargoes are now increasingly carried in containers of standard dimension i.e 8*8*20 feet unit known as - Twenty Feet Equivalent Unit (TEU). This container penetration in general cargo noticed remarkable increase of cargo lifting by containers from 20 per cent in1960s to more than 70 per cent at present. At the same time traditional general cargo vessels were replaced by specialized cellular container ships of ever-increasing dimension which has resulted in higher productivity and low transport cost. Leading container shipping line like "MAERSK SEALAND" has taken bold steps to container ships in excess of 8000 TEU of carrying capacity. Interested readers will be happy to know that MAERSK LINE has ventured to build triple Es carrier of 18000 TEU capacity which is likely to be inducted in trade soon. From above facts and figure, we can safely conclude that liner shipping is now virtually turned into liner container shipping. World fleet of liner vessels, primarily in the form of Container Ships and Roll-on / Roll-off Ships, are now capable to cater about 60 per cent of the goods by value being transported internationally by sea each year.

HOW TO START LINER SHIPPING

The pattern of liner services that has evolved over last century to meet the changing requirements of world economy is very extensive. The largest volume of trade linking three major industrial centers of the world are, North America, Western Europe, and Far East Asia. The following three major liner trade routes are operating to cover these industrial centers.

- The North Atlantic route covering the trade between north-west Europe, East Coast Canada and the United States.
- North America to the Far East route covering trade between East and West Coast of North America and the Far East, stretching from Japan to Singapore.
- Western Europe to the Far East route covering the trade between Western Europe and the Far East countries.

To start liner service, one of the above routes to be chosen. Then comprehensive study to be made to know the type and volume of cargo moving within the route per year and pattern of growth of trade. It is interesting to mention here that about 400 regularly scheduled liner services are operating round the world. To ensure regular sailing of vessel at declared schedule and earn stable freight on long term basis, Shipping Lines have developed Conference system. The first Conference was formed in August 1875 by the lines trading between the United Kingdom and Calcutta aiming to ensure charging similar rates, to limit the number of sailings, to grant no preferences to shippers and to sail on a given date whether ship is full load or not.

Again Shipping Lines work under different types of Conferences as mentioned below:

- *Closed Conferences:* The most common arrangement is the closed conference which restricts membership, sets freight rates for the conference and often fixes the trade share of each member of the Conference. This helps conference members to adjust capacity to demand and avoid unnecessary duplication of port calls. Inspite of many criticism against closed conference, it's existence for more than a century proves that this arrangement still fulfill the prime need of transport industry.
- *Open Conference:* Under this arrangement, membership is not restricted. Any shipping line can join in open conference and enjoy unit revenue set by the conference. Since there is no control on trade shares or number of ships to be employed in service by new member, there is always a risk of overtonnaging in open conference resulting in undercut of existing freight rate.
- *Outsiders:* There are Shipping Companies that set up liner services on a route without joining the conference. Outsiders can attract shippers in a route by offering lower freight, if the rate set by conference system is higher.

Once route is selected, then decision to be taken by shipping line whether to join in closed conference or open conference considering which conference can benefit them most. One of the important job of shipping line / conference system is to set up a reasonably workable tariff rate for all the commodities moving between the ports of a particular route where the Line serves. This is the most debatable area where conference system / member lines failed to evolve a unique pricing mechanism acceptable to all the shipping lines without any controversy. Experts on liner shipping have been working over a century on this issue, but no unique system could be developed as yet, as there are lot of economic and non-economic factors which are vulnerable to change in response to market conditions. Moreover the list of cargoes transported by liner companies are immensely diverse in nature, which makes the task of freight setting more difficult. We can have a look about the diverse nature of general cargo transported by liner vessel from the table below:

Commodities commonly shipped by liner service,		
SL No,	**Commodity,**	**Remark**
1	Metal manufactures	Important Liner cargo
2	Rubber	Important Liner cargo
3	Coffee & Tea	Important Liner cargo
4	Textiles	Important Liner cargo
5	Textile Fibres	Important Liner cargo
6	Beverage & Tobacco	Important Liner cargo
7	Machinery	Important Liner cargo
9	Simple manufactures	Plywood,buildingmaterials/
10	Cement	Mainly bulk but some liner
11	Timber(logs &lumber)	Mainly bulk but some liner
12	Steel products	Mainly bulk but some liner
13	Metal scrap	Mainly bulk but some liner
14	Oils & fats	Mainly bulk but some liner
15	Gypsum & pluster	Mainly bulk but some liner
16	Non-ferrous metal	Mainly bulk but some liner

Above table shows that liner cargo includes wide range of commodities and the list is ever increasing. So liner company has to formulate pricing policy considering features of each and every commodity separately and also different variable and constant factors linked with the services rendered. *The following basic items to be considered in general by liner company to set up freight tariff:*

- Freight charges is the first important item to consider which will cover cost of transporting the consignment from port A to port B. This charge is listed item wise in the conference 'rate book' which provides information regarding rate per freight ton(charged by weight or volume whichever is higher) for each commodity between ports or regions served by liner company. For some commodities, particularly those shipped in large volume, shipping line may negotiate with the shipper to fix up a separate price.
- Port charges. This includes expenses payable to the port authority when a vessel calls in port for cargo loading and unloading operation. This are generally separate because freight charges in the rate book

are often quoted on a regional basis. Within a region, ports may have different charges. Some conferences absorb port charges into the ocean freight.

- Service additionals. If the shipper undertakes additional services for the customer – for example, storage of goods, customs clearance or trans-shipment, then there would be additional charge for this.
- Cargo additionals. Some cargoes attract additional charges because they are difficult or expensive to transport – steel pipe over a certain length, heavy lift, or liquids that involve tank cleaning for example.
- Banker Adjustment Factor(BAF). It is difficult for shipping line to maintain a stable freight rate as per declared 'rate book', when sudden and unexpected increase occurs in the cost of bunker price in the international market. This leads to proportionate increase in the operating cost on long routes. To avoid revising the 'rate book', this is generally dealt with by a bunker adjustment factor, which is added to the freight.
- Port congestion surcharges. In a situation of prolong port congestion, liner company faces unscheduled delays in port for loading and discharging and it increases operating cost in terms of higher port charges and fixed operating cost to the vessel account. To compensate this financial loss, shipping line has to impose a congestion surcharge for cargo destined for congested port.
- Currency Adjustment Factor. The shipping line within the conference may face a problem that they submit freight invoice to the shipper in one currency but incur all their cost in another currency. If the rate of exchange of the currency through which shipping line is to settle their expenses, abnormally falls down compared to the currency rate of freight payment, then the line is subjected to great losses. Currency Adjustment Factor takes care of this adverse situation. It is based on an agreed basket of costs which keeps tariff revenue same, regardless of fluctuation in the tariff currency rate of exchange.
- Discount or loyalty rabate. A discount allowed by the conference for the genuine customers who are loyal to the conference for supporting.
- General rate increase. Due to cost inflation in the economy, sometimes shipping line has to raise or adjust freight tariff for each commodity proportionately which is known as General rate increase and is notified to the trade accordingly. This kind of general rate increase is sometimes negotiated with shippers / shippers council before implementation.
- Commodity box rate. In case of container freight, commodity box rate applies in general which means shippers to pay fixed amount per box irrespective of weight of its contents. This criteria can not be applied

to a special type of container which requires special treatment on board the vessel and thereby need to fix up higher freight. FAK(Freight of all kinds) is also used as fixed rate per box but this can not differentiate between high value commodities with low value commodities.

- Here pre and post shipment charges viz terminal handing charges, container service charges, LCL charges, port levies, container demurrage charges etc to be considered for freight calculation of a container. In case Inland transport services is required on carriers haulage, then cost to be included in the freight.

Next important job for newly established shipping line is to plan an ideal sailing schedule for the company which will ensure optimum utilization of the fleet in the selected route. Line has to collect following relevant information / data to plan a workable schedule.

- Who are competitors ? What is their fleet capacity – type of vessel / age. Is the service overtonnaged or undertonnaged ?
- Cargo flow – type and volume of cargo moving both in inbound and outbound leg. Seasonality of cargo.
- What is amount of cargo share among the competing lines. Is there any scope of slot sharing with existing operators ?
- Freight set by the conference is good enough to earn reasonable profit to survive.

With above information feedback, following criteria / factors to be considered for workable realistic schedule:

- The sailing schedule need to be realistic and reliable. Neither too tight nor too generous set-up give desired results.
- The most ideal set-up is to follow a fixed day and even a fixed hour departure / arrival of the vessel during a week. This may not be achievable, as cargo flows are not always sufficient to support a weekly sailing schedule.
- The tonnage to be used has to be suitable to carry all types of cargo offered by valued customers. If any cargo is refused on technical ground, it affects the image of the company. For example, some specific volume of 'Reefer cargo' is offered in the trade for some specific destination port at regular intervals. To ensure loading this cargo, identical ship having required reefer capacity need to be deployed.
- The speed of the vessel plays a vital role to obtain customers support in favour of the line because higher speed reduces transit time and helps shipper to fulfill contractual obligation to the buyer earlier and get the payment. For example, an outward voyage of 4000 nautical miles shall have following transit- time at different speed :

22 knots	7 days 14 hours
21 knots	7 days 23 hours
20 knots	8 days 8 hours
19 knots	8 days 18 hours
18 knots	9 days 6 hours

- Cargo offerings for both inbound and outbound, are of paramount importance. So schedule need to be designed in such a way so that ship's capacity can be fully utilized keeping minimum port calls. In the port rotation, there may be occasions when cargo offering from some particular port will be poor. In that case, it would be wiser to skip the port in that voyage and serve same port in alternate sailing.
- Since working on weekend i.e Saturdays and Sundays in port involves extra cost on overtime account, so ships to be at sea during weekends.
- It is normal that trade has seasonal peaks and troughs. At the end of the year, general cargo offerings from developed countries of the world, increases in volume compared to other months due to Christmas. Moreover commodities like coffee, cocoa, wool and fruits are seasonal in nature. So lines need to plan their schedule ahead in order to meet this increased seasonal demand of trade by placing more tonnage if necessary.
- There are some ports which have draught restriction and some are tidal ports where vessels entry and departure depend on tide. Placement of right size of vessel in the ports having draught problem and hassle free arrival / sailing in tidal ports should get top priority in schedule planning.

Shipping Line has to develop sound Agency networks in all the ports where the liner vessels will call for loading and discharging. This arrangement can be done either by opening their own local/regional office or through appointment of Agents. Since opening overseas office increases overhead cost of the company, so most of the companies now follow the principle of appointing agents.

The agents virtually represent the shipping line in a particular port or region and is responsible to do all the functions related to husbanding of ships calling at port as per instructions of Principal/Shipping line.

For their services, agents receive a commission from Principal for exports and imports which is generally calculated as a percentage of the freight or more specifically net freight including CAF (but often excluding bunker surcharges, less deferred rebate etc if any).

Commission for exports is generally higher than imports because agents has to undertake extra marketing efforts to procure export cargo. In case of import, their function is restricted to delivery of cargo only and no canvassing is required. The normal percentages of commission are :

5 per cent for export cargo
2.5 per cent for import cargo

A Standard Liner Agency Agreement is normally signed between the Principal and Agency house. This agreement provides modalities of functions and responsibilities in detail that agent is to perform and remuneration payable to them. The efficiency and image of liner service depend on how agents at different ports, are performing their assigned functions with professionalism, sincerity and dedication. An aggressive marketing strategy is to be adopted by shipping line with a view to grab volume cargo from global major buyers/ exporters/ importers to ensure optimum use of tonnage capacity and upgrade market share of the trade.

Cost classification in liner trade business : A shipping line when involves in trade by deploying their fleet of vessels in a particular route, then expenditure in different heads is incurred. Expenditures are broadly classified into two categories :

- *Fixed operating cost(FOC) :* This cost is fixed in nature and the shipping line has to bear the burden of cost irrespective of the fact whether ship is in employment or not. That means line has to incur this cost even if vessel remains idle or goes without employment. FOC includes following cost components.
- *Manning cost(crew cost)-* This includes basic salaries/other financial benefits payable as per contract, crew travel, repatriation cost, medical expenses etc.
- *Stores and lubricants :* It includes spare parts, deck and engine stores and lub oil which is require to keep the vessel always fit for commercial employment.
- *Repairs and Maintenance :* This cost is a recurring one and this is necessary to meet routine maintenance and repairs of the vessel as per recommendation made by Classification society through survey.
- Insurance cost covers risks related to hull and machinery of the ship, war risks etc. P and I Club to cover cargo claim and third party claims.
- Administration or Overhead cost includes expenditure of head office and other regional offices of the company. This constitutes a big amount in the fixed cost structure of a shipping line.
- *Capital cost/Depreciation :* The owner of the shipping line makes massive investment for purchase/procurement of ships which is the capital cost of the company. If owner purchases ships from his own fund, he is directly contributing "Equity" to his own company. Ship like other fixed assets, depreciates in value on yearly basis. To replace the ship at the end of its economic life, sufficient fund from revenue earnings has to raise and to be kept in separate account. Otherwise replacement of ship would be uncertain. In the shipping trade

depreciation cost is calculated by historical cost or straight line method. Let us assume purchase price of a new built container ship with 3-4000TEU capacity is around US$25m and economic life of such tonnage is 20 years. The depreciation cost per year would be $ 25milliion - $6million(estimated scrap value of the ship) / 20year = US$950,000. If ship is procured under bank finance or yard credit, depreciation cost per year would be on higher side.

- *Voyage cost :* This cost is variable in nature. It is directly related with a round voyage/trip of a ship in a particular route. Following variable cost components are included.
- *Port charges:* It includes expenditures on docking and warfage charges, mooring/unmooring, port dues, light dues, pilotage, tugs, garbage disposal etc. Since ship calls good number of ports in liner trade, port charges account for significant amount in the total voy cost.
- *Bunker charges:* It is also an important item of voyage costing. Ship has a standard fuel consumption rate per day at given speed in the sea. Based on this data, it is possible to calculate how much fuel will be required on the basis of distance in knots mile to cover from starting to the end of passage. It also includes cost of water purchased and used by ship's crew during voyage.
- *Cargo handling cost:* It is the loading and discharging cost paid to the independent agency or port authority who renders the service. Generally cargo handling cost is paid on per ton basis for general cargo and per tue basis for container as per declared tariff or mutual agreement.
- Canal dues are levied for the passage of Panama and Suez canal. The cost of transit is substantial.
- *Agency commission:* Amount payable to the appointed agents for rendering husbanding services to ship.
- *Taxes on freight:* Tax amount to be paid to the concern authority on freight earning as per law of the land.

Hope above description shall attract the attention of inquisitive readers to share the views that "Liner Shipping" acts as the Global Engine to connect countries and people all over the world for establishing an efficient, safe, low cost and above all environment friendly transportation network, which never exists before.

THE WORLDWIDE MARITIME NETWORK OF CONTAINER SHIPPING

Maritime networks are among the oldest forms of spatial interaction. Port hierarchies and the spatial pattern of maritime linkages can be considered as illustrations of wider ongoing processes, such as the regionalization and globalization of trade patterns and business cycles, thus revealing a certain political economy of the world (Vigarié, 1995). Lewis and Wigen (1999) argue that the meta-geography of the world system would be better understood from the maritime looking glass of basins, seas, and oceans. Following decades of adaptation and diffusion since the emergence of containerization, the global maritime container shipping network has become a reality (Frémont, 2007; Rodrigue and Notteboom, 2010).

The technological revolution of containerization has gradually produced new forms of relationships among countries, regions, and port cities, backed by a continuous pressure on transport costs (Limao and Venables, 2001) and an increasing power of shipping alliances and large carriers (Sys, 2009; Slack and Frémont, 2009). Investigating such changes would complement the lack of evidence about the spatial patterns of commodity chains (Leslie and Reimer, 1999), because ports compete not as individual places that handle ships but as crucial links within global supply chains.

While the main shipping routes and ports are well described in a number of studies, the structure and evolution of the global maritime network itself has not been fully documented. More extensive is the research on global airline networks due to their closer overlap with systems of cities. Despite the local dereliction of port-city linkages in recent decades, maritime transport remains absolutely necessary for globalization. Its crucial weight in world trade volumes (90 per cent) makes it a useful looking glass for analyzing the global economy and its geographic architecture.

In parallel, the spatial design of maritime transport not only follows trade demand but also possesses its own practical arrangements and network configurations, which also evolve over time. The concentration and regional polarization of flows by load centers and intermediate hubs towards other secondary ports are typical examples of such configurations. It is thus important to evaluate the respective influence of technological factors (*e.g.* carriers and infrastructures, industry changes) and territorial factors (*e.g.* geographic and trade proximities, socio-economic developments) in the formation of shipping networks, port hierarchies, and maritime regions.

The remainder of this chapter is organized as follows. Section 2 introduces the concept of port system and reviews the mechanisms shaping port competition, port selection, and port concentration, while describing the specificity and complexity of liner service networks. In Section 3, data on vessel movements (1996 and 2006) and the methodology for analyzing the global liner service network are presented, together with some results on the structure and geographic coverage of this network. Section 4 provides a closer look at the port hierarchy based on centrality measures and the geographic pattern of nodal maritime regions. The paper ends with a discussion of the research outcomes for further analysis of the global economy and its networks.

PORT SYSTEMS AND MARITIME NETWORKS

Port Choice and the Hierarchy in Port Systems

Traffic flows through ports are a physical outcome of route and port selection by the relevant actors in the chain. The most relevant service-related and cost factors explaining port selection by the main players of the transport chain (*e.g.* shippers, ocean carriers, and forwarders) are identified in the scientific literature on port choice. Port choice thus becomes a function of the overall network cost and performance. Notteboom (2009b) groups the factors together in the demand profile of the port, the supply profile of the port, and the market profile of the port.

Typical port choice criteria include factors such as:

- Physical and technical infrastructure including the nautical accessibility (*e.g.* draft);
- Terminal infrastructure and equipment, the hinterland accessibility and intermodal offer;
- Geographical location vis-à-vis the main shipping lanes and the hinterland;
- Port efficiency expressed as port turnaround time, terminal productivity and cost efficiency;
- Interconnectivity of the port (sailing frequency of deep-sea and feeder shipping services);
- Reliability, capacity, frequency and costs of inland transport services;
- Quality and costs of auxiliary services such as pilotage, towage, customs, etc.;
- Efficiency and costs of port management and administration (*e.g.* port dues);
- Availability, quality and costs of logistic value-added activities (*e.g.* warehousing) and port community systems;
- Port security/safety and environmental profile;
- Port reputation.

The aggregate outcome of port choice and supply chain decisions leads to a specific distribution of cargo flows in port systems. The search for regularities in the development of port hierarchies has mostly been done from a continental perspective considering ports as heads of land-based transport corridors willing to extend their hinterland coverage. Early works provided spatial models (Taaffe et al., 1963; Rimmer, 1967; Ogundana, 1970) suggesting a trend towards an increasing level of cargo concentration in port systems.

The concepts of maritime range (Vigarié, 1964) and port system (Robinson, 1976) originally comprised a set of adjacent seaports in close proximity that were interdependent through land and sea freight flows. However, most scholars have continued focusing primarily on hinterlands, due to the development of intermodalism and logistic chains around ports and the higher cost of land transport versus sea transport (Notteboom, 2004). The nature and performance of traffics is often explained by the situation of ports within land-based transport and urban systems (Ducruet et al., 2010c).

Although the development of peripheral ports (Hayuth, 1981) and offshore hubs has a maritime purpose for cargo distribution towards secondary ports (Slack and Wang, 2002; Notteboom, 2005), their emergence has been interpreted from the hinterland perspective of a port regionalization process leading to the formation of a regional load center network (Notteboom and Rodrigue, 2005). There remain important local deviations from general models of port system development due to path dependency and contingency (Notteboom, 2006a, 2009a).

The definition of port systems has often been limited to coastal morphology, geographic proximity, and administrative boundaries (Ducruet et al., 2009a, 2009b). Never have port systems been defined and delineated from the maritime perspective of inter-port linkages. This raises the question of whether physical factors and geographic proximity still play a role in the current spatial patterns of container shipping circulations. The concepts of maritime region and port region, which remain rather descriptive and vague in the literature (Ducruet, 2009), may benefit from the application of similar methods used by studies of other global networks, allowing for the definition of coherent groups of ports as well as the identification of leader ports. A close look at the current organization of liner shipping networks is necessary before applying specific network analytical tools.

DESIGN AND OPERATION OF LINER SERVICE NETWORKS

The development of liner shipping in the last 30 years has exceeded the growth of world trade volumes. The activity of this very dynamic branch of maritime transport is measured based on annual container port throughputs. Besides continuous growth in throughput volumes, we also observe a parallel increase in the concentration in the global port system, notwithstanding slight decreases in recent years, notably after the 2008 financial crisis that directly affected traffic volumes and distributions. Despite those conjectural changes, liner shipping remains built on a series of specific network configurations.

Container shipping features a complex combination of end-to-end services, line-bundling services, and pendulum services, which are connected to form extensive shipping networks. Port hierarchy in the container business is intrinsically linked to shipping lines' design of these liner service networks in terms of service variables such as service frequency, vessel capacity, fleet mix, vessel speed, and the number and order of port calls. Liner service design is a function not only of carrier-specific operational factors (*i.e.* lower costs) but also of shippers' needs (*e.g.* transit time) and willingness to pay for a better service.

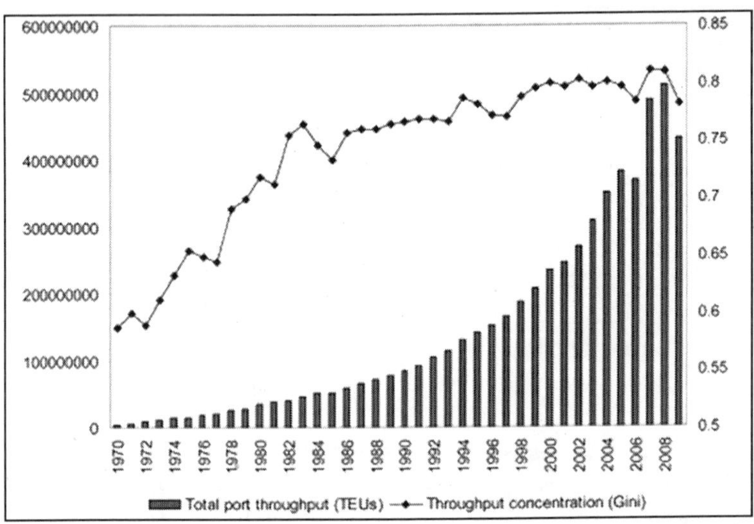

Fig. World Port Throughput and Concentration, 1970-2009.

In the last two decades, increased cargo availability has led carriers and strategic alliances among them to reshape their liner shipping networks through the introduction of new types of liner services on the main east-west trade lanes. The largest ships operate on multi-port itineraries calling at a limited number of ports.

The Europe–Far East trade provides a good example. Most mainline operators and alliances running services from the Far East to North Europe stick to line bundling itineraries with direct calls scheduled in each of the main markets. Notwithstanding diversity in calling patterns on the observed routes, carriers select up to five regional ports of call per loop. Shipping lines have significantly increased average vessel sizes deployed on the route from around 4500 TEU in 2000 to over 7500 TEU in early 2010. These scale increases in vessel size have put downward pressure on the average number of port calls per loop on the Far East–North Europe trade: 4.9 ports of call in 1989, 3.84 in 1998, 3.77 in October 2000, 3.68 in February 2006, and 3.35 in December 2009.

Maersk Line, MSC, and CMA-CGM are among the truly global liner operators with a strong presence in secondary routes. Their networks are based on traffic circulation through specific hubs. Productivity has been improved through the use of larger ships, new operational patterns, and cooperation between shipping lines. Container shipping lines have been very active in securing (semi)dedicated terminal capacity in the strategic locations within their liner service networks. An overview of the strategic ports in the worldwide liner network of Maersk Line. Shipping lines also rely on horizontal integration through operating agreements (*e.g.* vessel sharing agreements, slot chartering agreements, consortia and strategic alliances) and mergers and acquisitions. Alliance structures (cf. Grand Alliance, New World Alliance, and CYKH) provide its members easy access to more loops or services with relatively low-cost implications and allow them to share terminals.

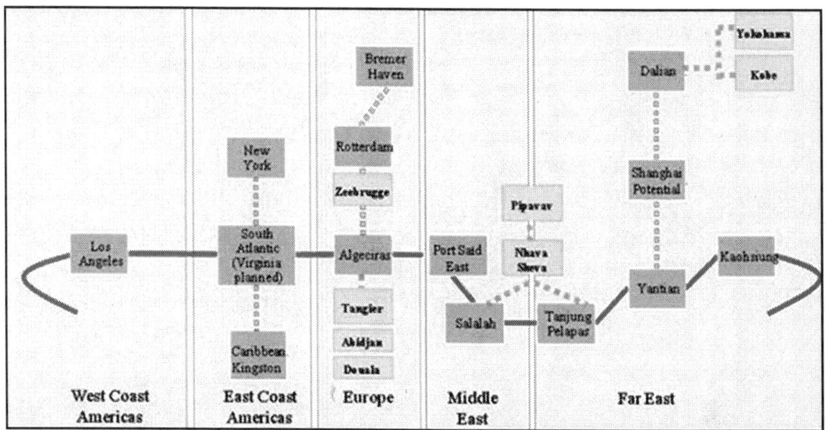

Fig. The Main Strategic Ports in the Liner Service Network of Maersk Line.

Note: Relay/Interlining involves trade route based transhipment at key network ports between deep-sea vessel strings. The aim is to transfer containers between mainline services, thereby adding new service options.

In the last few decades, extensive hub-feeder container systems and short-sea shipping networks came into existence to cope with increasing volumes and to connect to other port ranges (Rodrigue and Notteboom, 2010). The economics of transhipment and relay/interlining have resulted in the establishment of intermediate hubs with terminals owned, in whole or in part, by carriers or port operators. In some cases, intermediate hubs were developed within offshore location often on small islands with an implicit local cargo base (Rodrigue and Notteboom, 2010). The development of offshore hubs did not exclude transhipment activities at traditional gateway ports such as in the Western Mediterranean port system, where the distinction between hub ports and gateway ports has become blurred (Gouvernal et al., 2005).

The position of pure transhipment hubs is generally more unstable than that of pure gateway ports: once traffic volumes for the gateway ports are sufficient, hubs are bypassed and might even become redundant (Wilmsmeier and Notteboom, 2010). The location of transhipment hubs remains important, because they lower the deviation distance to/from main trunk lines (Zohil and Prijon, 1999). There remains a subtle combination between centrality (proximity to origin/destination markets) and intermediacy (insertion in carrier networks) in nearly every port (Fleming and Hayuth, 1994).

METHODOLOGY AND LINER SHIPPING NETWORK CHARACTERISTICS

In their recent review of the scientific literature on maritime network analysis, Ducruet et al.

(2010a) particularly stress the scarcity and fragmentation of empirical studies, which may be categorized among four main approaches:

- *Geographic coverage of carrier networks:* Regional or global distribution of the port networks for individual shipping companies based on service data (*e.g.* Coscon, Maersk) revealing their strategic choices;
- *Network connectivity:* Characteristics of a given network based on its topology, with reference to spatial analysis and graph theory, such as the pioneer study of Joly (1999) showing the tripolar organisation of the global maritime system based on Reeds zones, and other works on a regional level;
- *Network efficiency:* Modeling of port selection processes and search for the optimal location, for instance, of a transhipment hub lowering overall shipping costs;
- *Complex networks:* Description of the network' hierarchical structure on a global level comparing its properties with general models of small-world and scale-free networks.

This chapter wishes to further the interpretation of network structure, port hierarchy, and the dynamics influencing them. It gives paramount importance to the visualization of the network as a whole and of emerging regional patterns. This is based on a rarely used data source on daily vessel movements, which is more precise than service data and therefore more representative of the reality and complexity of liner shipping.

Data Overview

The methodology used for building the global liner network defines an inter-port connection by the circulation of vessels between the ports through a 365-day sequence of port calls. Thus, nodes (vertices) in the network are the ports, and links (edges) in the network are the connections realized by vessel movements. The years 1996 and 2006 were chosen, because 1996 marked the emergence of post-panamax vessels (*e.g.* the Regina Maersk of 6140 TEU was introduced in 1996) and the start of strategic alliance formation among shipping lines; 2006 saw the introduction of the first 10,000+ TEU vessels in a period of rapid container growth mainly triggered by the China effect in the world economy. Data was obtained from Lloyd's Marine Intelligence Unit (LMIU) that ensures most of the world fleet for all types of vessels. The obtained database covers approximately 92 per cent and 98 per cent of the world's fleet of container vessels in 1996 and 2006, respectively. Interestingly, the capacity and size of the fleet as well as the number of vessel movements have grown faster than the number of ports and operators, while the average vessel capacity has grown from 1906 TEU to 2413 TEU. Such evidence confirms the observed limitations for ports accommodating ever-growing vessels and traffic, which remain in the hands of horizontally and vertically integrated companies.

Table. Overview of the Database on Vessel Movements, 1996-2006.

	1996	2006	2006/1996
No. Ports	975	1,240	1.27
No. Vessel movements	176,439	390,740	2.21
No. Vessels	1,759	3,973	2.26
No. Operators	497	720	1.46
Total slot capacity (TEUs)	3,352,849	9,590,309	2.86
Share world fleet (% TEUs)	92.15	97.91	+7.75

The global network was modeled based on vessel characteristics, ports of call, and vessel movements. The first result is a global network composed of weighted and non-directed links between ports, which can be analyzed in two different ways. On the one hand, vessel circulations create a graph of direct linkages (GDL) based on the successive ports of calls (*i.e.* from port A to port B and from port B to port C).

On the other hand, it can be argued that two ports are also connected if they belong to the same liner service or loop, although they are not adjacent calls; a graph of all linkages (GAL) thus adds indirect linkages (*i.e.* from port A to port C). In the GDL, Le Havre and Tokyo are never connected by a direct link, whereas, in the GAL, this connection might occur inside a pendulum or round-the-world service. The GAL is the overlap of all individual complete graphs created by the circulation of each vessel.

These two dimensions of the same reality (GDL and GAL) may exhibit distinct features in terms of network structure and port hierarchy. In order to reveal the structural properties of the two graphs for each year of observation, we apply conventional measures derived from graph theory, which were originally applied to transport networks by Kansky (1963), Haggett and Chorley (1972), and Garrison and Marble (1974), and from complex systems theory, referring to the works of Barabasi and Albert (1999) and Watts and Strogatz (1998).

This set of measures provides clear evidence about the nature of the network based on topological properties.

One limitation of the data is that it ignores how many full or empty containers were truly handled by ships and ports. In reality, some vessels may not be fully loaded, since their passage in a port does not always include stevedoring activities (*e.g.* a port visit in the framework of bunkering activities). However, with reference to Joly (1999), the linear correlation between vessel traffic and port throughput is very significant: about 88 per cent and 87 per cent of total variance is explained by the regression in 1996 and 2006, respectively.

This verifies the good fit and quality of the LMIU data source with official port statistics for analyzing container ports and their position in liner shipping networks.

Network Structure

The important differences between the GDL and GAL approaches and between the two years of observation. In terms of network size, the GDL has fewer links than the GAL, which includes numerous indirect connections among ports, thus making it about 5 times larger (edges) and 12 to 13 times longer than the GDL for the same number of ports (vertices). In the GDL, the most central port in terms of maximum degree value connects about 18 to 19 per cent of all ports; in the GAL, it connects 48 to 51 per cent. Such differences in size have a strong influence on other network properties. Indeed, the GAL has about 5 to 6 times greater density, connectivity, and lattice degree compared to the GDL.

More robust measures proposed by physics complement such findings by revealing the polarized or scale-free structure of the GDL with power-law exponents higher than one (-1.35 in 1996 and -1.29 in 2006): few ports concentrate a large number of links (high degree centrality), while most ports have a limited number of links with other ports.

Due to its higher density, the GAL is more likely to be a small-world network: higher average clustering coefficients (0.74 and 0.73), higher transitivity (0.40 and 0.43), lower power-law exponents (-0.62 and -0.65), and smaller diameters (4 and 5) than the GDL indicate the tendency for a given port to have its direct neighbours connected to each other, thus forming tightly connected communities.

Thus, the GDL is more representative of hub ports dominating secondary ports, whereas the GAL represents densely connected maritime regions. Consequently, the GAL is more efficient than the GDL, because the inclusion of indirect links facilitates the circulation of flows in the graph, as reflected by its shorter average path length. Our results are similar to those of Hu and Zhu (2009) based on 2006 service data, both for the GDL (power-law exponent of -1.7, average clustering coefficient of 0.4) and the GAL (average clustering coefficient of 0.7).

Despite their fundamental differences in size and structure, the two networks share similar evolutionary paths. Network structure has remained somewhat resilient to the aforementioned industry changes (and their spatial consequences), as seen with the stable connectivity (gamma index) and clustering coefficients.

However, both networks have become more complex (cf. higher values for alpha and beta indices) due to the multiplication of nodes and edges, resulting in better efficiency as illustrated by the decreased average path length. One important trend that is only visible in the GDL is the decrease of the power-law coefficient, which seems to contradict the higher polarization of shipping networks for individual shipping companies as a result of service rationalization and a reduction of port calls per liner service.

Table. Topological Properties of the Global Maritime Network.

Index	Measure	Graph of direct linkages (GDL)		Graph of all linkages (GAL)	
		1996	2006	1996	2006
Network size	No. vertices	910	1205	910	1205
	No. edges	5,666	9,829	28,510	51,057
	Max. degree	165	226	437	610
	Avg. degree	12.787	17.027	64.178	87.521
	Total length (000s km)	5,159	10,813	71,835	130,927
	Traffic density (TEU/km)	331	407	125	183
	Max. edge length (km)	10,012	10,018	10,018	10,018
	Avg. edge length (km)	1,008	1,227	2,900	2,997
	Diameter	9	8	4	5
Cycles	Cyclomatic number	4,757	8,625	27,601	49,853
Lattice degree	Alpha	0.005	0.012	0.033	0.069
Complexity	Beta	6.226	8.156	31.329	42.370
Connectivity	Gamma	0.014	0.014	0.069	0.070
Scale-free	Power-law coefficient	-1.351	-1.293	-0.624	-0.647
Small-world	Avg. clustering coefficient (local)	0.540	0.545	0.744	0.734
	Transitivity (global)	0.266	0.266	0.404	0.435
Efficiency	Avg. path length	3.253	3.189	2.230	2.219

This decrease may be interpreted as the combined influence of bottom-up and top-down retroactions. Bottom-up phenomena include congestion issues at the port-urban interface and regional integration processes. On a local level, large ports face important limitations in terms of lack and cost of available land for further expansion as well as congestion and bottleneck effects at terminals situated within dense urban environments.

Port-city separation and the shift of modern terminals outside urban areas may be avoided in some cases through efficient planning policies (Lee et al., 2008). On a regional level, trade growth has multiplied the number of intra-regional shipping connections, thus making the network denser and more evenly distributed.

This is particularly true in emerging economies where maritime transport plays a crucial role (*e.g.* China, India, Brazil, and Middle East).

Top-down retroactions are found at the level of the competition among shipping lines. A number of shipping lines seek differentiation and competitive advantage by fully or partially controlling (semi)dedicated terminal facilities. However, this spatial concentration at the company level does not necessarily result in higher cargo concentration at port system level since individual shipping lines often opt for different locations to set up their hub ports (Cullinane and Khana, 1999; Frémont and Soppé 2007). Traffic thus becomes relatively more balanced among several hubs rather than one mega-hub. Even when dedicated hubs are developed, shipping lines can still follow a risk-spreading strategy over different ports in view of offering more routing options to shippers.

However, there are important variations in the position of individual routes and ports, as demonstrated in the next sections.

Geographic Coverage of the Network

The interplay between distance and flow intensity, where most traffic occurs across relatively short distances. This trend is more obvious in the GDL approach, where 78 to 79 per cent of worldwide vessel traffic occurs over links of 500km or less. Links of 100km or less support more than half of worldwide traffic in both years. Strong traffic links are likely to occur among adjacent seaports serving shared hinterlands (*e.g.* Antwerp/Rotterdam in the Benelux area) or acting as dual hubs (*e.g.* Busan/Gwangyang in South Korea), which often receive multiple calls for the same vessels or liner services. The share of links shorter than 500km is much lower in the GAL, because it includes many long-distance and high-density indirect maritime links between world ports such as Le Havre-Tokyo and New York-Singapore.

There is a noticeable increase in the traffic share of the 3000 to 5000km edges, caused mainly by the growing importance of trans-Pacific relations. Continued globalization and technological progress in the maritime industry are likely to be responsible for the increased share of the longest links (over 5000km) from 7 per cent in 1996 to almost 10 per cent in 2006. The increased share of shortest links (from 51 per cent in 1996 to 55 per cent in 2006) illustrate that long-distance links remain inferior to the number and weight of intra-regional linkages (*i.e.* short-sea shipping or hub-and-feeder services with a high sailing frequency).

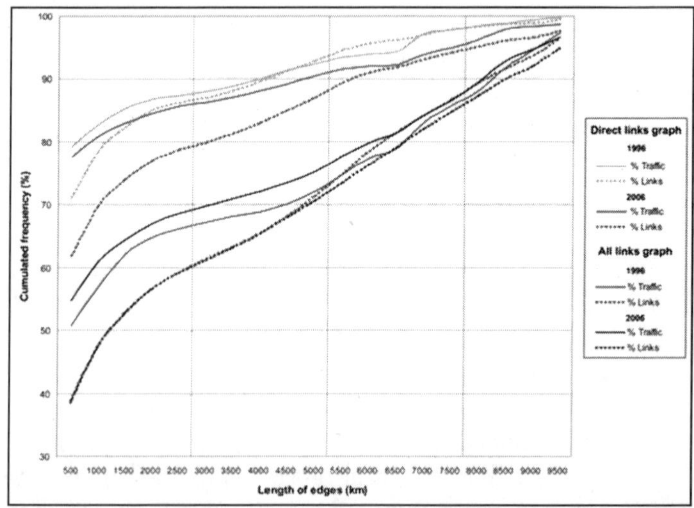

Fig. Edge and Traffic Distribution Over Distance in 1996 and 2006.

The application of the gravity model for estimating traffic flows by links and by ports. At the link level, the gravity model is able to estimate a non-negligible proportion of observed flows, although a majority of them cannot be explained by simple kilometric distance and port size. This result indicates that maritime networks are not completely disconnected from spatial matters, despite their low transport cost and high geographic flexibility. Obviously, important distortions, ranging from the aforementioned port selection factors to wider issues of geopolitics and natural barriers, remain important. More interestingly, results differ according to the type of graph and to the variable used to measure port traffic. The GAL always provides better results, with 35 to 40 per cent of actual flows being explained by the model, compared with 28 to 31 per cent for the GDL. Port throughputs are less relevant than vessel traffic for explaining the flows between ports. Still, almost one-third of the variance is explained by port throughputs in 2006 for the GAL.

At the port level, we summed the estimated traffic of the links for every port, thus generating a third measure of port traffic (*i.e.* estimated weighted degree). Higher coefficients are observed in line with the aforementioned high correlation between weighted degree (vessel traffic) and port throughput. The results for port throughput are closer to the estimated traffics than the results for weighted degree (62 per cent in 2006 in GDL and GAL), meaning that a large proportion of port activity may be estimated based on available port statistics and Euclidian distances between ports.

Table. Estimated Maritime Traffic Flows Based on Gravity Model.

Unit	Type of observed traffic	Direct linkages (GDL)		All linkages (GAL)	
		1996	2006	1996	2006
Links	Port throughput	0.145	0.184	0.259	0.308
	Weighted degree	0.285	0.309	0.397	0.354
Ports	Port throughput	0.533	0.620	0.570	0.615
	Weighted degree	0.458	0.514	0.414	0.687

Fig. N.B. values represent determination coefficients (per cent) of the power-law lines.

A look at the spatial distribution of the heaviest direct links provides interesting findings regarding the network's geographic coverage. The top 100 links represent 52 per cent and 39 per cent of total worldwide vessel traffic in 1996 and 2006, respectively. They connect primarily neighbouring ports and remain intra-regional rather than interregional.There is a clear dominance of three main poles: Asia, Europe, and North America. In each pole, a small number of ports constitute the backbone (*i.e.* East Asian corridor, North European range, and US East and West coasts). In 1996, only Buenos Aires, Santos, Jeddah, and Colombo stand out as main ports outside of these poles. The strongest inter-regional links run between Asia and the two other large poles, with Japan (*i.e.* Tokyo) and Singapore acting as turntables across the Pacific and the Indian Ocean, respectively. Most other inter-regional links generate less traffic, while some regions remain isolated (*e.g.* South Africa and Australia). The pattern in

2006 is similar, but there is an intensification of intra-regional links at the expense of inter-regional links. Busan has taken over as the key bridge between East Asia and North America, and Trans-Atlantic links has disappeared from the top 100 list. Such changes in the network structure and geographic coverage should also be analyzed from the perspective of port hierarchies.

CHANGING PORT HIERARCHIES

Centrality of Ports in the Network

The centrality of ports in the network can be approached at the local and global levels. Degree centrality is a local level measure counting for each port the number of connections to other ports. Betweenness centrality is a global level measure summing for each port the number of its positions on the shortest possible paths within the entire network. Degree centrality is a measure of connectivity, while betweenness centrality can be regarded as a measure of accessibility. The hypothesis is that hub ports will have both a high degree centrality and a high betweenness centrality, due to their role as inter-regional pivots in the global network. As defined by Fleming and Hayuth (1994), hub ports are those that welcome mother vessels for redistributing cargoes to satellite (and often secondary) ports via feeder vessel services.

The GDL and the port hierarchy. At first sight, the geography of the network appears similar over time, with Asia-Pacific centered on the Singapore-Busan axis and Europe-Atlantic with the Le Havre-Hamburg range. Surprisingly, large North American and Japanese ports are poorly represented despite their traffic volume due to their lack of hub/feeder activities. Inherent to the data, gateway (hinterland) functions of seaports are not included in the analysis. Results indicate that Singapore is the most central port of the global system, which echoes its rank at the top of throughput hierarchy in official statistics. The very high centrality of the Suez and Panama canals underlines the strong vulnerability of the global network, but they are not taken into account in the following analyses.

The reveals noticeable changes between 1996 and 2006. The lowered centrality of Houston and Port Everglades to Kingston, Jamaica in the Caribbean is a good example of the impact of hub-and-spoke strategies. Several ports have strengthened their positions based on their gateway functions, such as Santos, Brazil and Shanghai, China. In East Asia and the Mediterranean, an increasing number of ports have high connectivity (*e.g.* Gwangyang, Port Klang, Xiamen, Shenzhen in Asia; Marsaxlokk, Gioia Tauro in the Mediterranean), but this growth has not altered the established position of established pivotal hubs (*e.g.* Singapore, Busan, Algeciras, Gioia Tauro) and gateway ports (*e.g.* Barcelona, Valencia in Spain). Conversely, the position of some formerly central ports has lowered significantly, as in the cases of Los Angeles, Houston, New York,

Melbourne, Bilbao, North European range ports, Tokyo-Yokohama, Kaohsiung, and even Singapore.

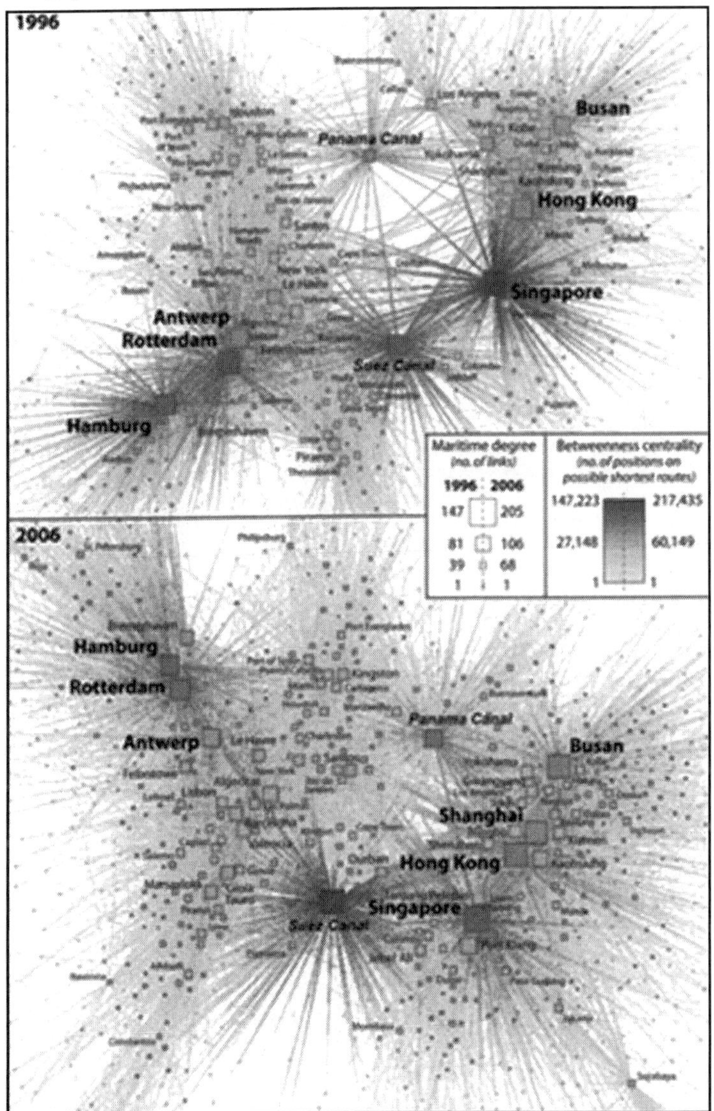

Fig. Visualization of the Global Liner Shipping Network in 1996 and 2006.

In contrast with recent literature (Yap, 2010), Hong Kong has maintained and even increased its position in the network. This trend is thus a good illustration of the globalization process with the shift of production from mature to emerging economies. Changes in betweenness centrality scores follow a similar geographic pattern with more drastic gaps among ports. We clearly see the strong effects of hub strategies at Kingston, Gioia Tauro, Dubai, and Busan as well as the emergence of large load centers in South Brazil and China. There is a clear North–South divide illustrating emerging economies and differentiating ports according to local and global changes in trade routes and port selection.

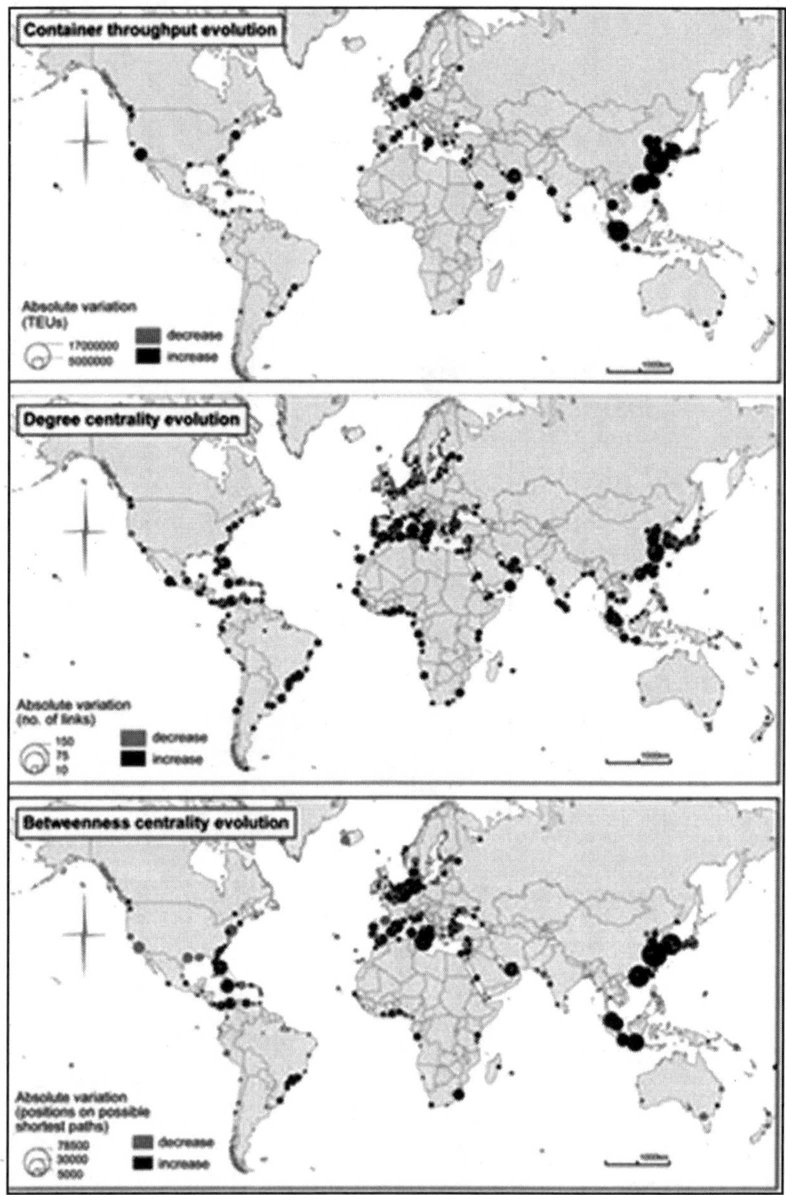

Fig. Changes in Throughput and Centrality, 1996-2006.

POLARIZATION AND NODAL REGIONS

The method applied originally by Nystuen and Dacey (1961) to telephone flows among Washington State cities in the U.S. has been extensively applied to many transport networks, but this is the first time that it has been applied to maritime transport. The method allows for delimiting so-called nodal regions by focusing on the strongest associations between city pairs, which are believed to reflect the hierarchy of central places in which subordinate nodes (satellites) are under the influence of independent (dominant) nodes through a transitive principle: an independent city also dominates the satellites of its satellites. Due to its higher average clustering coefficient, this algorithm is applied to the GAL to reduce the likelihood that geographic proximity is the main explanatory factor behind the delimitation of nodal regions.

A small number of nodal regions form the world maritime system and tend to merge or to split with each other over time. Indeed, the global network is highly polarized by a few large entities concentrating 58 per cent and 69 per cent of all ports in 1996 and 2006, respectively. Singapore and Hong Kong's combined nodal regions include 39 per cent in 1996 and 50 per cent in 2006 of all ports, while Hamburg and Rotterdam maintain their 19 per cent share. This complements the sole indicators of centrality and better highlights the increasing influence of Asia on the world economy.

Hong Kong is the independent port of the largest region centred on Asia due to its role as a gateway for South China and centrally located hub in East Asia. Hong Kong's ramifications remain focused on East Asia in 1996, except the link with Los Angeles, but they extend much further in 2006 with the inclusion of important Caribbean and Mediterranean ports. Despite their traffic size, other large Northeast Asian ports remain under Hong Kong's influence due to double calls and hub dependence (Yap, 2010). Some of them have also extended their influence, such as Busan and Shanghai, while Taiwanese and Japanese ports have seen a significant reduction in their influence.

Comparatively, Singapore possessed a widely diversified tributary area in 1996 due to its pivotal role between Europe and Asia, as reflected by its ramifications covering Southeast Asia, South Asia, the Middle East, and large parts of the Mediterranean. This pattern did not change in 2006, notwithstanding the increase in the number of ports under its influence. In fact, a number of large subordinate ports such as Incheon, Surabaya, and Port Klang extended their own tributary areas in response to the overwhelming dominance of Singapore and Hong Kong. The extensions of the latter two ports towards the Mediterranean reflect the importance of the Europe–Asia trade link with a continuous and regular alignment of transhipment hubs during the last two decades. The port hierarchy does not always overlap traffic volumes due the dominant gateway function of some ports compared with their limited transhipment activities (*e.g.* Antwerp, Bremerhaven, Le Havre, Shenzhen, and Tokyo).

Although European ports appear as subordinates of Asian ports in 1996, this is no longer the case in 2006, as the core region has split in two between

Europe and Asia. This change can be interpreted in two ways. On the one hand, each region has reinforced its internal connectivity, making it a distinct entity stemming from regional integration forces. On the other hand, the so-called global shift (especially in the manufacturing sector) has placed Asia at the forefront of the global scene, thus relegating Europe and the rest of the world to the periphery.

A closer look at the geographic coverage of Rotterdam and Hamburg, the two main ports of the European nodal region, reveals their respective specialization. In 1996, Rotterdam primarily covered the British Isles, Iceland, the Iberian Peninsula, and the Canary Islands, while Hamburg turned towards Scandinavia and the Baltic regions, with Antwerp as a large subordinate. Despite the stability in the number of subordinates and geographic coverage in 2006, Rotterdam extended to Africa and the Black Sea, while Hamburg reached across the Atlantic through Antwerp, Liverpool, and Le Havre.

Geographic proximity and regional integration seem to explain the delineation of most nodal regions, except for the giant Asian region, and despite the absence of a comparable transatlantic region. Physical geography that reinforces the internal connectivity of basins may also be responsible for the limited North–South linkages across Europe.

Several secondary nodal regions remained in 2006, such as the one centered on New York, which integrated the region comprising Kingston and Rio Haina. Another important region expanded in 2006: the one from Santos primarily bound to Brazil ports but embracing Venezuela and some Caribbean ports. One may interpret such changes under the context of NAFTA and MERCOSUR arrangements due to growing North–South trade among the Americas.

Some nodal regions have become detached from large ones, such as the region of Lisbon, with strong links to the Azores, the region of Constantza in the Black Sea, and the region of Izmir and Ambarli in Turkey. Others have remained rather stable in their size and geographic distribution, such as the West Mediterranean range polarized by Barcelona and the West African range polarized by Abidjan, despite a drop in the number of its subordinates that were caught by Algeciras on one side and the Asian region on the other. The independent port has shifted in some regions: Melbourne and Buenaventura have replaced Sydney and Callao (*i.e.* Oceania and the Latin American West Coast).

Conversely, some formerly detached regions have been integrated within a larger one, such as the East Mediterranean range (Piraeus) and the region of Cape Town (Southern Africa) shifting to the Asian region as well as the Belem and Puerto Cabello regions shifting under the influence of Santos (Brazil). Such phenomena depict the expansion of ocean carrier networks, making the world system increasingly interconnected.

CONCLUSION

This chapter presents an analysis of the global liner shipping network in 1996 and 2006, a period of rapid change in port hierarchies and liner service configurations. While it refers to a wide literature on port system development, shipping networks, and port selection, it is one of the only analyses of the properties of the global container shipping network. The paper examines the network structure and the relative position of ports based on daily vessel movement data covering all of the world's container fleets. The application of graph theory and complex network analysis provide a number of important and rather novel results about ports and liner shipping networks.

Although such networks are highly dynamic due to changes made by market players in port and hub selection and the changing geography of container demand, we observe a certain level of robustness in the network structure. While transhipment hub flows and gateway flows might slightly shift among nodes, topological properties remain rather stable. The increasing size and complexity of the network occur in parallel with its decreasing spikiness caused by simultaneous bottom-up and top-down retroactions.

The analysis confirms the strong influence of geography and distance on the distribution of traffic, showing the dominance of intraregional links and demonstrating good applicability of the gravity model for estimating inter-port traffic. As in previous analyses of other global inter-city networks, maritime linkages retain an important regional dimension (Derudder and Taylor, 2005), but there is a striking absence of strong transatlantic linkages compared with the global pattern of airline networks (Cattan, 2004). The overarching importance of the Asia–Pacific area in the maritime network is best illustrated by delineating the ramifications of nodal regions. This was also made evident when mapping the changing centrality of ports. While the Old World (Atlantic, Northern hemisphere) versus the New World (Asia-Pacific, Southern hemisphere) would be a too simplistic interpretation of our results, the role of a changing world geography cannot be ignored. As such, analyzing the global liner shipping network provides a useful and necessary complement to the study of globalization and regionalization processes, which are often approached through other types of global networks.

Further research in this field may benefit from the inclusion of land-based networks (*e.g.* road, rail) as a means of considering hinterland accessibility. Currently, a worldwide database of vessel movements over the contemporary period (1946-2010) for all types of vessels is being built to expand the analysis of the global maritime network's dynamics.

5

Supply Chain Integration of Shipping Companies

SUPPLY CHAIN INTEGRATION

Most OEMs no longer compete solely as autonomous corporations. They also compete as participants in integrated supply chains. This revolution, which is changing the ways products are designed, produced, and delivered, has the potential to alter the manufacturing landscape as dramatically as the industrial revolution or the advent of mass production. This chapter describes the changing nature of supply chains and efforts to optimize their performance.

In the past, OEMs typically drove down the cost of purchased materials through aggressive negotiations, imposing terms and conditions that minimized supplier profitability and often left suppliers in a weakened condition. More recently, OEMs have begun to adopt a strategic partnership approach, which recognizes that increased, sustainable benefits can accrue from long-term relationships between participants in the supply chain (a win-win situation). This approach considers total life-cycle costs over multiple iterations of a product, with the goal of increasing mutual benefits for all participants in the long run.

SUPPLY CHAIN MANAGEMENT

In this era of competition among supply chains, the success of a corporation is increasingly dependent on management's ability to integrate the company's networks of business relationships. Supply chain management has been defined as the integration of key business processes, from raw-material suppliers through end users, that provide products, services, and information that add value for customers and other stakeholders (Lambert et al., 1998).

Supply chain management makes use of a growing body of tools, techniques, and skills for coordinating and optimizing key processes, functions, and relationships, both within the OEM and among its suppliers and customers, to enable and capture opportunities for synergy. An OEM's competitive advantage is highly dependent on this integrated management function. Supply chain management attempts to combine the best of both worlds, the scale and coordination of large companies with the low costs, flexibility, and creativity of small companies.

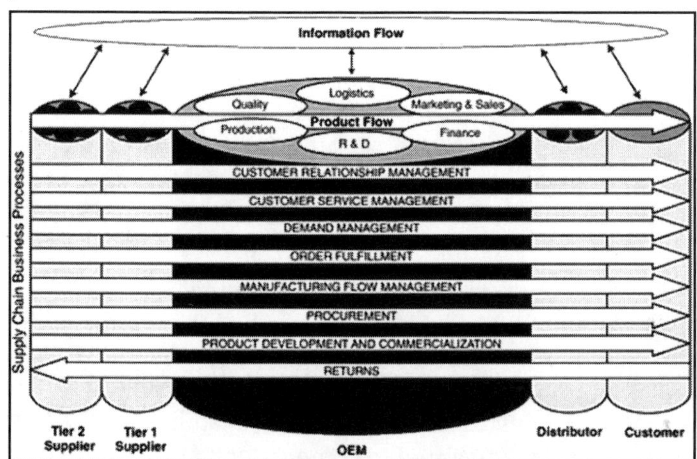

Fig. Supply Chain Management: Integrating and Managing Business Processes Among Participants Throughout the Supply Chain.

The focus of supply chain management must evolve in response to changing business environments and evolving product life cycles. Different interactions among participants are required during each phase of the product life cycle, from inception through recycling. The supply chains for products in new markets must be flexible to respond to wide fluctuations in demand (both in quantity and product mix). Products in mature, stable markets require supply chains that can reliably deliver products at low cost. Thus, effective supply chain management must be responsive to these changing conditions to ensure that the supply chain evolves accordingly.

For example, marketing excellence used to be the primary source of Procter and Gamble's (P and G's) dominance of the consumer products industry. However, as P and G expanded its product and service offerings in response to market opportunities, the increased complexity of these offerings created difficulties in meeting the needs of retail partners and customers. Traditional marketing strategies involving in-store sales and price promotions created great variations in product demand. To meet heavy short-term marketing-induced peaks in demand, P and G invested in huge manufacturing capacities, inventories, warehouses, and logistics capabilities.

In response to these problems, P and G modified its supply chain focus and remade itself through a series of innovative initiatives. Working both internally and with suppliers and customers, the company created a heralded partnership with Wal-Mart, virtually eliminated price promotions, and streamlined its logistics and continuous replenishment programmes. These initiatives reduced variations and uncertainties in demand, thereby reducing the need for surge production capacities and large inventories. Thus, by evolving their primary supply chain focus from marketing to production, inventories, and logistics in response to changing business requirements, P and G was able to reduce costs, meet customer demand, and build strong, coordinated relationships with retail partners and customers.

CONCEPT OF INTEGRATION

An integrated supply chain can be defined as an association of customers and suppliers who, using management techniques, work together to optimize their collective performance in the creation, distribution, and support of an end product. It may be helpful to think of the participants as the divisions of a large, vertically integrated corporation, although the independent companies in the chain are bound together only by trust, shared objectives, and contracts entered into on a voluntary basis. Unlike captive suppliers (divisions of a large corporation that typically serve primarily the parent corporation), independent suppliers are often faced with the conflicting demands of multiple customers.

All supply chains are integrated to some extent. One objective of increasing integration is focusing and coordinating the relevant resources of each participant on the needs of the supply chain to optimize the overall performance of the chain. The integration process requires the disciplined application of management skills, processes, and technologies to couple key functions and capabilities of the chain and take advantage of the available business opportunities. Goals typically include higher profits and reduced risks for all participants.

Traditional unmanaged (or minimally managed) supply chains are characterized by (1) adversarial relationships between customers and suppliers, including win-lose negotiations; (2) little regard for sharing benefits and risks; (3) short-term focus, with little concern for mutual long-term success; (4) primary emphasis on cost and delivery, with little concern for added value; (5) limited communications; and (6) little interaction between the OEM and suppliers more than one or two tiers away. Integrated supply chains tend to recognize that all parties should benefit from the relationship on a sustainable, long-term basis and are characterized by partnerships with extensive and open communications. A well integrated system of independent participants can be visualized as a flock of redwing black birds flying over a marsh. Without any apparent signal, every bird in the flock climbs, dives, or turns at virtually the same instant. That is an integrated system! Supply chain members, in a similar manner, must react coherently to changes in the business environment to remain competitive.

Supply chain integration is a continuous process that can be optimized only when OEMs, customers, and suppliers work together to improve their relationships and when all participants are aware of key activities at all levels in the chain. First-tier suppliers can play a key role in promoting integration by guiding and assisting lower tier suppliers. In an example of multi-tier integration, Wal-Mart thoroughly integrated P and G's Pampers product line into its supply chain. P and G, in turn, worked with 3M to integrate its production of adhesive strips with Pampers manufacturing facilities.

Forces Driving Increased Integration

The following worldwide trends and forces are driving supply chains towards increased integration:

- Increased cost competitiveness. Having substantially improved the efficiencies of internal operations, OEMs are seeking further cost reductions by improving efficiency and synergy within their supply chains.
- Shorter product life cycles. The Model-T Ford, for example, was competitive for many years. A personal computer (PC) is state of the art for less than a year, and the trend towards shorter product life cycles continues.
- Faster product development cycles. Companies must reduce the development cycle times of their products to remain competitive. Early introduction of a new product is often rewarded with a large market share and sufficient unit volumes to drive costs down rapidly.
- Globalization and customization of product offerings. Customers the world over can increasingly afford and are demanding a greater variety of products that address their specific needs. Mass customization has become the new marketing mantra.
- Higher overall quality. Increasing customer affluence and tougher competition to supply their needs have led to demands for higher overall quality.

These increased demands on OEMs for improvements in product design, manufacturing, cost, distribution, and support are being imposed, in turn, on their supply chains.

CASE STUDY: DELL COMPUTER AND FUJITSU AMERICA

Dell Computer Corporation's success in the past few years and its growth relative to the rest of the PC industry made daily headlines throughout the 1990s. Based on the premise that bypassing resellers, building products to order, and reducing inventories would result in a lower cost, more responsive business, Dell has grown into one of the largest forces in the industry. Nevertheless, it is squeezed into such a narrow business niche that, from some perspectives, its very survival seems tenuous. Dell competes with many capable and, in some cases, lower cost competitors, has virtually no proprietary technology, and must deal with exceedingly robust suppliers, including Intel and Microsoft. The heart of Dell's success is its integrated supply chain, which has enabled rapid product design, fabrication, and assembly, as well as direct shipment to customers. Inventories have been dramatically reduced through extensive sharing of information, a prudent choice given the risk of technological obsolescence and reductions in the cost of materials that can exceed 50 percent a month. Even with reduced inventories, Dell's strategic use of information has made possible a dramatic reduction in the elapsed time from order to delivery, giving Dell a significant competitive advantage.

Component inventories are monitored weekly throughout the supply chain and, when there are deviations from plan, the sales force steers customers, by means of discounts, if necessary, towards configurations for which there are adequate supplies. Thus, abundant, timely information is used to work the front and back ends of the supply chain simultaneously.

Speed is a critical factor in the computer industry, especially in the area of inventory. In the late 1980s, Dell measured component inventories in weeks. In 1998, they were measured in days. They may soon be further reduced through real-time deliveries so that, as components are used, they are automatically and immediately replaced. The reduction in inventory not only lowers requirements for capital, it also enables rapid changeovers to new product configurations because no old parts must be used up. Faster time to market for new products translates into increased revenues and profits. The change in emphasis from inventory levels to inventory velocity throughout the supply chain has been made possible, in part, by the Internet.

In Dell's new virtual corporation, inventories are reduced by use of timely information; emphasis on physical assets is being replaced by emphasis on intellectual capabilities; and proprietary business knowledge is being increasingly shared in open, collaborative relationships. This extensive integration of the supply chain can be viewed as a shift from vertical corporate integration to a virtually integrated corporation (Magretta, 1998). Vertical integration was essential in the early years of computer manufacturing when the supplier base was not well established and assemblers had little choice but to design and build components and assemble the entire end product in house. Proprietary component technologies were a main source of competitive advantage, although in some cases they had little to do with creating value for the customer. As the industry matured, multitudes of component suppliers became eager to invest and compete in terms of price and innovation.

Leveraging investments by these suppliers has freed Dell to focus on delivering complete solutions to its customers. However, because these components are available to all PC assemblers, it has become harder to compete in terms of end-product differentiation. Thus, a high premium has been placed on speed and process efficiency, blurring the traditional boundaries between supplier, manufacturer, and customer. For instance, peripherals, such as monitors, keyboards, speakers, and mice, need not be gathered in one location prior to shipment to the customer. Manufactured by separate suppliers and labeled with the Dell logo, shippers gather them from all over North America, match them overnight (merge-in-transit), and deliver them as complete hardware sets to customers as if they had come from the same location.

Dell's virtual integration has the following characteristics:

- Use of rapid, seamless communication to build direct relationships between customers, OEM, and suppliers
- A clear definition of what Dell does best (*i.e.*, core competencies, including branding, marketing, and selling through direct channels), with partnerships for the rest (capital-intensive and labour-intensive component fabrication processes and services). This enables Dell to be highly selective in its capital investments and to focus on activities that create the most value for customers and shareholders
- Selection of partners who are best in their respective fields, inviting them to become intimate parts of the business, and holding them to the same exacting quality and performance standards as in-house segments of the business
- Use of a minimum number of suppliers, to whom Dell is highly loyal as long as they maintain their leadership in technology, quality, cost, and delivery
- Use of the Internet, not just as an add-on to the business, but as an integral part of a strategy to eliminate boundaries between companies and promote effective integration
- Less emphasis on guarding intellectual assets and more emphasis on using assets rapidly before they become technologically obsolete

By using a highly integrated supply chain, Dell has enjoyed many of the advantages of vertical integration while simultaneously benefiting from the investments, innovation, efficiencies, and specialization of highly focused suppliers. Although the Dell model does not fit every situation, Bottom of Form the lessons of Dell's experience can be extracted and adapted to many other supply chain situations, even for SMEs.

By 1998, the success of the Dell model, as might be expected, was causing problems for competitors, including Fujitsu America, which had large inventories and high shipping costs (Washington Post, May 2, 1999). Customers had to wait 10 days for laptops, while competitors were delivering in five. In response, Fujitsu moved its distribution center from Portland, Oregon, to Memphis, Tennessee, and turned distribution over to FedEx Corporation, the parent company of Federal Express. In direct response to orders, FedEx coordinates the shipment of components from worldwide suppliers, oversees the assembly of PCs, and ships them out, all in three or four days. By early

1999, the cycle time on the ground was eight to twelve hours, and the goal was to reduce it to four hours. Fujitsu has essentially eliminated geographic proximity as an issue and has made maximum use of the benefits of globalization, including low cost. Even with the premium price of express shipping, this modification of the Fujitsu supply chain saved the company millions of dollars, slashed inventories by about 90 percent, and increased profits by 25 percent. Most important, these changes have enabled Fujitsu to compete effectively with Dell for Internet sales directly to consumers. However, as is evident from these examples, these innovations in supply chain integration can also impose large burdens on suppliers in terms of responsiveness, inventories, and management of their own supply chains.

COSTS OF INTEGRATION

The costs, complexities, and risks of fully integrating and managing a highly integrated supply chain can be as substantial as the costs of integrating and operating a corporation of comparable size. Thus, most supply chain integration efforts to date have been very limited in scope.

Some of the major costs are listed below:

- Time devoted to managing, training, and support
- Effort devoted to becoming a better customer
- Investment in supply chain integration software and compatible information systems throughout the chain
- Opportunity costs (*i.e.*, investments in supply chain integration may necessitate foregoing other business opportunities)
- Risks of production stoppages

Because the extent of interconnectedness and interdependency makes highly integrated chains increasingly vulnerable to disruptions, the risk of production stoppages should not be overlooked. A highly integrated, interdependent supply chain that consists primarily of sole-source suppliers practicing just-in-time manufacturing with minimal inventories is highly reliant on the timely delivery of quality components and services. Failure by one participant to deliver can rapidly bring other parts of the chain to a halt. This happens, on occasion, even to the best suppliers and logistics providers.

Automakers, for example, who are under constant pressure to reduce costs, have tightened their supply chains to the point that they typically have less than a one-day supply of parts at final assembly facilities. Thus, a breakdown anywhere in the supply chain has the potential of bringing production to a halt (*e.g.*, strikes at two GM parts plants in 1998 resulted in the shutdown of virtually all assembly operations within days, and flooding in 1999 at a single supplier in North Carolina reduced operations at seven DaimlerChrysler and three GM assembly plants to half-shifts due to shortages of a single part). Potential threats, including storms, power outages, terrorism, computer hackers, disruptions in communications, and equipment breakdowns, can be very difficult to predict and costly to prepare for. In another example, the earthquake that shook Taiwan in September 1999 showed how a power supply disruption in one country can have worldwide reverberations through an entire industry. Damage to two electric power substations was the primary cause of a shutdown of Taiwan's computer-chip industry, which resulted in shortages of components and higher costs in the supply chains of OEMs around the world.

Supply chain participants must individually and collectively assess the probability of production-stopping events and their tolerance for risk, which must be balanced against the savings from increased sole-sourcing, tighter integration with remaining suppliers, and reduced inventories and production capacities. Thus, although good communications and resource sharing can be helpful in preparing for and responding to disruptions, supply chain, participants must be careful to avoid unacceptable levels of risk in their zeal for integration. Recommendation. Small and medium-sized manufacturing enterprises should develop operating strategies based on an appropriate balance between supply chain performance and risk; assess the probability and effects of potential threats to their supply chains; and maintain sufficient (though sometimes expensive) slack, redundancy, and flexibility to keep the potential threats at manageable levels.

BENEFITS OF INTEGRATION

The most sought-after benefit, or return on investment, in supply chain integration is the cost savings that result from reductions in inventory. Inventories can be reduced by increasing the speed at which materials move through the supply chain and by reducing safety stocks. For example, if the costs of maintaining inventory are approximately 1 percent per month and if an integrated supply chain can reduce inventory levels by 30 percent, the savings, shared among the participants, can be substantial. Another common benefit of supply chain integration is a reduction in transaction costs. If information sharing can reduce the number of transactions and if electronic systems can reduce the cost of each transaction from the $150 cost of a traditional transaction, each participant can realize substantial savings (LaLonde, 1997).

Reductions in supplier redundancy can reduce product costs by increasing production levels at remaining suppliers and reducing the costs of managing the supply chain. Although this can also increase investment and management burdens on suppliers, the delegation of responsibility and authority to entities closer to the action can result in improved decision making, as long as good communications are maintained throughout the chain.

Other potential benefits of supply chain integration are listed below:

- Reduced friction, fewer barriers, and less waste of resources on procedures that do not add value

- Increased functional and procedural synergy between participants
- Faster response to changing market demands
- Lower cost manufacturing operations
- Lower capital investment in excess manufacturing capacity
- Shorter product realization cycles and lower product development costs
- Increased competitiveness and profitability

SUPPLY CHAIN TECHNOLOGY: INTEGRATING THE OLD AND NEW

New supply chain technology can power up existing operations, streamline inventory, and increase revenue—if implemented correctly. Making sure new solutions integrate with existing technologies and processes is crucial. Here's how it's done. Integrating new technology into existing operations can help significantly increase customers service, reduce costs, and streamline supply chains. The new technology must be fully synthesized with existing policies, practices, and people, however, to tap its full power.

Collections Etc., a privately owned catalog company located in Elk Grove Village, Ill., took the steps required to synthesize the old and the new when it revamped warehousing operations to handle significant growth. Collections, which sells giftware direct to consumers, previously maintained three warehouses—two housed picking and packing operations, while the third stored goods and replenished the pick-and-pack facilities.

When the company decided to consolidate its different facilities, it began building up infrastructure and staff to support the change. Collections also developed a deep understanding of its current status, explains Bruce Getowicz, operations manager for the catalog company. This required getting a full picture of order profiles, shipping trends, fill rates, back-order rates, and productivity. Collections hired Sedlak Management Consultants, a supply chain and distribution consulting firm based in Highland Hills, Ohio, to study its existing operations, including volume, activity, and production rates. Then, armed with a good baseline of its operation, Collections began envisioning the new facility.

The company gave Sedlak its three- to five-year growth projections, and asked the consulting firm to plan its new distribution center. The distribution center uses new technology, including a warehouse management system (WMS) from Manhattan Associates, handheld scanners, conveyors, and narrow aisle high-bay storage. One of Collections' goals was to move the majority of its warehouse workforce to the new DC. Finding a new facility less than 10 miles from the other location helped make that possible. Collections also invested time to ensure that associates—some of whom had not worked with computers before—were comfortable with the new technology. "We started conversations early on with our warehouse group. We held two open discussions about five months before the new building was operational," says Getowicz. During these meetings, associates saw the building layout, learned about new processes, and were introduced to the new technology. Two months before the system was scheduled to go live, managers and super users received WMS training. Shortly after, associates and group leaders began weekly training sessions with the new system, working with detailed instructions developed by Sedlak and the Collections team. Four weeks before the facility went live, Collections began formal tours with employees. In addition, the company conducted two mock go-lives. In the first, conducted three weeks before actual go-live, 20 people performed operations—picking, scanning, and moving product—for two hours. A second mock go-live, conducted one week before the launch, involved more than 30 associates. Both exercises served the dual purpose of getting associates comfortable with the technology, while helping to resolve minor systems issues before actual go-live.

Collections went live with the WMS in April 2004, roughly 120 days before the beginning of its peak holiday season. It also selected a phased implementation. The initial go-live brought 15 percent of activity from an existing facility into the new distribution center. The company gradually increased the percentage of activity in the new DC until it was completely transitioned. Thanks to careful preparation, go-live went smoothly, Getowicz reports. "Peak season last year went well, but we still weren't in full stride with production—we were at 90 percent," he says. "About six months after the initial implementation, we hit full stride." The company will continue to fine-tune operations in the future to maintain optimum performance. Integrating new supply chain execution technology into an existing operation can present significant challenges, notes John Pulling, chief operating officer of supply chain software vendor Provia Software Inc., Grand Rapids, Mich.

Companies that merge old and new systems correctly take the following steps to mitigate risks and maximize success, he says. RE-ENGINEER PROCESSES. Adding new technology without re-engineering related processes won't reap maximum results. The magnitude of the re-engineering effort depends on the type of technology being implemented. Installing a transportation management system (TMS), for example, will generally involve less process re-engineering than implementing a complete supply chain management suite. Regardless of the type of technology, however, companies should conduct a full process review early on. "Conduct a high-level process review, document the business' current state, and identify ways the new technology can streamline operations," Pulling recommends. Next comes the process redesign.

Improving data quality can be a big part of process re-engineering. "Companies need to do an analysis to understand how good their data is, and put a plan together to fix what needs fixing," Pulling says. PLAN THE

IMPLEMENTATION TIMING. "Implement the system at the easiest time of year for the business," Pulling advises. If an implementation bumps up against peak season, for example, it is best to wait. "Companies cannot go live with a new technology a few weeks before busy season," Pulling warns. "It creates havoc and puts too much pressure on everyone involved." Companies should also consider carefully the pros and cons of a "big-bang" approach versus phasing in the new technology, he says.

The Surfactants Business Unit of chemical manufacturer Akzo Nobel, for example, is tackling transportation improvement in two phases. During the first phase, ChemLogix LLC, the company's third-party logistics provider, is automating shipment rating, prepay-and-add customer billing, freight cost accruals, and freight bill audit/settlement using an on-demand TMS from Nistevo. In addition, Akzo's customer service staff are using the Nistevo application through a web browser to determine freight rates for customer quotes. During the second phase of the transportation initiative, ChemLogix will use the Nistevo application to automatically plan, execute, and track Akzo's truckload, bulk, and LTL shipments.

American Electric Power (AEP) is also taking a phased approach to implementing its modular, web-based TMS, e-CTMS from Memphis-based Continental Traffic Service Inc. (CTSI). "As a small transportation group, we've been successful using a phased-in approach, buying separate modules rather than buying a complete package and trying to ramp up all at once," reports Ted Lunsford, senior transportation and logistics coordinator for AEP. Based in Columbus, Ohio, the company is one of the largest electric utilities in the United States. Primarily an inbound shipper using thousands of suppliers, and shipping to several hundred locations, AEP faces myriad possible shipping lane combinations. When implementing the new technology, which helped automate its previous manual environment, "we started slowly and waited until we felt comfortable that our first TMS piece was running smoothly," Lunsford explains. "Then we started the next phase. We wanted to make sure we didn't overwhelm our users with too many changes at one time."

AEP began using an online routing guide in mid 2004, then added an online load posting site for truckload and flatbed shipments in spring 2005. By using these modules, the company's transportation professionals have significantly reduced their contact with suppliers and internal shipping facilities. This frees them to work on strategic projects. AEP is now phasing in benchmarking and freight modeling tools that will further facilitate transportation management.

INVEST IN CHANGE MANAGEMENT. The challenges of implementing new technological tools go far beyond the systems themselves, according to Pulling. Addressing the change management aspects of implementation is where difficulties may arise. "Change is difficult for people, no matter how well you manage it," Pulling notes. That's why investing in planning, communicating, and training is key for a successful transition from old to new. "To address change management formally, someone within the organization should be tasked with handling it," Pulling says. He considers it a near full-time job within a major systems implementation. "In addition, rolling out technology that affects multiple aspects of the supply chain requires change management people for each function or place where the technology is being implemented," he says. Companies that give lip service to change management but don't invest the necessary resources often pay the price with less-than-optimal results. To maximize the likelihood of a successful implementation, companies need to develop a communications plan that spells out a change management approach, including the process for gaining buy-in from those the change affects. Rather than waiting until the technology has been selected, employees should be involved in the early stages of the change, says Pulling. Otherwise staff members may feel steamrolled, and resent having to make the new technology work despite the fact that they weren't involved in its development.

Also, companies can increase buy-in success by identifying informal leaders in the organization and bringing them onboard early in the process. Hy Cite Corporation, a distribution, marketing, and financial services company based in Madison, Wis., used this approach when it replaced its manual warehouse with a new distribution center and new technologies in spring 2005. The company identified subject matter experts who would act as change agents, explains Arin Brost, Hy Cite's vice president of information systems. "They become your evangelists," Brost says. "You have to find the people who will continually talk about the benefits of the change." Communicating with supply chain partners that will use the new system was also key for the company. Hy Cite, which uses the direct sales model to market its cookware, cutlery, crystal, china, and housewares, recognizes that its distributors are critical partners, so it informed them in advance about its new distribution center.

"We explained that we were making the change to support our growth, and so that we could continue to service them at the highest level," notes Brost. Distributors were pleased to learn that the new facility would enable a shorter order cycle time, and are happy with the results. Ted Lunsford e-mailed and faxed details on AEP's new web-based TMS to his company's top 600 suppliers, who would be the system's major users. In addition to telling suppliers about upcoming changes and providing screen shots, the company also included a web link in all its purchase orders, so suppliers had the information each time they received a PO.

These efforts have paid off. "We are now getting close to 1,000 hits per month on our online routing guide," Lunsford reports. Lunsford also trained the company's truckload and flatbed carriers on using the e-CTMS web site and sent them samples of the e-mail notifications they would receive when loads are posted. Response from suppliers and carriers alike has been positive.

PLAN THE IMPLEMENTATION TIMING. As a go-live date approaches and work still remains to be done, "companies are often tempted to cut training time," Pulling says. "It's one of the biggest problems software vendors face."

Like change management, companies often pay lip service to training, but don't commit to it. "Taking staff out of production environments and pushing them into training is a big dollar commitment," says Pulling. Companies that have been through an implementation will usually admit that they didn't train enough, he says. Many companies have their technology vendor train the entire staff, but a train-the-trainer approach—where the systems vendor trains super users, who then train other users—is also effective. This approach transfers the knowledge to the company, and ensures that it has the in-house capacity to train new users in the future.

Hy Cite, for example, made sure its associates were fully trained on its new warehouse management system and processes. The company used its WMS vendor, HighJump Software (a 3M Company), to train its systems staff, supervisors, managers, and super users. Then super users, working with a consultant, trained associates. Two months of preparation and training helped Hy Cite associates get acclimated to using handheld devices. Hy Cite brought small groups of associates into the new facility for a half day of training. This involved pushing production data and packages through the new WMS, enabling associates to train in a real-world test environment.

"This provided us with two benefits," Brost reports. In addition to giving associates hands-on experience with actual data in a test environment, "it gave our systems administrators and developers a chance to watch the data flow," he says. BE OPEN TO CHANGING YOUR GO-LIVE DATE. "Customers will forgive you for being late; they'll never forgive you for being bad," Pulling says.

"If your company is not on schedule to meet a go-live date, it is not okay just to say to the team, 'You have to speed things up,'" he adds. "There's a natural tendency to do that, but sometimes you are simply too far behind schedule to catch up." Companies not prepared to meet an initial implementation date should consider changing it.

Avoid last-minute surprises by building milestones in your project schedule. "Add success criteria that serve as go/no-go points in your project plan, and make them visible," Pulling advises. If these criteria aren't met, think seriously about changing your go-live date.

INTEGRATING RFID INTO YOUR OPERATION

Suppliers to retailers such as Wal-Mart and Target are integrating new RFID technology into existing operations to meet their customers' RFID compliance standards. Atlanta-based Newell Rubbermaid, for example, is a chosen vendor for both the Wal-Mart and Target RFID initiatives. The company started its RFID effort in August 2004.

"Our initial strategy was to use the 'slap-and-ship' approach," explains Jason C. Vag, director of global RFID for the consumer products giant, which produces household names such as Rubbermaid products, Calphalon cookware, Little Tykes toys, Graco baby strollers, and Irwin Industrial Tools. Newell Rubbermaid went the slap-and-ship route for several reasons. "Not only had we not done RFID before, few people in the world had done it. Our plan was to keep it simple and minimize the complexities of the installation," Vag says.

In addition, Newell Rubbermaid wanted to give RFID technology time to mature before undertaking a broader initiative. The company assembled a crossfunctional RFID team that included both divisional and corporate resources—including business, IT, and financial representation—as well as external consultants and software vendors. In fall 2004, team members traveled to several RFID testing facilities and vendors to evaluate available solutions.

The company chose to implement RFID technology in a California distribution center that handles Graco baby strollers, selecting a handful of RFID-friendly SKUs. It sent product to an RFID testing facility for tag placement testing in the fall of last year. Graco conducted its final technology testing in the DC in November, and went live with RFID in mid-December 2004. "When an RFID order came through, we segregated it, ran it through a slap-and-ship line, then married it with the rest of the order," Vag says. Go-live occurred as expected, and the company ran the RFID initiative status quo for the first six months. In mid-2005, Graco expanded its initiative, fully integrating RFID orders into its warehouse management system. To do this, it had to upgrade the Manhattan Associates' RFID module it used during the initial phase, and integrate it with Manhattan's WMS.

Interestingly, the process required little change management or training, according to Vag. It has been nearly a seamless transition for the users on the floor, who pick to a label. Labels for non-RFID orders are produced by a regular printer; labels for RFID orders are printed by an RFID printer. Other than the change in labels, picking and shipping processes are the same, he explains. Graco has implemented RFID in a second DC, and is now rolling it out through other divisions. "Eventually, all our divisions will be fully RFID-enabled," Vag says.

GETTING READY FOR RFID

Use of RFID technology is expected to grow as RFID tag costs drop, standards are adopted, and the technology's benefits become more established. Most companies implementing RFID will need to integrate the technology with their existing bar-code technology. "Bar codes are not going away in the foreseeable future," says Frank LaBarbera, director of RFID product management for Accu-Sort Systems, Hatfield, Pa.

Clothing manufacturer Garan Inc., which makes the popular Garanimals line, for example, recently installed an automated RFID and bar-code system in its distribution center in Jena, La. The new technology, Accu-Sort's FAST Tag In-Motion system, enables Garan to automate the application of bar-code labels and RFID tags, which previously were applied by hand. Today, all pick-pack products at Garan's DC run through the system. Cartons processed on the line receive a bar code and a retailer-compliant shipping label. The system determines which cartons need RFID tags, and applies them as appropriate.

Whether implementing RFID with existing bar-code technology as Garan did, or using RFID as a standalone technology, companies need to prepare for the changes RFID will bring. Here are six steps that help companies get ready for implementing RFID technology:

- Get smart and get involved. "Talk with RFID experts, attend trade shows, and network with people who have been through an RFID implementation," advises Vag of Newell Rubbermaid. Because "the best way to gain knowledge is to do it," Vag suggests purchasing an RFID test kit to gain experience using RFID with your products in your environment.
- Consider using external resources. Despite tremendous advances in the past two years, RFID technology is still maturing. Depending on your organization, it may make sense to work with outside resources such as consultants and technology vendors as you explore your RFID options.
- "In our company, it made sense to bring in a third party," Vag notes. "We didn't have the expertise internally, so we used external resources." Newell Rubbermaid worked with consulting firm Tompkins Associates to gain a fuller understanding of the RFID market and where it's heading, and observed various RFID hardware and software at Tompkins' Emerging Technology Center in Orlando.
- The company also worked with Tompkins to develop its RFID rollout strategy, and partnered with consulting firm Scott Sheldon LLC of Medina, Ohio, on RFID integration. "There's a full spectrum of RFID technology to consider, such as antennas, tags, and printers," says Mark Buffum, partner, systems integration, for Tompkins. Take advantage of investments other companies have made, such as consultants' and systems vendors' testing laboratories, to observe the various solutions in a realistic environment, Buffum suggests.
- Understand the current environment in your facilities. "We'll go to a customer site and conduct a materials handling site survey," says Garan's LaBarbera. This involves mapping the materials handling process, as well as understanding the systems, infrastructure, read points, and performance.

- "You have to understand the existing infrastructure so you can minimize any disruptions. Because RFID is a disruptive technology, you want to develop it so that it interfaces with existing systems," he says. The site survey also involves a spectrum analysis to verify that an RFID system will work in a particular environment. Because of factors such as interference from an existing RF system, "just throwing an RFID system into an existing infrastructure won't work," LaBarbera says.
- Conduct a prototype. "Start with a simple prototype that won't impact your operations," advises Buffum. Consider using a low-visibility product that will have little impact on your client base as you work through start-up issues.
- The prototype should not disrupt a company's existing operation. When conducting the prototype, "make sure you have a fail-safe switch," LaBarbera recommends. Accu-Sort's team, for example, will go into a facility in the early morning to install technology for a pilot. They also have a backup plan in place if they determine that the system is not ready to operate. Integrating RFID technology into an existing operation works well for slap-and-ship prototypes involving a limited number of SKUs. If you're looking to get a broader understanding of how RFID technology works with a group of SKUs that are representative of your entire product line, consider using a controlled environment in your facility or at a testing laboratory, LaBarbera says.
- Look for flexible solutions. Because RFID technology is developing so rapidly, and because companies will likely be reading both bar codes and RFID tags well into the future, a scalable, flexible system is best. "Look for technology that can do more than one thing, such as read the different generations of tags," LaBarbera advises.
- This may mean taking a modular approach so that you can plug in modules as needed. "Today, you may tag one line. Tomorrow, if you need to tag other SKUs, and need to automate another line, you don't want to disrupt the layer, you just want to plug in another module," he says.
- Manage expectations. "RFID is still a developing technology, so it's important to have an understanding of not only its benefits, but its limitations," LaBarbera says.

Make sure your team and your executives understand all the elements that can affect RFID's performance—such as tags, tag placement, product characteristics, and RF interference. Companies should also be realistic about the payoff they'll see initially. Companies that are implementing RFID simply to comply with customer requirements may miss some opportunities. "If you have to implement RFID, and are going to make the investment, look for ways to bear fruit from it," says Buffum. Use that information to develop a business case and identify return on investment, he suggests.

During the first year of its RFID implementation, for example, Newell Rubbermaid identified potential payback from two main areas: reducing chargebacks by having visibility to what product was actually received by the customer, and increasing product availability during promotional periods. "With RFID tags, we can track where a product is in the supply chain. We know when we shipped it, when it reaches the retailer's distribution center and the back room of the store, and when it is placed on the sales floor," Vag says.

As a result, if product hasn't been pushed out to the sales floor in time for a promotional effort, Newell Rubbermaid will be able to contact its customer and get the product out on the floor. That may have a significant, positive impact on the company's top line—which is just one benefit companies can achieve when synthesizing the new with the old in business logistics.

A SYSTEMS PERSPECTIVE ON SUPPLY CHAIN MEASUREMENTS

The interest in managing supply chains is growing rapidly among companies around the world. Major forces behind this development are increasing competitive pressure and a belief that working cooperatively in supply chains can create a competitive advantage. Firms abandon the old antagonistic approach to doing business in favour of a more integrative management style focused on coordinating activities along the supply chain in order to attain or sustain their competitive position.

Coordinating activities in a supply chain, however, is difficult. The difficulties are partly due to the complexity induced by the large number of related and interdependent activities in the supply chain. The fact that the effects of certain actions are separated from their cause both in time and place increases complexity, and is made even worse by the functional division of responsibility along the supply chain. Understanding the interdependencies and the complex causal relationships in a supply chain is therefore crucial to the successful management of these activities. It is important to realize that what you do not understand, you cannot manage.

Systems thinking offers a method for describing and analyzing problems in such contexts, and is therefore well suited to solving the complex and dynamic socioeconomic problems found in logistics systems today. However, the problems reported by many organizations show that the use of systems thinking is insufficiently developed, although it has been with us for several decades. Senge (1992) elaborates on this theme, and claims that firms seem more concerned with detail - as opposed to dynamic - complexity. If firms deal only with detail complexity, they are obstructed from seeing how relations of different kinds reach beyond their own firms and change over time. The nature of the problems reported indicates that many organizations act as autonomous units instead of components of a larger system, and thus neglect the width and scope of their interdependencies with other firms.

Unfortunately, the lack of systems thinking also influences how firms approach another important area: the design of performance measurement systems. A performance measurement system plays an important role in managing a business as it provides the information necessary for decision making and actions. Although this area has been pointed out many times as strategically important, it still is not sufficiently understood (Keebler et al., 1999; Atkinson et al., 1997; Vitale and Mavrinac, 1995; Eccles, 1991). The lack of systems thinking becomes especially disturbing when measurement systems are applied to supply chains.

PURPOSE

The purpose of this chapter is to explain supply chain performance measurement problems from a systems perspective. One important objective is to show if and how the problems are a result of insufficient systems thinking. Given the exploratory nature of this chapter, areas for future research are suggested in order to contribute to the body of knowledge within logistics.

METHOD

This chapter is based on an extensive literature review across disciplines such as management, quality and logistics, in addition to observations from a case study of six firms composing part of a supply chain in the home furnishing business in Sweden. IKEA, a multinational company in the home furnishing business, acted as host, providing access to organizations within IKEA as well as to suppliers of finished goods. Several echelons of the supply chain were included, ranging from retail outlet stores to manufacturers' plants.

The following organizations were included in the study:

- A sales organization;
- A wholesaler;
- A product development organization;
- A purchasing organization; and
- Two key suppliers.

Each organization within IKEA was a separate legal entity dedicated exclusively to IKEA operations. The fact that several echelons of the supply chain were included promised that problems and phenomena related to collaboration beyond dyadic relationships were examined.

Validity has been gained mainly by using triangulation of data sources and research methods, but also by adopting member checks and debriefing by peers. Regarding the collection of data, both semi-structured interviews and documents were used in addition to a questionnaire. Each of the three data collection methods is presented in greater detail below:

1. A total of 33 semistructured in-depth interviews were conducted by a single researcher, preceded by a test of the interview guide on three respondents from IKEA. The interviews were conducted with respondents at various levels within each of the organizations until saturation was reached. The interviews, lasting between one and three hours, were recorded and transcribed, leading to more than 250 pages of single-spaced data. A manual method for the categorization, clustering and analysis of interview data was used.
2. Documents showing such things as strategic business plans, financial reports, performance reports, supplier evaluation criteria and worker compensation criteria were collected when available. The purpose was to collect information that could be used to complement, contrast or verify the information provided through interviews.
3. A questionnaire was used to assess the extent to which the actors in the supply chain had a consistent view of priorities, and whether the respondents found that they were measuring the right things or not. The questionnaire was designed to follow the ideas of the Performance Measurement Questionnaire developed by Dixon et al. (1990).

OUTLINE OF THE ARTICLE

In the following section, "Supply chain fundamentals", a brief description of supply chain fundamentals is presented. The next section, "Typical measurement problems", encompasses a discussion of common measurement problems. The section "Adopting systems thinking to measurements" provides an introduction to systems thinking and its application to supply chain performance measurement, which is further developed in the following three sections - "Fragmented supply chain measurement activities", "Behavioral patterns", and "Structure determines behaviour". Some insights are presented in "A new view of measurement systems" before the final section, "Concluding discussion", which provides concluding remarks and suggestions for future research.

SUPPLY CHAIN FUNDAMENTALS

In the following discussion a supply chain is viewed as a number of organizations - at least three - working cooperatively with at least some shared objectives. To understand how these firms interact, it is important to notice how the management of such supply chains differs from classical materials and manufacturing control.

Oliver and Webber (1982) have described the fundamentals of supply chain management as follows:

- The supply chain is viewed as a single entity, not fragmented areas of responsibility for functional areas such as purchasing, manufacturing, distribution, etc.

- A direct consequence of the first statement is that supply chain management calls for - and depends upon - strategic decision making.
- Supply chain management includes a different perspective on inventories, which are used as a balancing mechanism of last, not first, resort.
- Supply chain management requires a new perspective on systems. Organizations must be integrated, not simply interfaced.

The result of a study covering more than 100 manufacturers, distributors and retailers conducted by Andersen Consulting and presented in 1997 (Anderson et al., 1997) supported the concept presented above. The study showed that companies that have successfully implemented supply chain management have two things in common. First, they think about the supply chain as a whole. Overcoming the inward-looking, self-focused attitude is thus a crucial element in supply chain management. Second, they pursue tangible outcomes focused on revenue growth, asset utilization and cost reduction.

In order to succeed, the firms adopted a number of principles that required them to look at the supply chain from their suppliers' suppliers to their customers' customers. The segmentation of customers, the customization of the logistics network, the cross-functional planning process, the postponement of product customization, and development of enterprise-wide systems for control and monitoring all required the supply chain members to adopt a holistic view of the supply chain. Neither of these initiatives would have been possible without viewing the supply chain as one entity.

However, the firms in the study reported difficulties in a number of areas. Assessing customer profitability was hard, partly because they lacked the adequate tools to understand both their own and their customers' costs. Furthermore, the independent, self-centered forecasting routine applied by firms was identified as incompatible with excellent supply chain management, and was replaced by cross-functional planning systems and processes. In order to deal with high inventory levels and out-of-stock situations, distributors started sharing information with the manufacturer, leading to improved fill rates, asset turns, and cost metrics for all concerned.

Unsuccessful companies had an equally consistent profile. Those companies were functionally oriented and narrowly focused. The problem was not a lack of ideas about what to do, but instead about how to coordinate the efforts in order to avoid "dying the death of a thousand initiatives". The functional orientation and narrow focus that obstruct the coordination of activities for those companies suggest that they lack a holistic perspective, and that systems thinking in those supply chains is underdeveloped. In essence, the study shows that those firms that have succeeded have adopted a holistic view of the supply chain, recognizing that the outcome that counts is that of the entire supply chain, not that of single organizations.

TYPICAL MEASUREMENT PROBLEMS

Research scientists have shown an increasing interest in improving the measurement systems design during the last few years (Keebler et al., 1999; Vitale and Mavrinac, 1995; Caplice and Sheffi, 1995; Kaplan and Norton, 1992; Eccles, 1991). They have questioned traditional performance measurement for several good reasons, not least because of its inability to allocate resources to areas important to future success, *e.g.* the development of employees' competency, capabilities and skills (Vitale and Mavrinac, 1995). A few important problems are briefly described in the following paragraphs.

Strategy and Measurements are Not Connected

One problem that deserves attention is the lack of connection between strategy and measurements. Adams et al. (1995) report that many measurement initiatives are not derived from strategy and are therefore not supporting the business. Although it seems obvious and natural to base a measurement system on the company's strategy, Eccles (1991) claims that a surprising number of companies do little to measure the variables described in their strategies. Because of the missing connection, measures and measurement activities seem focused on internal functions instead of overall company performance and customer needs. For instance, a firm may measure productivity throughout its own facility and closely track that goods are shipped on time, but pay little or no attention to whether the goods actually arrive at the customers' facilities when promised or needed.

Furthermore, because of the weak link to strategy, different divisions and functions have developed their own metrics in isolation and linked local reward incentives to those measures. This might lead them in different directions. Thus, the missing connection between strategy and measurements promotes an internal focus, which becomes an obstacle to developing supply chain measurement systems. However, not all strategies are successful. Regardless of how well a measurement system is connected to strategy, it will not turn a losing strategy into a winning one.

A Biased Focus on Financial Metrics

Many companies still rely too heavily on financial figures as their key performance indicators, which unfortunately are better at showing the result of yesterday's actions than indicating tomorrow's performance. Financial metrics have served as a tool for comparing firms and evaluating a firm's behaviour over time, and the information was primarily designed to meet external evaluators' needs.

Today the situation is quite different. People inside the organizations have more responsibility, and financial information is not decision-relevant to them (Atkinson et al., 1997). The lagging nature of financial metrics makes them less useful for proactive actions. What meaningful actions to manage a situation can be taken when the report finally arrives two weeks after the event? Furthermore, the usefulness of financial information is reduced by the aggregation of data over time and place, which makes it even more difficult to understand.

Success in business today is not solely determined by a strong cash flow or meeting a financial budget. Instead, developing competency, capabilities and skills in areas such as team-based problem solving and innovation are much more important, yet not easily measured in financial terms (Vitale and Mavrinac, 1995). Some firms have started to regularly report how much time and other resources are invested in employee development programmes, or how well the firm's competency profile meets future demands. Therefore, describing the complex and dynamic characteristics of a supply chain in financial terms alone is no longer sufficient, as it provides too simplified a view of the supply chain. Nonetheless, accounting-based information plays an important role in strategic planning and for monitoring financial results, although it is less suitable for controlling and improving activities (Johnson, 1990).

Too Many Isolated and Incompatible Measures

The number and variety of metrics used in organizations tend to increase over time, and require more and more resources to produce. Because metrics once introduced are too seldom removed, they soon become obsolete as strategy and underlying activities continue to change. For instance, why do firms continue giving top priority to goods handling efficiency and fill rate in trucks, when what the customers really need are timely and accurate shipments of goods? A common conclusion is that measurement systems have measured too many things and the wrong things. The negative impact of insufficient measurement systems can be severe. For example, Baldwin and Clark (1992) claim that a major cause of the USA's competitive decline is due directly to the managers' use of inappropriate performance measurement systems.

The Problems in a Supply Chain Context

The problems described earlier are mainly those reported by single organizations. However, it seems reasonable to assume that similar problems will occur and negatively affect management actions in supply chains (Holmberg, 1997). This assumption is based on the prevailing lack of systems thinking, and the increased complexity in supply chains encompassing several organizations with different corporate cultures, different policies and different routines. Using a single-firm management style when managing a supply chain is therefore likely to obstruct supply chain integration.

The idea proposed in this chapter is that the measurement activities in supply chains are not managed as one system, but as several independent systems. To make this point clearer, the next section will deal with some of the basic ideas in systems thinking and discuss measurement activities from that perspective.

ADOPTING SYSTEMS THINKING TO PERFORMANCE MEASUREMENT

Logisticians often claim to use systems thinking when managing the flow of goods and information from point of origin to end consumers, but few authors explain why or how the concept is used. Perhaps the lack of openness and clarity is unintentional. Nevertheless, it obstructs both research scientists and practitioners from developing a deeper understanding of how complex problems can be approached, understood, and solved.

The Systems Concept

The idea of a system is generally expressed as encompassing interconnected components separated from their environment by a system border. Checkland (1993) provides the following definition: The central concept system embodies the idea of a set of elements connected together, which form a whole, this showing properties which are properties of the whole, rather than properties of its component parts.

The rationale for using systems thinking is that it provides a method for describing, analyzing and planning complex systems of different kinds (Gustafsson et al., 1982). This method offers a way of understanding problems and communicating this understanding to others. Systems analysis helps us depict real world systems by using a structured way of building models. The general approach is to define components (rules, policies, phenomena, machines, people, etc.), decide what components should be included in the system, and define how the components are related.

A simple systems analysis could be to look at the order fulfillment process, including the ordering of products, the picking of orders, and the shipment of goods to the customers. If we decide to look only at what happens in the warehouse, we would optimize the routines for the consolidation of goods on pallets so that the handling of goods in the warehouse becomes as efficient as possible. That would improve the productivity of that isolated unit. If, on the other hand, we were to consider what happens to the goods once they arrive at the customer's plant, the decisions and actions would perhaps look different. The customer may want to have the goods sorted in a specific manner, because they are sent to different locations in the customer's plant. Not sorting the goods may make the distributor's operations efficient, but it induces increased costs for the customer. Consequently, viewing the wholesaler's and the retailer's operations as one entity provides opportunities for improvements not possible if each were analyzed separately. Thus, within systems thinking, qualitative data and metaphors can be used to depict what the components look like and how they are related. Because not every possible component can be included in the system for practical reasons, only closely related components relevant to the issue at hand are chosen. For example, although handling equipment plays an important role in the warehouse, describing how this equipment is serviced and maintained does not necessarily add much value to the discussion of order fulfillment.

Analyzing Measurement Problems from a Systems Perspective

Checkland's statement captures the problems in supply chain measurements quite well. Because measurement activities are generally not considered as a set of connected components, the properties on the whole are not recognized. The total cost concept may serve as an example. If, for instance, the cost of transportation and the cost of inventory in a firm were managed separately instead of jointly, the entity "total cost" encompassing both components would not exist. Thus, we would, for example, not be able to discuss the trade-off between the two cost components, which means that an important opportunity for improvement is lost.

One important shortcoming of many firms is their inability - or unwillingness - to widen the scope of their measurement activities. When limiting their focus to a single organization and neglecting to consider local measurement activities as part of a greater whole, they miss an opportunity to capitalize on how the measurement system could contribute to improving supply chain performance by taking waste out of the supply chain, not just moving it somewhere else.

For example, when firms use sales to intermediate customers as a measure of performance and actively try to maximize sales, they delimit the perspective and cut themselves off from the ones setting the pace in the supply chain. Because sales to intermediate customers does not show whether a final consumer pays for the product or not, it may lead to increased inventory build-up and higher costs. Measuring local productivity and local costs has the same effect, *i.e.* an increased risk of sub-optimization of the supply chain. Again, it is important to adopt a wide enough scope of measurement activities to remove - or at least reduce - inefficiencies in the supply chain.

A Systems Analysis Framework

The following discussion is aimed at positioning measurement problems and initiatives in a framework based on systems thinking, suggesting that adopting a systemic view of the supply chain can assist in improving performance. The framework is based on Senge's (1992) ideas about what kinds of explanations to phenomena firms use, depending on how well they have adopted systems thinking. Firms not recognizing the relationships between phenomena within the context in which they operate characterize the first and lowest level of adoption. Those firms turn to event explanations, which means that they generally (re)act on single events, and find themselves victims of circumstances. Whatever happens to them is perceived as resulting from external factors, which they assume cannot be controlled or influenced. This kind of firm tends to develop a self-centered and inward looking attitude, partly due to an insufficient exchange of information with its trading partners. Because the firms perceive the components (people, resources, phenomena, etc.) as independent units, their operations become fragmented and their behaviour reactive, partly because the firms look only within their own organizations for explanations or solutions.

Firms at level two are concerned with describing behavioral patterns, *i.e.* how phenomena change over time and place, *e.g.* seasonal variations over a year and the fluctuations in demand across a supply chain. Thus, the firms recognize some kinds of relationships between phenomena, and do not consider them as being totally independent. Consequently, it becomes important for them to collect information although it cannot always be fully utilized or understood. Because they know from experience what may happen - albeit not exactly when it will happen - they can plan better to cope with things bound to happen. Yet, they generally do not know how to prevent them from happening because they do not understand the underlying engines of change.

At the third level, which is considered the most developed one, firms deal with how structure determines behaviour. Those readers familiar with the Beer Game may remember that the problems people experienced in supplying beer throughout the supply chain were not caused by people wanting things to go wrong. Instead, the problems were largely caused by the isolation of each echelon in the supply chain. No information except orders was provided, which forced each member of the supply chain into a reactive behaviour. The structure that determines behaviour is composed of both tangible things, *e.g.* computers and communication equipment, and intangible things such as policies, culture and values. Understanding how structure determines behaviour is crucial to the successful restructuring of supply chain measurement systems leading to a predicted and desired outcome.

The following three sections are intended to illustrate how typical measurement problems and activities can be positioned in the framework presented above. This is done in order to argue that adopting a systemic view of supply chain activities may induce desired behaviour. The description of typical firms is sometimes quite categorical for the purpose of clarity. In reality, firms are likely to be less "typical".

FRAGMENTED SUPPLY CHAIN MEASUREMENT ACTIVITIES

Many activities and tasks are carried out in a firm's daily operations. For instance, goods are received from suppliers and put into warehouses, customer orders are registered, products are picked and shipped, and invoices are sent. Sometimes it all works well and customers receive the products they have ordered when they expected to, but sometimes it does not.

Managers in charge of the operations sometimes introduce metrics to allow them to be in control. When a specific problem or activity has received management attention for a while, it is usually corrected. Attention is then automatically focused on other and more urgent problems. While new metrics are defined to monitor the new problems, the old metrics are kept because the problem might turn up again. Consequently, the number of metrics increases while consuming more and more resources, but adding little value.

Understanding what goes on in a firm or in a supply chain can be quite difficult, which to some extent can be explained by the flow of information being delimited and fragmented both within and across firms. Not to add to the confusion, fragmentation within a firm will henceforth be called "internal fragmentation", whereas fragmentation across firms will be called "external fragmentation".

Internal Fragmentation

Understanding the meaning of a single metric might be easy, but the meaning of the metrics in combination and their effect on overall company performance is hard to intuitively understand. One problem is that "controller figures" based on financial accounting systems, and expressed in financial terms, are not easily compared with "engineering figures" focused on the movement of bits and pieces resulting in volumes and flows. For example, it is not obvious how the loading or unloading of goods or the productivity in order picking influence the operational result of a distribution center. Other factors such as goods handling damages, delivery quality or inventory accuracy greatly influence the performance of the operations as a whole. Furthermore, the use of financial accounting information promotes a functional perspective within an organization, mainly because resources are allocated from the top down, whereas goods and services flow horizontally through the firm.

The fragmentation is reinforced by different conceptions of performance, which negatively influence communication between people. Top management and controllers - being affected by external stakeholders - often use financial information for assessing the performance of the firms, while people on the shop floor prefer other kinds of information. The concept of performance clearly varies between different levels in an organization, which causes difficulties in integrating measurements across the operational, tactical and strategic levels.

External Fragmentation

Fragmentation across firms, for example in supply chains, means that not much information is shared. The self-centered attitude of firms and their unwillingness to look beyond their own firms creates a barrier to improving performance. The following example from IKEA may illustrate the point.

Starting at the retail end of the supply chain, a retail outlet manager claimed to be "squeezed" between the customers and the supplying organization, and claimed that both costs and sales were given equal (top) priority in his organization. The message he received from the top management was "... focus on sales, sales, sales to 100 percent and focus on cut, cut, cut (costs) to 100 percent". Because each store had a fixed budget (in absolute figures, not as share of revenues), it was difficult to improve sales by *e.g.* hiring more sales personnel. The only way to free resources was to focus on productivity in the store, which reinforced the focus on internal matters.

The supplying wholesale organization, being under constant pressure to reduce costs, had an equally strong focus on productivity. Operating on a margin of a few percent of revenues did not allow for extravagant service to the retailers. A request from a retailer to have tailored shipments encompassing unique mixtures of products and lower than normal delivery quantities was not received well by the wholesale organization. One reason the request did not lead to a meaningful discussion was the lack of (comparable) performance figures. Each party, for example, measured productivity in their own way. Because the retailer's request was not accompanied by an estimate of expected savings, no trade-off calculation could be made.

At the procurement side of the supply chain, the purchasing organization was focusing on keeping the purchase price low as it was driving costs throughout the supply chain. Aside from measuring purchase price development, suppliers' delivery performance was also closely monitored. Due to a complex order system, delivery plans were not very well coordinated with real customer demands, which forced suppliers to deliver goods according to plan whether IKEA needed the products or not. Behind this strange behaviour was a measure of supplier delivery performance linked to a bonus system in the purchasing organization. Thus, individual interests negatively influenced supply chain performance. This counterproductive connection was later identified and removed.

Although the main part of the IKEA supply chain was controlled by IKEA itself, firms within the supply chain adopted a self-centered behaviour, which was reinforced by the way performance was monitored. The retail outlet manager being "squeezed", the wholesaler having his hands tied by a small operating margin and the purchasing organization driven by purchase price, all to some degree point at event explanations to their situation. In order to break up this state of affairs in the IKEA supply chain, it is necessary to widen the scope of their perspectives. Otherwise, the retailer will continue to look for solutions to his problems within his own organization, the wholesaler will remain focused on internal operational efficiency without considering the effect on the retailer, and suppliers will continue fighting unsuccessfully for ideas which make sense and which might improve supply chain efficiency.

BEHAVIORAL PATTERNS

Understanding what happens in a supply chain and why it happens can be difficult for firms with limited information about what is going on in other parts of the supply chain. One way of reducing this problem without changing the underlying causes is to exchange more and other kinds of information. With sufficient and carefully selected information provided by measurement systems, it becomes possible for firms to understand better what is going on and what is about to happen. As mentioned in the framework, firms cannot prevent it from happening, but can plan and act to reduce its negative effects. Consequently, within supply chain management literature, information exchange is viewed as an absolutely necessary and indisputable component in any successful supply chain, having a tremendous impact on firms' operations.

Coordination Through Information Exchange

Information sharing is without question important, but depending on what information is shared, when and how it is shared and with whom, information seems to have different functions in the supply chain. The literature reports that firms usually start sharing sales information such as point-of-sales (POS) information in order to coordinate activities. The case study at IKEA showed that information used for coordination purposes was generally captured in one part or firm of the supply chain - most often downstream - and distributed to the other parts of the supply chain. Such information can, when provided in a timely fashion, make it possible for one process to respond to the needs and limitations of another process, which is an important part of the integration process (Alter, 1996).

POS data were shared among IKEA organizations in the case study, whereas suppliers received POS data only occasionally and often too late to be useful. For the majority of suppliers, sales information came indirectly in the form of orders, which more often than not were distorted from the journey through IKEA's order system. Unmotivated fluctuations in order quantities, which showed no similarity with the fluctuations in real consumer demands, forced suppliers to alternate between high and low capacity utilization of plants. Consequently, suppliers were obstructed from running their operations as efficiently as they knew was possible, partly due to the way information was shared.

Recognition of Relationships

Relationships between phenomena, *e.g.* between goods availability in retail outlets and delivery lead-time, are seldom explicitly described or explained.

Instead, those measures are presented in the same performance report with no explanation as to how they are related. The "logic" connecting them, which is not openly or widely communicated, is "owned" by a few people within the organization who have the necessary training, knowledge and understanding of the organization. The rest of the users of the information are thrown upon their own resources to interpret it and turn it into actions.

The one organization in the IKEA case study possessing the overall responsibility of the supply chain developed a performance model called "the product management model".

This model consisted of measures within five different areas:

1. Product range;
2. Cost;
3. Quality;
4. Availability; and
5. Service.

The areas of measurement were identified as important to the consumers during the buying process, which in turn represented the logic connecting the five areas. Consumers were assumed to fancy a wide and attractive product range, assess whether the products offered value for money or not, and whether the product was available in stock to take home. Although the measures were logically related, no explicit descriptions of how they were connected were provided, *i.e.* no cause-and-effect relationships were explicitly or widely described or communicated. This meant that each manager had to develop his/her own idea of what created business success.

The product management model illustrates an organization's ambition to make explicit the priorities of the supply chain. Still, the model was only moderately well received and used by managers, who instead turned to self-developed tools and reports. An inherent weakness of the model was that it did not manage - or was never intended - to make explicit the relationships between the different dimensions of performance.

One important thing to notice is that the scope of measurement activities encompassed several organizations, and IKEA no longer viewed the phenomena as isolated, but as interrelated. Although no relationships were made explicit, the different dimensions of performance were considered part of a greater whole, which is fundamental in systems thinking. For instance, inventory levels in different parts of the supply chain were monitored and reported, which made it possible to reduce the total amount of inventory in the supply chain. Instead of clear definitions of the relationship between, *e.g.* customer service measures and measures of inventory levels and the like, IKEA relied on safety stock calculations, rules of thumb and experience.

The view of measurement activities presented earlier has developed into a new measurement structure.

STRUCTURE DETERMINES BEHAVIOUR

Firms that have moved beyond event explanations and descriptions of behavioral patterns have expressed an ambition to do better, to get ahead of the problems. They have experienced a need to describe how the different activities in the firm - or across firms - are related. What they intuitively know about their business may have been discussed before, but not explicitly described. They know that they want to use the information derived from the measurement system to induce behaviour that is supportive of a strategy (Adams et al., 1995). Furthermore, they have realized that they still lack a crucial and often ignored step in developing a useful measurement system: the definition of a business performance model that contains the often-implicit relationships between management actions and results (Eccles and Pyburn, 1992).

A New Understanding of Relationships

Some interesting things have happened recently in measurement system design. First, firms have started using their strategy as a base, as strategy determines the scope and focus of the measurement system (Adams et al., 1995). Second, firms are balancing different dimensions of performance, *e.g.* service quality, innovation skills and costs to reduce the negative impact and reactive behaviour induced by financially oriented metrics. Third, instead of looking only at the result, firms define causal relationships between the result and the engines of the result.

The complex network of interrelated activities in supply chains makes it difficult for managers to describe and understand how those activities are related and how they influence each other. This is not unusual, because many situations in management and economics can be described as high-order non-linear systems, and intuitive solutions to such complex problems are extremely difficult to find (Forrester, 1991). For example, how does the work scheme and compensation programme in an order-picking group in a warehouse influence the firm's customers' ability to serve their customers? These kinds of questions do arise in a supply chain context, but common tools and techniques provide little help in answering such questions.

It is difficult not only to adequately depict these kinds of relationships because so many factors influence the result, but also to communicate them to others (Senge, 1992; Forrester, 1991). When measuring performance in this context, it is much too easy to escape the problem by focusing on single units' performances instead of relating the measurements to overriding objectives. Single, fragmented measures provide little information because the context is missing. For example, is a 10 percent increase in productivity in unit A good or bad? Well, it depends, for example, on whether the overall performance in terms of service quality and costs has improved. At best, such information is useless, but improperly designed performance measurement systems may even be quite harmful and obstruct decision makers' learning processes (McNann and Nanni, 1994).

Performance Models

A perhaps well-known model showing important relationships is the balanced scorecard, created by Kaplan and Norton (1992) in the early 1990s. Besides introducing a concept of balancing four different dimensions of performance, they use cause-and-effect relationships to describe how the four dimensions of performance are connected. The model is claimed to be not merely a measurement tool, but moreover a management system to clarify and translate strategy and vision into strategic objectives. This is important, as managers tend to develop their own understanding of what the strategy means to themselves individually. It is also a tool to communicate and link strategic objectives and measures in the organization. The process of planning, setting targets and aligning strategic initiatives is facilitated by the balanced scorecard, which ultimately aims at enhancing strategic feedback and learning. An illustration of how the four different dimensions of performance can be linked by cause-and-effect relationships.

This model has become quite popular, possibly because it provides a long-awaited tool to relate different dimensions of performance. Critics (for example, Neely et al., 1997) claim, however, that the model fails to answer one of the most important questions of all: what are the competitors doing?

Whereas Kaplan and Norton use a linear cause-and-effect relationship in their model, Senge (1992) uses a different technique in which he turns the linear cause-and-effect relationships into circular loops. The technique of closing the loop plays an important role as it challenges people's desire to oversimplify relationships. The idea of closed loops may not be that controversial after all, although people often stick to linear cause-and-effect relationships. People are likely to accept the idea that improved financial results offer an opportunity to reinvest the money in the business, and, for example, improve internal processes, reward employees and stimulate innovative ideas. Thus, there is a link from what seemed like an end, to what can be viewed as engines of success.

Both models serve the same purpose, *i.e.* to uncover the "mechanisms" of the business. The models make it possible to connect different phenomena and thus describe - albeit in vague terms - how they interact. Of course, the number of links can be high, and the need for simplification obvious. Nevertheless, the models provide a means of communicating the ideas about such things as how sales can be increased or how overall productivity can improve by adopting non-obvious solutions. For example, improving profitability might be easier if resources are spent on removing the obstacles to increased profitability, *i.e.*

the increased distribution costs, instead of allocating resources to increased marketing efforts. Worth mentioning is an initiative taken to improve supply chain performance through a measurement called the SCOR model.

The model is developed by the Supply-Chain Council (SCC), an independent, not-for-profit, global corporation, and based on a process view of the supply chain using four distinct management processes:

1. Plan;
2. Source;
3. Make; and
4. Deliver.

The process reference model integrates the well-known concepts of business process re-engineering, benchmarking, and process measurements into a cross-functional framework. Each of the four processes at the top level is successively divided into sub-processes, first at a configuration level, then at a process element level. Finally, at the fourth level and beyond the scope of the SCOR model, activities are defined by companies individually. Measures are defined for all processes at the three top levels, and firms provide information about how they perform while receiving a benchmark in return against which they can compare their own performance. This model provides not only an opportunity to see how the firm is doing, but also a common frame of reference and a common language across the supply chain.

Measurements Across Organizations at IKEA

The above mentioned performance models aimed at reflecting the structure of the underlying system. In the IKEA case, one such model had been used for years, even before the ideas about supply chain wide measurement systems emerged in business literature. The system in question was a cost calculation system covering parts of the supply chain, which enabled managers to estimate the (average) cost of distribution from purchase of finished goods until delivery to stores. Although the model was by no means perfect (more of that in a moment) it provided a tool for analyzing the cost structure at a high level of detail across several firms in the supply chain.

Whereas the sharing of POS information from the retail outlet enabled firms upstream in the supply chain to respond better and faster to changes in customer demands, it provided merely an opportunity for coordinating existing processes. In contrast, cost information as provided by the above mentioned cost calculation system made it possible to compare one part of the supply chain with another, as information was collected from each of the organizations. Other examples of such information are inventory levels and lead time.

Capturing and exchanging cost information is a sensitive and debated issue, where many firms want to reveal their partners' cost structure, but not give away their own. IKEA was no exception to that rule. In the case study, costs were captured only in the mid-part of the supply chain, leaving suppliers and retail stores out. Because no detailed cost information was provided from the retail stores (only figures of gross margin and generic information about cost structures), the effect of direct deliveries from suppliers to stores was difficult to assess. A number of other problems or shortcomings were related to measuring costs the way IKEA did. One obstacle to comparability of figures was that costs were mixed with mark-ups at each organization in the model. Another problem was that figures in the system were calculated as average figures, which made it impossible to distinguish one product from another.

Measuring and comparing, *e.g.* costs, for the purpose of removing inefficiencies from the supply chain is often difficult, partly because it requires significant alignment of data structures, which to some degree is dictated by government rules and regulations. Many firms are not likely to have the systems or capabilities in place to make this alignment without great efforts. An even greater obstacle is the lack of trust and firms' willingness to share proprietary information. It seems true though that exchanging this kind of information among partners does facilitate analyses and discussions that may lead to structural changes influencing the firms' competitive positions.

Returning for a moment to the other measures that crossed the IKEA supply chain, measuring inventory levels was uncontroversial and a rather technical matter. The firms in the case measured inventory in retail outlets and distribution centers, but did not include suppliers' stock. In general, this information was primarily used for capacity planning purposes and, of course, to avoid gross overstocks. Measuring lead times, however, was a bit more difficult. The most prominent difficulty with sharing lead-time information was that data could not be captured at all points where they made sense (*e.g.* when goods arrived at retail stores), and those data were captured in the wrong format (the highest level of detail was "day" instead of "hour"). The result was that variances in lead time to stores could not be analyzed or fed back to transporters to improve performance, for example.

Collaborating on performance measurements means, among other things, that the firms are getting closer to each other. It also means that the borders become less distinct. Getting access to information beyond a single firm makes it possible for firms to fight event explanations, and act in accordance with wider objectives, *e.g.* that of a supply chain. In essence, sharing information as illustrated above is supportive of the integration process.

6

Logistics Strategy in Container Shipping

THE NATURE OF LOGISTICS

The growing flows of freight have been a fundamental component of contemporary changes in economic systems at the global, regional and local scales. These changes are not merely quantitative with more freight in circulation, but also structural and operational. Structural changes mainly involve manufacturing systems with their expanded geography of production, while operational changes mainly concern freight transportation with its geography of distribution, namely intermodal transport systems. As such, the fundamental question does not necessarily reside in the nature, origins and destinations of freight movements, but how this freight is moving. New modes of production are concomitant with new modes of distribution, which brings forward the realm of logistics; the science of physical distribution.

Logistics involves a wide set of activities dedicated to the transformation and distribution of goods, from raw material sourcing to final market distribution as well as the related information flows. Derived from Greek logistikos (to reason logically), the word is polysemic. In the Nineteenth century the military referred to it as the art of combining all means of transport, revictualling and sheltering of troops. Today it refers to the set of operations required for goods to be made available on markets or to specific locations.

The application of logistics enables a greater efficiency of movements with an appropriate choice of modes, terminals, routes and scheduling. The implied purpose of logistics is to make available goods, raw materials and commodities, fulfilling four major requirements related to order, delivery, quality and cost fulfillment. Logistics is thus a multidimensional value added activityincluding production, location, time and control of elements of the supply chain. It thus enables a better managerial level of space-time relations and as such an important aspect of transport geography. Logistics acts as the material and organizational support of globalization requiring acomplex set of decisions to be made concerning an array of issues such as the location of suppliers, the transport modes to be used and the timing and sequencing of deliveries.

Logistics and supply chain management are becoming increasingly blurred and are often used interchangeably. Previously, logistics tended to focus on on transportation and warehousing aspects, while supply chain management would consider sourcing and well as final distribution. In recent years the meaning of both has converged. Thus, we consider logistics and supply chain management as similar. Activities comprising logistics include physical distribution; the derived transport segment, and materials management; the induced transport segment.

Physical distribution is the collective term for the range of activities involved in the movement of goods from points of production to final points of sale and consumption. It must insure that the mobility requirements of supply chains are entirely met. Physical distribution includes all the functions of movement and handling of goods, particularly transportation services (trucking, freight rail, air freight, inland waterways, marine shipping, and pipelines), transshipment and warehousing services (*e.g.* consignment, storage, inventory management), trade, wholesale and, in principle, retail. Conventionally, all these activities are assumed to be derived from materials management demands.

Materials management considers all the activities involved in the manufacturing of commodities in all their stages of production along a supply chain. It includes production and marketing activities such as production planning, demand forecasting, purchasing and inventory management. Materials management must insure that the requirements of supply chains are met by dealing with a wide array of parts for assembly and raw materials, including packaging (for transport and retailing) and, ultimately, recycling discarded goods and commodities. All these activities are assumed to be inducing physical distribution demands.

The close integration of physical distribution and materials management through logistics is blurring the reciprocal relationship between the derived transport demand function of physical distribution and the induced demand function of materials management. This implies that distribution, as always, is derived from materials management activities (namely production), but also, that these activities are coordinated within distribution capabilities. The functions of production, distribution and consumption are difficult to consider separately, thus recognizing theintegrated transport demand role of logistics. Distribution centers are the main facilities from which logistics are coordinated.

Distribution Center. Facility or a group of facilities that perform consolidation, warehousing, packaging, decomposition and other functions linked with handling freight. Their main purpose is to provide value-added services to freight, which is stored for relatively shorts periods of time (days or weeks). DCs are often in proximity to major transport routes or terminals. They can also perform light manufacturing activities such as assembly and labeling. A warehouse is a facility designed to store goods for longer periods of time.

Therefore a distribution center tends to focus on the demand while a warehouse is more driven by the supply.

Since it would be highly impractical to ship directly goods from producers to retailers, distribution centers essentially act as a buffer where products are assembled, sometimes from other distribution centers, and then shipped in batches. Distribution centers are established in part to deal with to different forms of asynchronisms in freight distribution such as different paces of production and consumption. Distribution centers commonly have a market area in which they offer a service window defined by delivery frequency and response time to order. This structure looks much like a hub-and-spoke network.

The wide array of activities involved in logistics, from transportation to warehousing and management, have respective costs. Once compiled, they express the burden that logistics impose on distribution systems and the economies they support, which is known as the total logistics costs. Costs are however not the only consideration in supply chain management since supply chains can also be differentiated by time, reliability and risk level. The nature and efficiency of distribution systems is strongly related to the nature of the economy in which they operate.Worldwide logistics expenditures represent about 10-15 per cent of the total world GDP. In economies dependent on the extraction of raw materials, logistical costs are comparatively higher than for service economies since transport costs account for a larger share of the total added value of goods. For the transport of commodities, logistics costs are commonly in the range of 20 to 50 per cent of their total costs.

The emergence of logistics in contemporary supply chains is based upon continuous improvements in transport and inventory management costs, leading to lower cycle and lead times. Cycle time. The amount of time required from the receipt of an order to when this order is completed (assembled) and ready for delivery. Often labeled as the completion rate and is mostly linked with the function of production in the manufacturing sector. Often labeled as the level of responsiveness of production.

Lead time. The time it takes for an order to be fulfilled, which includes preparation, packing and delivery to a designed location. Often labeled as the arrival rate and is mostly linked with the function of distribution, mainly its efficiency and reliability. Often labeled as the level of responsiveness of distribution. Before the emergence of online purchases, customers were rarely exposed to the concepts of cycle times and lead times since goods were directly purchased at a store. The customer was seeing the outcome of cycle and lead times, but not the process. An online transaction, particularly if it concerns a complex and customizable good (*e.g.* a computer) commonly includes the time it takes for the order to be ready for shipment and the delivery time from the distribution center to the customer's address.

DRIVING FORCES IN SUPPLY CHAIN MANAGEMENT

Lean supply chains, as a managerial concept, is often labeled as seminal in the emergence of modern supply chains where inventory levels are kept at a minimum and where a large share of the inventory is in constant circulation. Typically the manufacturing sector has 6 to 8 inventory turns per year. In the electronics sector, this can even be more frequent with 10 to 20 inventory turns per year. During the 1980s, the application of flow control permitted to reduce inventories in time-sensitive manufacturing activities from several days' worth to several hours. Much of these efforts initially took place within the factory, while supply and output flowed as batches from suppliers and to distributors. In the 1990s, with the convergence of logistics and information and communication technologies (ICT), this principle was increasingly applied to the whole supply chain, particularly to the function of distribution.

Another important requirement was containerization, which conferred substantial flexibility to production systems in addition to the container being its own storage unit. The expansion of standard transport infrastructure such as highways, terminals and airports was also essential for the development of modern logistics. Logistics and integrated transport systems are therefore related, particularly because of the container which has concomitantly become a unit of load (transport), production and distribution. Thus, the physical as well as the ICT elements of technological change are being underlined as it helps strengthen the level of control distributors have over the supply chain.

The technological dimension of logistics can thus be considered from six perspectives:

- Transportation modes. Modes have been the object of very limited technological changes in recent decades. In some cases, modes have adapted to handle containerized operations such as road and rail (*e.g.* doublestacking). It is maritime shipping that has experienced the most significant technological change, which required the construction of an entirely new class of ships and the application of economies of scale to maritime container shipping. In this context, a global network of maritime shipping servicing large gateways has emerged.
- Transportation terminals. The technological changes have been very significant with the construction of new terminal facilities operating on a high turnover basis. Better handling equipment lead to improvements in the velocity of freight at the terminals, which are among the most significant technological changes brought by logistics in materials movements. In such a context, the port has become one of the most significant terminals supporting global logistics. Port facilities are increasingly been supported by an array of inland terminals connected by high capacity corridors.
- Distribution centers and distribution clusters. Technological changes

impacted over the location, design and operation of distribution centers; the facilities handling the requirements of modern distribution. They serve different purposes depending on the combination of fabrication, storage and distribution functions they perform within their supply chains. Modern distribution centers tend to consume more space, both from the site they occupy and the building area. From a locational standpoint, distribution centers mainly rely on trucking, implying a preference for suburban locations with good road accessibility supporting a constant traffic. They service regional markets with a 48 hours service window (lead time) on average, implying that replenishment orders from their customers are met within that time period. They have become one floor facilities designed more for throughput than for warehousing with specialized loading and unloading bays and sorting equipment. Cross-docking distribution centers represent one of the foremost expressions of a facility that handles freight in a time sensitive manner. Automation is also pushing forward the productivity level of distribution centers. For instance, it is possible to fully automate the sorting, storing and palletizing processes in a distribution center. Another trend has been the setting of freight distribution clusters where an array of distribution activities agglomerate to take advantage of shared infrastructures and accessibility. This tends to expand the added-value performed by logistics.

- Load units. Since logistics involves improving the efficiency of flows, load units have become particularly important. They are the basic physical management unit in freight distribution and take the form of pallets, swap bodies, semi-trailers and containers. Containers are the privileged load unit for long distance trade, but the growing complexity of logistics required a more specific level of load management. The use of bar codes and increasingly of RFID (Radio Frequency Identification Device) enables a high level of control of the load units in circulation.
- Information technologies. Consider the vast array of information processing changes brought by logistics. The commodity chain is linked with physical flows as well as with information flows, notably through Electronic Data Interchange (EDI). Producers, distributors and consumers are embedded in a web of reciprocal transactions. Standardization of Internet-based applications enabled corporations to establish interfaces with their customers. While these transactions mostly take place virtually, their outcomes are physical flows. The commercial diffusion of Global Positioning Systems (GPS) is now allowing for the identification and routing of vehicles and therefore a

better utilization of these assets. The outcome is often more efficient production and distribution planning with the additional convenience of tracking modes, shipments and inventories and thus giving a greater visibility for customers.

- Ecommerce. Ecommerce offers advantages for the whole commodity chain, from consumers being exposed to a wider range of products to manufacturers and distributors being able to adapt quickly to changes in the demand. Ecommerce generates a lot of home deliveries parcel movements that are carried by conventional postal services as well as specialized parcel carriers. In the United States, about 70 per cent of home deliveries are made by the United States Postal Services, while the remaining 30 per cent is carried by private parcel companies. Fulfillment (warehousing, packaging) costs account for 10 to 12 per cent of the revenue of ecommerce, while shipping and delivery costs added up another 10 per cent. Ecommerce is also inciting shifts in retail freight distribution with the setting of new fulfillment and sortation centers. As retail sales get partially replaced by online sales the need for conventional retail space declines while the footprint occupied by distribution center increases.

For logistics, ICT is particularly a time and embeddedness issue, particularly because of ICT, freight distribution is within a paradigm shift from inventory-based logistics (push) to replenishment-based logistics (pull). Demand, particularly in the retailing sector, is very difficult to anticipate accurately and is prone to cycles. A closer integration between supply and demand enables a more efficient production system with fewer wastes in terms of unsold inventory. Logistics is thus a fundamental component of efficiency improvements in a market economy.

DISTRIBUTION SYSTEMS

In a broader sense distribution systems are embedded in a changing macro- and microeconomic framework, which can be roughly characterized by the terms of flexibility and globalization:

- Flexibility implies a highly differentiated, strongly market and customer driven mode of creating added-value. Contemporary production and distribution is no longer subject to single-firm activity, but increasingly practiced in networks of suppliers and subcontractors. The supply chain bundles together all this by information, communication, cooperation, and, last but not least, by physical distribution.
- Globalization means that the spatial frame for the entire economy has been expanded, implying the spatial expansion of the economy, more complex global economic integration, and an intricate network of global flows and hubs.

The flow-oriented mode affects almost every single activity within the entire process of value creation. The core component of materials management is the supply chain, the time- and space-related arrangement of the whole goods flow between supply, manufacturing, distribution and consumption. Its major parts are the supplier, the producer, the distributor (*e.g.* a wholesaler, a freight forwarder, a carrier), the retailer, the end consumer, all of whom represent particular interests.

Compared with traditional freight transport systems, the evolution of supply chain management and the emergence of the logistics industry are mainly characterized by three features:

- Integration. A fundamental restructuring of goods merchandising by establishing integrated supply chains with integrated freight transport demand. According to macro-economic changes, demand-side oriented activities are becoming predominant. While traditional delivery was primarily managed by the supply side, current supply chains are increasingly managed by the demand.
- Time mitigation. Whereas transport was traditionally regarded as a tool for overcoming space, logistics is concerned with mitigating time. Due to the requirements of modern distribution, the issue of time is becoming increasingly important in the management of commodity chains. Time is a major issue for freight shipping as it imposes inventory holding and depreciation costs, which becomes sensitive for tightly integrated supply chains.
- Specialization. This was achieved by shifts towards vertical integration, namely subcontracting and outsourcing, including the logistical function itself. Logistics services are becoming complex and time-sensitive to the point that many firms are now sub-contractingparts of their supply chain management to what can be called third-party logistics providers(3PL; asset based). More recently, a new category of providers, called fourth-party logistics providers (4PL; non asset based) have emerged.

While many manufacturing corporations may have in-house transportation departments, increasingly the complex needs of the supply chain are being contracted out to third parties. Depending on the strategy and costs corporations can outsource in whole or in part their transport and supply chain operations. Third party logistics providers (3PL) have emerged from traditional intermediaries such as the forwarders, or from transport providers such as FEDEX or Maersk. Both groups have been at the forefront of the intermodal revolution that is now assuming more complex organizational forms and importance. In offering door to door services, the customer is no longer aware or necessarily concerned with how the shipment gets to its destination, namely the modes used and the routing selected. The preoccupation is with cost, reliability and level of service. This produces a paradox, that for the customer of intermodal services geographic space becomes meaningless; but for the intermodal providers routing, costs and service frequencies have significant geographical constraints. The effectiveness of intermodal transport systems is thus masking the importance of transportation to its users.

Logistics is thus concomitantly concerned by distribution costs and time. In addition, many dimensions are added to the function of distribution.

While in the past it was a simple matter of delivering an intact good at a specific destination within a reasonable time frame, several components have become linked with distribution:

- Distribution time, notably the possibility to set a very specific ETA for deliveries and a low tolerance for delays.
- The reliability of distribution measured in terms of the availability of the ordered goods and the frequency at which orders are correctly serviced in terms of quantity and time.
- The flexibility of distribution in terms of possible adjustments due to changes in the quantity, the location or the delivery time.
- The quality of distribution concerns the condition of delivered goods and if the specified quantity was delivered.

GEOGRAPHY OF FREIGHT DISTRIBUTION

Logistics has a distinct geographical dimension, which is expressed in terms of flows, nodes andnetworks within the supply chain. Space / time convergence, a well known concept in transport geography where time was simply considered as the amount of space that could be traded with a specific amount of time, including travel and transshipment, is being transformed by logistics. Activities that were not previously considered fully in space / time relationships, such as distribution, are being integrated. This implies an organization and synchronization of flows through nodes and network strategies:

- Flows. The traditional arrangement of goods flow included the processing of raw materials to manufacturers, with a storage function usually acting as a buffer. The flow continued via wholesaler and/or shipper to retailer, ending at the final customer. Delays were very common on all segments of this chain and accumulated as inventories in warehouses. There was a limited flow of information from the consumer to the supply chain, implying the producers were not well informed (often involving a time lag) about the extent of consumption of their outputs. This procedure is now changing, mainly by eliminating one or more of the costly operations in the supply chain organization. Reverse flows are also part of the supply chain, namely for recycling and product returns. An important physical outcome of supply chain management is the concentration of storage or warehousing in one facility, instead of several. This facility is increasingly being designed as a flow- and throughput-oriented distribution center, instead of a warehouse holding cost intensive large inventories.

- Nodes and Locations. Due to new corporate strategies, a concentration of logistics functions in certain facilities at strategic locations is prevalent. Many improvements in freight flows are achieved at terminals. Facilities are much larger than before, the locations being characterized by a particular connection of regional and long-distance relations. Traditionally, freight distribution has been located at major places of production, for instance in the manufacturing belt at the North American east coast and in the Midwest, or in the old industrialized regions of England and continental Europe. Today, particularly the large-scale goods flows are directed through major gateways and hubs, mainly large ports and major airports, also highway intersections with access to a regional market. The changing geography of manufacturing and industrial production has been accompanied by a changing geography of freight distribution taking advantages of intermediary locations.
- Networks. The spatial structure of contemporary transportation networks is the expression of the spatial structure of distribution. The setting of networks leads to a shift towards larger distribution centers, often serving significant trans-national catchments. However, this does not mean the demise of national or regional distribution centers, with some goods still requiring a three-tier distribution system, with regional, national and international distribution centers. The structure of networks has also adapted to fulfill the requirements of an integrated freight transport demand, which can take many forms and operate at different scales. Most freight distribution networks, particularly in retailing, are facing the challenge of the "Last Mile" which is the final leg of a distribution sequence, commonly linking a distribution center and a customer (store).

Since cities are at the same time zones of production, distribution and consumption, the realm ofcity logistics is of growing importance. This issue is made even more complex by a growing dislocation between production, distribution and consumption, brought by globalization, global production networks, and efficient freight transport systems and logistics. This dislocation has incited a growing emphasis on issues related to supply chain integration so that in spite of acute geographical separation physical and managerial processes have minimal friction. How challenging individual countries are perceived to be in the setting and management of supply chains can be assessed, as done by the Logistic Performance Index.

It underlines that logistical costs in developing countries tend to be higher, which undermines economic development for the main following reasons:

- The regulatory complexity of distributing goods in developing countries involves higher logistic costs and is inciting distributors to maintain higher inventory levels to cope with uncertainty. Custom regulations are complex and prone to delays and road transportation can be subject to arbitrary tolls and inspections. This is reflected in higher final goods or component prices that are assumed directly or indirectly by consumers.
- Labour and infrastructure productivity in developing countries tend to be lower, which in many cases doubles logistics costs. The advantages of cheap labour can often be counterbalanced by lower levels of productivity. This also impacts the reliability of freight distribution with unreliable lead times and deliveries.
- Modal and intermodal capacity is inconsistent. While several terminal facilities, particularly ports, are modern with capacity on par with global standards, hinterland transportation can be problematic with road segments unable to effectively handle trucks of standard capacity.

In such a context, reforms have been advocated to promote the effectiveness of logistics services and therefore break a vicious cycle in which several developing countries are entangled in. This involves a series of reform, pending the capacity to overcome political constraints and the inertia (and commonly rent seeking behaviour) of established stakeholders, concerning service providers, infrastructure investment as well as the administrative and regulatory environment.

HOW TO PACK A SEA SHIPPING CONTAINER WITH HOUSEHOLD CONTENTS

So that's it, your decision is irrevocable, you've decided to relocate overseas. You've been hesitating between selling your household contents and travel light, then buy everything back again; or packing a container to ship overseas.

The former option demands less efforts, but induces a big money loss, as second hand personal effects drop a lot in value for anyone else than you. The latter option takes a lot of energy if you do it yourself, but allows to preserve the entirety of your household, except some consumables. If you own enough, this option is still the cheapest. Also, priceless is the feeling or living in a known setting again. If this is what you're after.

I've tried both, and today I'll share with you my own experience with packing a 20' shipping container with my personal effects for a half-the-world-away trip. As always, there are the when, where, what and how considerations to take before you start anything.

THE HOW AND THE WHAT

The Decision Making Process

It may not be worth packing a full container load if you don't own much. Shipping a container is costly. Not only the hiring and insurance costs, but also time off work may add to the bill if you don't have any, or not enough paid leave.

Practical Case

You live in a studio apartment and own for about $10,000 worth of furniture, white goods and clothes and clothes, for a total volume of about 12 m3. You're considering moving from Australia to Europe. If what you own is less than 20 cubic meters, you may consider option A: container sharing, as option B: full container load (FCL), could cost you not less than $4,800 in shipping and insurance (actual values, taken from an actual quote, 2012, from Adelaide, Australia).

I don't know how much container sharing is these days, but it's a cost that is proportional to the volume occupied by your stuff. The base unit is the m3. A number of years ago, I paid about $300 per m3. It might have gone up. If you're considering option C: selling everything and buying it back in Europe, you might get $2000 of your effects if you're lucky, and pay about $7000 to buy everything back in Europe, where your purchasing power in Australian dollars is higher than the Euro.

The total cost of these three options is:

- *Option A:* $3600 + pickup/delivery cost to and from the harbour
- *Option B:* $4800 (includes pickup, delivery and road delivery at destination)
- *Option C:* $5000

In this case, option A, container pooling, is what you should choose.

Now, in a different scenario where you're a bit older, with more stuff at home, let's suppose your total household contents total up $50,000 for a volume of 25 m3. Option A: container pooling, is now getting expensive as you've got a larger volume. It could cost you $7500.

Selling could bring you $10000, but will require a lot of time and efforts to organise the sales, given the number of items. Buying everything back in Europe may cost you $32000. Here, option C: FCL, would cost you about $5200. The difference with the previous scenario option C, is that you insured your content for a higher value. The insurance component is about 2 per cent of the declared buy back value in the destination country.

The total cost of these three options is:

- *Option A:* $22000
- *Option B:* $7500
- *Option C:* $5200

In my opinion, you should take into account the time taken to organise the sale or the packing, and also the cost of hiring a vehicle, or someone to pick up your load and take it for container sharing if you choose option A.

Enquiring About Shipping in a Container

You'll realise there are a few transport companies who do this in your area, at very different prices. My belief is that for this type of job, you can't say you benefit from a lot of post-sale value added. It's basically raw service all across the board: drop-off, pickup, transport, customs clearing, transport, delivery. Therefore you should choose the cheapest.

THE WHEN

Iso-Hemisphere Relocation

If the shipping route stays all in one hemisphere, I advise yo to rather pack and ship in the nice season. Especially if your place can get really humid at packing time. You would store gaseous water in these extended days when packing, and it may condensate every night inside the container even though you haven't finished yet. Imagine your quilts, sheets, clothes, couch, covered in dew every night . . .

If you can't choose the date yourself, pack at home before taking out to the container. Take your items out into the container during the warmer hours of the day, and close the container doors tightly before night time to avoid inside condensation. This is particularly true up in Queensland, when dew starts to form about an hour before sunset in autumn and winter. Use an excess of plastic bin bags to wrap your items made of fabric; tightly pack your couch in large plastic sheets, like it is when a furniture shop receives it.

TRANS-HEMISPHERE RELOCATION

If you relocate into another hemisphere, it's a different story. I think it's preferable to pack in a dry week in autumn or the start of winter, if there are any, so that your container arrives in the other hemisphere in the warm season. There's physics behind this. I'll try to explain my theory.

To pass from one hemisphere to another, the ship will cross the inter-tropical belt, traditionalist humid. The atmosphere inside of it might then get humid, but it's acceptable as it's still warm. Then, as the ship sails further along north, the outer atmosphere will either dry up if it's heading to the warm season, or cool down if it's heading to winter season. In the former case, it's a win, as any humidity collected inside the container through the equator will escape the container as outside is drier and warmer (remember that the tropics are warmer and drier than the equator in summer, except if the ship's destination is India or Asia, at monsoon time). Therefore your stuff should arrive dry. On the other hand, if the ship is heading towards winter after crossing a humid equator, the humidity collected inside the container may never leave it and even condensate as the temperature inside the container is dropping. Your stuff may then arrive wet. Then again this is just a theoretical case that is likely to happen, but some specific climatic conditions may hinder these predictions.

PACKING IN THE RAIN

This situation is not welcome at all, especially if you have to walk some distance between your place and the container. It might pay to have your container delivered 10 days prior to departure, so that you wait and jump on the dry days of that period that may occur. This is the method I used for my personal relocation, as it was autumn and rainy. It turned out that waiting 3 days with the container tightly closed, not doing anything but packing inside the house, was the best option as the weather become clear, sunnier, colder and drier a few days later.

THE HOW

Preparing Your House Contents for Shipping

- All these years, as a general rule since your mind is set at travelling, keep the original boxes as much as you can in your life. If you need to move, or sell, or break up . . . they will be second to no other package, and they will save you a lot of time will effectively protecting your goods.
- Starting months in advance, collect as many boxes, wrapping, material for padding, plastic, foam, polystyrene, in various shapes and sizes, to make a large collection of material you'll eventually use at packing time. In my case, I would do furniture shop bins, science university bins (they often have large boxes with a lot of padding as they order expensive apparatus, devices and computer systems), and also ask hospitals for those 40x30x25 boxes that they get when they order sets. They need hundreds of them each month, and you'll help them by taking them away from their place.

- Identify what you really want to take abroad. Any broken items that are not worth spending energy on? Low valued bulky items that you'll spend less on buying back than transporting? Are you really still using all of your clothes? Is now a good time to change your mattress? Take this opportunity to "cut the fat" and short-list what you really want to move.
- You might consider spoiling a few friends of neighbours with the "blacklisted" items that you don't take with you, and in return, they'll help you with practical considerations in the last days before you go: use of their washing machine, oven . . .
- Project yourself in your target environment: will your bulky items fit? Will they be able to work in the new electrical environment or with the new water supply? Have you prepared some power adapters?

You can do it yourself by buying a few female power-boards in your country of origin; then you'll buy a few male plugs in the country of destination. Putting them together only needs a screwdriver, a cutting tool to strip the plastic off the wire ends, and about 15' of work per power-board. Will you're destination place be big enough to accommodate everything? Will your washing machine be able to be plugged with the same input diameters for water supply, or just with cold water as some countries only have a cold water input.

- Allow yourself a backup solution to live in those few, yet important days when you'll have to unplug, clean and dry the fridge, put away the couch, put away the dishes, the micro-wave oven, etc . . . You will be enough tired with the relocation, so anything that could help you being more relaxed will be welcome.

GETTING THE CONTAINER DELIVERED

Approach transport companies a couple of months before your sought relocation date, to allow them to secure a space for a container on-board a vessel, and a secure the container itself, as well as the right type of truck to deliver it to your place. If your place has a narrow access, they may need a tilt-tray truck. They can be rare to find in some cities. If they have no access to your front door for such a big can, they might envisage delivering the container on the street (contact your local Council for prior approval; the permit could be refused and make your move a nightmare).

Your neighbour may be helpful if they enjoy a better street access than you do. They could maybe host the container for a few days on their front yard, or driveway. Consider the distance to carry heavy objects from your place to the container before choosing an option or another. If what you need is street delivery, you'll find out that your local council may need a public liability of a no-BS sum of $10m. Do you have the proper insurance policy for that as part of your house insurance. IF you don't have a house insurance, it might be a problem, and maybe your favourite neighbour can use theirs to ask the permit in their name. Allow yourself enough time with the container at your door or in the neighbourhood. You'll find out that 3 days is the least you'll need to pack it seriously. It should be free to have it a week ahead or more, so use this time wisely if you can. When the transport company says it is now ready to bring you the container, think of the positioning of the doors: will they open wide enough to allow you to move around with heavy or bulky objects? If a tilt-tray truck is to be used, the maximum tilt angle, seen on picture 1 of this chapter, announces that the whole contents may fly inside the container, and remain unstable and shaky for the rest of the trip as early as pick up time. Therefore it's a good idea to think ahead and consider an opening-forward delivery, where the doors of the container are facing forward when the truck holds the container on its tray. This way the heavier items, typically put at the back of the container first, will prop against the back wall at pick up and delivery at the harbour. It's always a better option than propping against the smaller boxes of the container.

LIGHT AND TEMPERATURE INSIDE THE CONTAINER

With the deadline approaching (pick up time is set, and dictated by the vessel's closing time), you might get caught up working undue hours inside the container. I myself put three days at about 16 hours of work a day to meet the deadline. I was mainly working in the afternoon and all night. Therefore your working conditions inside the container are essential. Make sure you've got a good halogen lamp that you can easily hook at the door lock catches at the door of the container. Allow yourself a good rest after each day of work as the next might be just as hard or more. Drink plenty of water if you pack in summertime as the temperature and humidity conditions inside the container might turn your work into a real physical challenge. It can be anecdotal to mention it, but if you leave in snake infested areas, you might want to tightly close the doors after you've worked, as the tin will get quiet, and could look like a reliable shelter for our legless friends.

GETTING STARTED AND GETTING YOUR FIRST SECTION UP.

Here we are, your can has been delivered in the morning, and you chose to have it delivered about a week prior to collection, to allow you plenty of time to assure a quality packing and securing. The first thing to do is to open it to air it. Who knows what it was used for just before becoming yours for a few weeks. It might stink and will contaminate all your effects. Then proceed with sweeping the inside thoroughly. A clean interior is quick to get and will save you time in cleaning every single item after unpacking. Get the floor covered in cheap yet clean carpet. You can find cheap cut-outs that won't sell, or collect some at some unlikely places, like after an expo, or a sport competition. I got mine from after the Australian Swimming Championship 2012! They had dunked entire rolls of thin clean carpet. When you think they hold some prestigious Olympic champion DNA as we speak . . .

Spot where the anchor points are inside the container. There are plenty, up and down. Think of how much rope you'll need. I personally got 120m of rope at just over 20c per meter. I'll explain later in this chapter how to use it.

After unplugging your white goods, give them a good clean and make sure they are dry. Short list other heavy items you will pack first at the back of the container. These pieces must go first as they are mostly square; they increase compactness, they are hard to move eventually, and they will prop against the back wall and side walls to the cyclic movements of the boat, therefore you should better have them really compactly arranged against each other. The idea is to put up a "wall" of them at the back, and get to a square shape, like at

Tetris game if you know it. You must ensure the white goods are dry and their doors are left slightly open (insert a thick piece of cardboard, foam, or use any other valid trick to ensure they are not completely closed, otherwise you will get blue cheese upon arrival!).

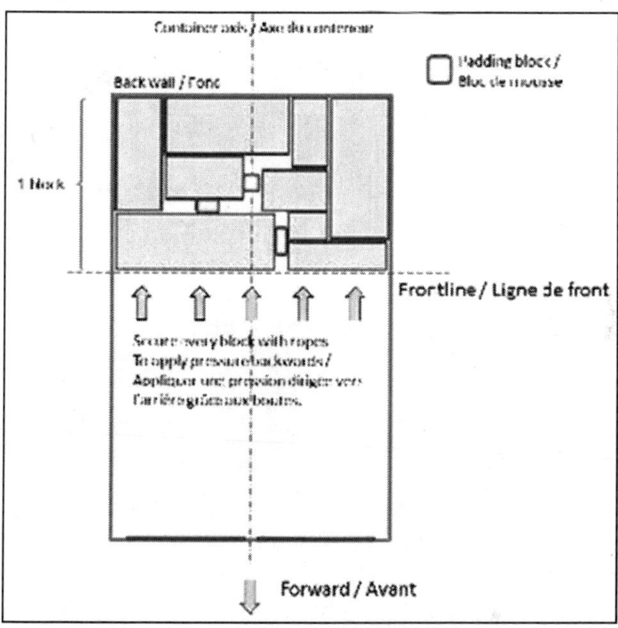

I was mentioning Tetris earlier; well, like at Tetris, once you get a full row, *i.e.* a front line, the whole block shifts up. It is a similar game here inside the container: once you get a front line, *i.e.* a line perpendicular to the axis of the container, it is a good time to secure that block tightly with a rope, or ropes. Anchor your rope further back, and make it restrain that block before going to the back of the container again. This way it will prevent the block from moving forward. You already know it won't move back since because of the container back wall, neither will it move on the sides thanks to the container side walls. As a result, that block shouldn't move at all. It's not always possible to attain 100 per cent compactness. Therefore you should use padding blocks. In the weeks prior to moving, I got all shapes and sizes from Harvey Normanbins. Make sure you pick dry days to pick them from the bin . . .

BOX TIME, RANDOM SHAPED ITEMS, AND FINALISING

Box time can start earlier, in the previous section, along with the heavy items: some boxes can fit in some corners, gaps, or pigeon holes if you have shelves for example. In that case they would act as the yellow padding blocks seen on the arrangement diagram. But only a minority will go there anyway, the major part will come in the last sections. By definition, once all the heavier items are at the back, there only remain the lighter ones, unless you're household has only heavy items . . . Seriously, as you go you will form a kind of massive wedge that ends at the container doors. Do not stack boxes as much possible. It is not a good idea as they can easily slip off and fall, breaking their own contents or other contents. Bear in mind the ship will literally rock and roll for days or weeks, sometimes for over a month (like in my case).

In you really have to stack boxes, place the heavier as low as possible, to avoid rolling (on the ground if possible). If you have a large number of same size boxes, you should build a consistent low block, like a slab on the floor, with them. If they contain incompressible stuff, like books, they can themselves bear a lot of weight, meaning you will be able to put random shapes over them at the very end. If you have too many too small boxes, gather them in a larger strong box. (I'm thinking of small office items, stationery, etc . . .). This way you'll contribute to the compactness by using large square volumes, that can endure pressure from all sides. At all times you must think: "can this item move sideways, and back and forth, while the ship will be rocking and rolling?". Compactness is the keyword.

Welcome to the Third Dimension

Another important rule is:

- "have I used the third dimension of the space (*i.e.* the height) as much as I could ?"

Remember, a container is only worth its actual volume if you use the third dimension of the space. If you use the first metre up only, you'll be only looking at 13m^2 or so, vs 33m^2 if you use the whole height. But with the wedge arrangement I was talking about, what you really use if more like 17^2 anyway, as you can't really stack smaller boxes up to the top. If there are small business around your place, go and ask them if it's possible, for a couple of bucks, that they wrap some of your most square little boxes on pallets. This way you can go up in height and take advantage of the third dimension.

LAST, RANDOM SHAPE OBJECTS

Everybody has got some in their household. I am thinking of prams, hoists, garden tools, sport equipment, all those things that hardly fit in a box, or, if they do, are a waste of compactness (that damned keyword . . .). My belief is to stack them up, in the antiwedge, *i.e.* the empty space above the solid wedge. The advantage is that that empty wedge could be as much as $10m^3$ or more.

These items are sometimes heavy. In my case I had a Concept2 ergometer to pack, it's both quite heavy, and very odd shaped. I unfortunately couldn't keep the boxes at the time, so I had to pack it either in a corner, or on top of everything. I had just enough room to pack it in the corner just behind the front door, but I could have stacked it on top of everything too, with appropriate securing. Once the bottom wedge is all compact and secure, it is not an problem to stack bulky items on that, provided they don't press too much at one spot in particular. Of course I don't want to see a washing machine or a dishwasher on there, since it's heavy and square such items should go to the back, but bikes, pram, hoists, rakes, brooms, all these things could go at the top, with appropriate wrapping and securing.

Avoid pressure points by lying them on a long flat side if they have one. Weight is not a problem if it's evenly distributed along a large surface. Weight divided by surface is a physical quantity that defines pressure. The higher the contact surface the lower the pressure. The lower the pressure the less damage. No punching or puncture in short.

LISTING, INSURING AND TRACKING YOUR CONTENTS

At this stage the job is done. In my case I spent about 35 hours of work in 2.5 days to pack the container. At some point I had to reorganise items to optimise the arrangement. My biggest time spending was done to prepare the items at home before dragging them into the container, not to arrange the container itself.

The Container Content List

As you were packing, you have numbered, labelled, and maintained a n electronic spreadsheet of all the boxes and "loose" items inside the container. Electronic management will save you time, as you will send this list to the carrier, to the insurer, and keep the source for you to show the customs at arrival too. You will need at list 3 columns: box number, description and replacement price at destination. This latter value is important to describe for each and every line, as your spreadsheet software will be useful to sum up the whole amount. This whole amount can be used by the insurer in case a drama occurs, but before that it will simply be used to evaluate the veracity of your home contents value declaration when you choose your cover level.

The destination Customs will also use this value to let your container to go through without (or with . . .) any levy. Depending on the destination, you should check with the Customs if you have to produce a relocation declaration to prove this is your home contents, so that you are not charged import tax on your own stuff! For example, Australia may ask to see your visa to assess if your relocation is genuine. France may ask for a relocation declaration that the French consulate will send you once you return your consular registration card and give them a destination address; they may need a utility bill and a letter from the person who will host you at destination, or your destination lease, or any document proving your move is a genuine relocation.

Insuring Your Contents

The carrier is about to send their truck to come and pick your canned life. You can wait as late as this moment to organise insurance, but it will be less of a worry if you already had had this done. In Australia, like most things, a few minutes only over the phone were all it took to get the contents insured. You will need to tell them the container number that appears on the metal plate on a door of the container; also e-mail your contents list, and agree verbally, or by a written declaration, that you are ok with the Terms and Conditions of the insurance policy. Be prepared that any damage done to your items by themselves, as in, following rocking, rolling, mis-packing, loose securing, etc, will be at your own expense, and can't be claimed against. The carrier's responsibility is only engaged if they make a mistake, or a natural even provokes a loss (storm leading to your container rolling overboard). Expect to pay a 2 per cent premium or so of the total sum insured for that one way trip. It's both a lot if nothing happens, and a negligible sum if your container gets sea sick and disappears overboard . . .

TRACKING YOUR CONTENTS

Very soon should the carrier send you a bill of lading, a marine word for "voyage document" for your container. It recalls the properties of the trip, such as the vessel name, the origin and destination addresses, the container identification, the contents (very summarised) and the total mass. You can use a good marine web site to track the ship, or even better, track the container by using its number. It can happen that your container gets a stopover of connecting ship . . . Like ours in Singapore.

And Vice-Versa

If you ever have to do the entire process the other way, like returning "home", take into consideration that packing your container will take days; it can pay to secure the doors properly overnight; or pack it at night precisely to assure some presence at that quiet time, or do turns with your family or friends to never leave the container alone at night. Some cities can harbour the dodgiest people who will certainly help you unpack in a couple of hours without you knowing, instead of packing . . . know what I mean?!

I hope this chapter will help you improve planning and think of the steps you may take to achieve your goal, from the decision making process "is it worth doing all that?", to the "Pfeeew, now sitting on the plane to destination, that's a good thing done. A beer please!". For the road, bear in mind the whole process unroll at destination, less securing and optimising, so it should really take less time. However, if you're moving to one of these very dense cities, I will think of you, while your container is blocking half of that narrow street with all the cars honking as you unpack, in that summer shower, and no one helping!

Preparing for the Delivery

I passed on the maybe long and complicated task to find a apartment or a house, with a street or driveway that allows the easy delivery of your container by truck; so not the 1st district of Paris basically . . . If like me you're moving to a social country like France, with tenants being overprotected and virtually free from being evicted even if they stop paying their rent for years, you'll find that finding a place demands guarantees you may not have immediately at this stage, such as a permanent job for more than 3 months that pays at least 3 times the amount of the rent. But this is another topic . . .

So that's it, you've secured a place, well you need to organise the oncarriage from the delivery harbour to that place now, and well before the container hits the harbour. In my case, I changed my mind about the target city, and the oncarriage extra cost was in excess of EUR 800, as the harbour was far from the city. You might plan well if you can't afford this extra cost.

Getting Your Container Customs Cleared

You will first deal with the Customs intermediate (who's a private company who works at the terminal) who gets hold of the container before clearance by the Customs. You'll pay them in advance so that they can clear your load quickly when the container gets to the harbour. You may have to send them your container content list, and your certificate of change of residency, to benefit from the GST waiver. This certificate may be obtained from your local Consulate provided you have been living at least 6 months in the country and have been using your equipment for at least 12 months.

If you were registered with them, it may be obtained free of charge. Within a few days they will send it to destination. You must make sure you have this document if the Customs at destination need it. Remember, all this communication takes time. The port authorities will only allow you to freely park your container for up to four days at the terminal. Past this period of grace, the daily fee will be increasing, and quite deterring. What you want to do is to get the ball rolling from when your container gets to the port. To achieve this, you'll want to coordinate the Customs agent and the carrier so that they communicate with each other (each has got to know the contact number of the other.

THE HIDDEN OPPORTUNITY IN CONTAINER SHIPPING

The container-shipping industry has been highly unprofitable over the past five years. Making things worse, earnings have been exceptionally volatile. Several factors are responsible, notably trade's spotty recovery from the global financial crisis, and redoubled efforts by corporate customers to control costs. Some of the pain is self-inflicted: as in past cycles, the industry extrapolated the good times and foresaw an unsustainable rise in demand. It is now building capacity that appears will be mostly unneeded.

These problems are real and significant, and largely beyond the power of any one company to address. But shipping companies cannot afford to throw up their hands and accept their fate. Hidden beneath these issues (and driving them to a degree) is another set of challenges that shipping lines can readily take on. Across the enterprise, in commercial, operations, and network and fleet activities, shipping lines have opportunities to improve performance. In sales, for example, carriers often confuse their costs with the value received by customers and fail to charge a premium for services for which shippers will pay more. In operations, many lines treat bunker as just another cost of doing business. In fact, fuel presents many opportunities, not just in procurement, but also in consumption. In network design, more than a few shipping companies use outmoded approaches to design their routes; new and more powerful systems use algorithms to make better, more effective decisions about networks.

With a little bit here and a little bit there, companies that take on a full programme of initiatives can boost earnings by as much as 10 to 20 percentage points—enough to reverse the recent trend, and return to profit. To realize that kind of upside, however, firms must also ready their organizations for change. That's a non-trivial challenge: in many ways, very little has changed in container shipping since the first crane hoisted the first box in 1956. Companies need to find ways to help employees embrace new ways of working and must be prepared to bet on the future. Carriers that embrace change will be better prepared than their rivals to make the best of the current business cycle and to thrive in the next one.

THE INDUSTRY'S BLEAK ECONOMICS

Transport is often seen as the harbinger of the broader economy. It certainly fulfilled that role in the recent economic crisis, as business fell off precipitously. However, shipping is now also a kind of lagging indicator: its performance is trailing the broader, somewhat erratic global recovery.

A big part of the problem is that the industry continues to add capacity. By 2015, the typical vessel delivered will handle about 10,000 20-foot equivalent units (TEU), five times more than ships built in the 1990s. Not surprisingly, pressure to fill this capacity and capture the efficiency benefits of larger vessels has led to hasty decisions by carriers. In turn, profits have become exceptionally volatile. Record losses in 2009 were followed by strong profits in 2010?and significant losses again in 2011.

- The market is saturated, and the industry is now in a race for market share. The quest to take share is squeezing out smaller players and has started another wave of price wars. Shipping companies are forsaking their guidelines on pricing, both in spot rates and general rate increases, and choosing not to enforce contracts with customers.
- Companies are pricing at their marginal cost. That's not necessarily bad; in fact, it's the right decision for many. But for others it is irrational, and when everyone does it, the industry suffers. Many shipping companies have ineffective cost-management systems. When they use these to determine pricing, they are pricing at a fraction of full costs; fuel, for example, is only partially priced into many charters. In effect, companies are passing on all of the cost savings they have achieved in recent years to customers.
- Innovation in service offerings is sporadic. Most carriers offer the same or similar service to all customers, regardless of need. Carriers are missing opportunities to charge premiums for value-added services (for example, intermodal and guaranteed delivery times) and are unable to monetize innovations.
- Fleet changes have made network designs outmoded. Most companies' networks do not adequately maximize profits. For example, the arrival of the new ultralarge container ships has already triggered cascading effects on smaller ships. Although feeder ships are benefiting from this trend, mid-size Panamax vessels and others have been squeezed out. This will have a significant effect on shipping lines, which carry a large portion of Panamax vessels on their balance sheet.
- Conflicts between asset managers and transportation companies are producing suboptimal business decisions. Many carriers are caught in conflicts with owners of ships they manage. Carriers want to manage the transportation business for profit; owners want to manage for maximum value of their assets. Many suffer from a conflict between the asset-management and transportation mind-sets. Without fundamental changes, such as industry consolidation or new external

shocks, we see the trend of overcapacity and industry losses continuing for the next three to five years. We project that supply/demand imbalances will persist, with revenues and pricing remaining under pressure as larger vessels launch and global GDP grows only moderately.

ORGANIZATIONAL CHALLENGES

Of course, executives are aware of many of the problems the industry faces. And most know the solutions—nothing we describe in this chapter will be earth-shattering for container-line executives. But getting their organizations to act on them is difficult. Shipping companies are deeply conservative; change comes only slowly. Many companies discount anything that is "not invented here." One operations head found that an unconventional trim, one or two meters "by the head," cut bunker consumption by 3 percent. But when captains and masters balked, the executive found no support elsewhere to drive his cost-saving idea. Most lines also have few analytical resources, either in the corporate center or the business units. Decisions are often undertaken and forecasts made with only a minimum of information, much of it often borrowed from external providers that also supply their competitors.

In part, the industry's conservatism is born of a long history of boom and bust. These cycles make it difficult to provide meaningful performance-based incentives to executives and staff. But that hinders motivation; employees become uninterested in challenging the status quo or in making changes in the way they work.

Other problems crop up in companies' structures. Most are organized by function, for good reason. But ensuring cooperation can be difficult when departmental budgets are involved. The maintenance organization pays for cleaning of hulls and propellers, but the resulting savings in fuel go to purchasing.

AN AGENDA FOR GREATER PRODUCTIVITY

Some of the challenges that companies face?the supply/demand imbalance, and swings in demand?are systemic, and beyond the ability of any one company to fix. But the rest are readily addressable. Container lines can and must deploy three sets of actions–commercial, operations, and network and fleet–to improve their performance. Taken together, these three elements typically improve a line's earnings by 10 to 20 percent. Companies have a huge incentive to act first—once the whole industry has moved to a greater level of productivity, the benefits will likely be passed on to customers once again through competition. Several lines are already well advanced on the journey to greater productivity; smart lines can beat the competition by being quicker and more thorough in their implementation.

Commercial

In their marketing and sales, shipping companies need to shift from a cost-plus approach to one that emphasizes value. Lines should get paid full value for the services they provide. A comprehensive commercial programme, covering the full gamut of commercial activities from pricing strategy to contracting strategy to uptake management, can deliver immediate bottom-line impact. In our experience, companies can improve return on sales (ROS) by 1 to 2 percent within 9 to 12 months.

The approach has many elements; three stand out. First, a "model ship" analysis can help carriers understand which customers contribute most to profits. One global container line used market information to develop its model. Based on this analysis, the company created targeted sales campaigns to pursue and capture high-contributing customers. The campaigns lifted ROS by about 2 percent in several regions and trade lanes.

A second element is better commercialization of "last mile" customer services, including detention and demurrage. Many shipping lines have made strides in this area, but more can be done. One global shipping line created a rigourous performance-management system to ensure accurate invoicing and expedited collection of detention and demurrage. It also standardized tariffs across different countries and trades. These two steps lifted detention and demurrage revenues by 15 percent.

Third, and perhaps most important, lines can improve their pricing discipline to ensure that they reap the full benefit of their value-selling approach. We see clear improvement potential for lines across all elements of the pricing process, from strategic pricing to transactional pricing to the systems and tools used to support the front line. Sometimes it is right to follow the market and price close to marginal cost to fill the ship. But lines need to identify the peaks in prices (they do happen, even in today's oversupplied market) and the times that they have privileged capacity, and ensure that they are charging to capture both events. This requires building flexibility into contracting, so that in the peaks a carrier's ships are not full of low-yielding cargo contracted at annual rates. Carriers can also extract higher prices from customers in certain industries, to whom smooth and reliable transport and the resulting stable inventory are quite valuable.

Operations

Even more than commercial levers, operational improvements are squarely in the shipping company's wheelhouse; they are entirely under the carrier's control. That makes them an excellent source of improvement in both profitable and unprofitable periods. And, given that many lines are already well down the implementation path, it's an imperative for all. Three levers account for most of the costs and thus deliver most of the impact: bunker management, procurement, and asset utilization. The improvements we sketch out below can drive a five- to ten-percentage-point rise in earnings.

Bunker management. Rising fuel prices have made bunker the largest cost item for shipping lines, more than fleet or overhead, and often exceeding 40 percent of all costs. Fuel bills can be reduced in many ways, some well known (optimizing vessel speeds, more frequent hull and propeller cleaning), others less so (unconventional trimming "by the head," inventory management). Lean terminal operations is one that many carriers overlook. Faster turnarounds in port save time, which ships can use to steam at lower speeds at sea. Ports can automate intermodal dispatch of both incoming and outgoing cargo and better integrate planning and IT systems with inland operators. That work falls mainly on port operators, of course, but shipping lines can make it happen through tough negotiations with competitive ports, service-line agreements that cement the deal, and guarantees of berth availability.

Finally, though bunker is a commodity, companies can achieve savings through better sourcing processes, drawing from a wider range of suppliers and using lower-quality fuels where available. Reducing bunker costs through these moves typically improves earnings by two to three percentage points. For example, one global shipping company optimized the hundreds of millions of dollars of bunker inventory it carries in the ships, saving about 3 percent of total bunker costs from just this one lever.

Procurement. For most lines, the next biggest operations opportunity is in procurement. Beyond bunker, lines should be concerned with three other categories. First, terminal costs can be reduced. Negotiations with competitive port operators, as discussed above, will help in some cases; in others, greater use of requests for quotation (RFQs), and a clean-sheet analysis of ports costs, including accessorial fees, such as storage, security, handling, transshipments, and re-efer monitoring can deliver savings. A few carriers are taking these moves a step further, and tightening their relationship with terminals. Colocated teams can jointly optimize operations; well-structured incentives and penalties can align interests.

The same analyses can also produce savings in intermodal costs (including feeder vessel hires), the second big category. Lines should understand suppliers' costs for trucking, rail, and feeders, and use the information for advantage in negotiations. Market analysis can help lines know when prices are at their lowest and establish the correct pricing structure to reduce total cost of ownership. One global carrier rolled out a new online bidding system for trucking services in North America; it eased the system in with workshops for vendors. The initiative is now delivering savings of about 10 percent of intermodal costs.

Third, RFQs and similar approaches also work well in containers and logistics, at time of purchase and also in maintenance and repair. A review of the total cost of ownership can reveal some surprising anomalies; the container with the cheapest purchase price often costs the most in the long run. Companies can get more strategic by building price forecasts of dry containers, which can help them decide when to pull the trigger on new purchases and negotiate those in progress.

Asset utilization. Stowage planning and container-fleet management are crucial levers to optimize asset utilization. Done well, a company can even reduce its fleet. New software tools can help with stowage planning. A "cockpit" can help companies develop smart metrics and use them to guide the company. A target performance analyzer shows the deviation between planned and actual stowage. A move validator uses a heuristic to calculate the "right" number of crane moves for the given load, which can then be compared to the number of moves on the bill.

These tools must be combined with careful execution. Since stowage is a tension point between operations (which wants certainty) and commercial (which prizes flexibility), companies need to clearly define processes, handovers, cutoff times, and so on. Best-practice companies finalize their load lists two to three days before sailing and rely on solid forecasting and prediction systems, standard rolling processes, and exception-handling routines.

NETWORK AND FLEET

Network and fleet improvements take longer than commercial or operational moves and require strategic timing. Two moves in particular can boost earnings by six to eight percentage points. "Own or lease?" The question has long lain at the heart of container-shipping strategy. From our analysis, the industry typically relies too much on leasing. While leasing may be the only option for many cash-strapped liners that already have substantial debt, other lines should take advantage of this by owning more of their fleet. Leasing does provide a little more flexibility to change vessel deployment. But that breathing room often comes at too high a price.

Shipping lanes or "trades" provide another interesting test. Shipping lines must choose whether to deliver direct or transship at an interim hub. The decision depends on several factors such as size of ship and distance. The tradeoffs have changed with today's larger vessels and expensive fuel. But lines have not always made the necessary changes to their networks. Leading lines are building new network tools to solve these knotty challenges.

MAKING IT HAPPEN

As they take up the complex agenda outlined above, lines will also want to make changes to their organization that will give them the best chance for success. Five tactics can help a container-shipping line unleash its full potential.

- Build cross-functional teams. Teams that bring together critical functions make better decisions on the trade-offs facing carriers. For example, one global line recently established an exception-management team with representatives from operations and commercial. Its mandate is to decide tricky questions that come up in vessel operations. Should a vessel speed up to get to Hong Kong and take on transshipment cargo, or should it skip the port and sail at a lower speed? The exception-management team considers both the commercial and operational impact and makes the right choice for the company.

- Challenge the legacy. Companies can shake things up by bringing in new and controversial points of view. External experts can challenge established practices. Companies must innovate; a systematic approach to finding and testing new ideas can help. Innovation is possible across the enterprise, in products and services, the organizational and business models, and especially in the digitization of key operational processes. It is not too far-fetched to imagine that within three years, new technology start-ups can develop a superior, data-based understanding of cargo flows to threaten container lines. Already, new IT-enabled businesses are making inroads into logistics and freight-forwarding markets; others aim to automate processes for ocean-freight booking and invoicing. In anticipation, leading carriers are investing in devices and software to track containers in real time. At a minimum, all carriers need to monitor developments in this space.
- Create a performance culture. Programmes to transform business practices may start strong but typically fade after a few months or years. To sustain the improvement, shipping lines must build a rigourous and regular performance-management system. Weekly dialogues can improve transparency and help senior managers make more informed decisions.
- Redesign incentives. Employees need both monetary incentives and recognition to energize a transformation journey. We have helped the transformation leaders of global shipping companies think through incentive programme design and rollout. Programmes can include new key performance indicators and bonus pools in addition to recognition awards and ceremonies. It is important to balance the right mix of monetary and non-monetary incentives to achieve the desired behaviors.
- Invest in analytics. Dedicated analytics teams can help senior managers understand the financial impact of both high-level issues including corporate strategy and pricing. Analysts can also help with tactical issues including network design (utilization, vessel deployment, string strategy); terminal productivity (port bottlenecks,

terminal operations); bunkers (speed profiles of vessels, optimal speeds), and market intelligence and forecasts (industry-wide utilization on given trades, rate trends, mid- and long-term outlooks). Automatic identification system (AIS) data can be invaluable to the analytics team; some leading shipping lines are developing AIS-based models of utilization and other measures of productivity.

IMPORTANCE OF MARINE CONTAINER LOGISTICS STRATEGIES

Since the beginning of containerization , the shipping industry has shown enviable developments in increased productivity, vessel capacity, speed ,safety, reduction in service time and cost. Despite these achieved efficiencies, marine container logistics has been suffering from severe trade imbalances between the major trading regions..

Projections indicate that the container fleet size as well as the vessel size will continue to increase as the order book of all major carriers are quite big , though the present economy slow down will delay the release of new builds further. This is a clear indication that the volume of empty container need to be handled in future will increase considerably.

The problem of trade imbalances and repositioning of empty container will continue to be a serious transportation logistics issue. As per the available stats regarding strong trade imbalance between Trans pacific , Trans Atlantic and Asia Europe trades , the exports from Asia , the world's factory, to America and Europe are 15 per cent and 9 per cent respectively. Whereas the imports from the respective regions to Asia is 5 per cent and 3.5 per cent only.

India's container handling capacity for international and domestic traffic is expected to reach 21 million in 2014, up from 9.1 million in 2008 according to Frost and Sullivan analyst's report " Strategic Assessment of Containerization Trends in India". Our container trade registered an impressive double digit growth of 23 per cent during the year 2007-08. With Indian trade growing 11-12 per cent per annum, the insufficient port and other related infrastructures, will result in increased port congestions at major ports and will adversely affect container shipping industry.

Similar to the international container shipping industry, Indian ports too face serious trade imbalances and equipment storage, repositioning issues. The problem of import , export imbalance is very high in southern ports of Cochin , Mangalore and Tuticorin due to seasonal cashew imports from Africa. The east coast ports, Chennai and Kolkata too have similar issues. To minimize the port / depot congestion and the equipment dwell time , carriers are forced to make logistic vessel calls to evacuate the excess equipments. Due to insufficient port / depot infrastructure and poor logistics management strategies of the carriers, the whole process of evacuation used to be cumbersome , time consuming and expensive. This situation demands for an empty container management strategy which rationalizes the repositioning, storage and maintenance of empty containers in major importing regions.

India's productivity growth is very strong and this is surely an indication of the robust growth of container shipping industry as well. In the present economic scenario, India is emerging into the spot light due to the stable economy and steady growth rate. Also the upcoming Vallarpadam International Transhipment Terminal and the proposed Vizhinjam terminal is expected to position India as a transshipment hub .To maintain the present momentum and ensure the future growth, the container shipping industry must take measures to strengthen the overall logistics chain.

THE CONTAINER SHIPPING MARKET

The growth in global trade and freight distribution has led to a demand for new containers. Each year, about 2 to 2.5 million TEUs worth of containers are manufactured, the great majority of them in China, taking advantage of its containerized export surplus. Production peaked to 3.9 million TEU in 2007 with the global inventory of containers estimated to be at 28.2 million TEUs. This approximately implies 3 TEUs of containers for every TEU of maritime containership capacity. The standard 20 foot container costs about $2,000 to manufacture while a 40 footer costs about $3,000. Therefore, a twenty foot container costs $1.71 per cubic feet to manufacture while a forty foot container costs $0.80, which underlines the preference for larger volumes as a more effective usage of assets. Even so, the twenty foot container remains a prime transport unit, particularly for the shipping of commodities such as grain where it represents an optimal size taking account of weight per unit of volume capacity of containers, around 34 metric tons.

China accounts for more than 90 per cent of the global production of containers, which is the outcome of several factors, particularly its export-oriented economy and its lower labour costs. Considering that China has a positive trade balance, notably in the manufacturing sector which highly depends on containerization, it is a logical strategy to have containers manufactured there. This enables a free movement since once produced a new container is immediately moved to a nearby export activity (factory or distribution center), then loaded and brought to a container port. A long distance empty repositioning is therefore not required for the newly manufactured container. Every container utilization strategy must thus take into account production and location costs.

The great majority of containers are either owned by maritime shipping companies or container leasing companies. With the beginning of containerization in the 1970, a container leasing industry emerged to offer a flexibility in the management of containerized assets, enabling shipping companies to cope with temporal and geographical fluctuations in the demand.

Following a period of growth correlated with the ebbs and flows of global trade, the leasing industry went through a period of consolidation in the 1990s, on par with the container shipping industry. An important trend in recent years has been the growing share of container ownershipattributed to maritime shipping companies, which reached 59.8 per cent in 2008.

This growth can be explained by the following:

- Containers are an asset that maritime shipping companies make available to service their customers. Providing containers help increase the utilization rate of containerships.
- A growing level of intermodal integration and control where maritime shippers are interacting with port terminal operators (some directly operate port terminals such as APM) as well as with inland transport systems such as railways and inland ports. In such a context, controlling container assets enables a more efficient use of the transport chain.
- The rising cost of new containers, the repositioning of empties and systematically low freight rates along several trade routes, have made the container leasing business less profitable. Ocean carriers also have a greater ability to reposition empty containers since the control a fleet and can reposition their containers when capacity is available. It is also not uncommon that a whole containership will be chartered to reposition empties.

About 60 per cent of the equipment available for location is controlled by five leasing companies having fleets exceeding 1 million TEU each. If the 13 largest leasing companies are considered, they account for 90 per cent of the global container leasing market and controlled the equivalent of 10.7 million TEU. Shipping and leasing companies often have contradictory strategies in the usage of their container assets. From the point of view of shipping companies, their containers are assets enabling a more efficient usage of their ships through a higher level of cargo control. They consequently maximize their ship usage, which are their main assets and the container a tool for this purpose. From the point of view of leasing companies, containers are their main assets and the goal is to amortize their investments through leasing arrangements.

These arrangements come into three major categories that differ in terms of length of the lease and who is responsible for the repositioning of empty containers. In the past, maritime shippers relied extensively on leasing but recent trends underline their more active role in the management of container assets, particularly because a container spends a large share of its life span idle or being repositioned.

Chassis fleets are also an important element of the market as they are necessary to carry containers by road and sometimes within terminals, particularly rail. A breakdown of the chassis ownership reveals that shipping lines (70 per cent) and leasing companies (10 per cent) have the bulk of the assets. What remains is owned by railroads (8 per cent), truckers (8 per cent), and terminal operators (4 per cent). The high share of chassis ownership by shipping companies is related to their high share of container ownership, particularly if they are as well involved in terminal operations. In this case a chassis pool enables to offer intermodal services such as moving containers in and out of stack and providing drayage operations for their customers.

EMPTY CONTAINER FLOWS

A container is a transport as well as a production unit and can move as an export, import or repositioning flow. Once a container has been unloaded, another transport leg must be found as moving an empty container is almost as costly as moving a full container. Shipping companies need containers to maintain their operations and level of service along the port network they call. Containers arriving in a market as imports must eventually leave, either empty or full. The longer the delay, the higher the cost. Repositioning thus begin immediately after a container has been unloaded and it is important since it involves costs that must be assumed by the shippers and are thus reflected by the costs paid by producers and consumers. Also, they represent development opportunities for export markets as every disequilibrium tends to impose a readjustment of transport rates and can act as an indirect export subsidy. Firms taking advantage of this may reduce, likely temporarily, their transport costs.

An increasing number of containers are repositioned empty because cargo cannot be found for a return leg. The outcome has been a growth in the repositioning costs as shippers attempt to manage the level of utilization of their containerized assets. The positioning of empty containers is thus one of the most complex problems concerning global freight distribution, an issue being underlined by the fact that about 2.5 million TEU of containers are being stored empty, waiting to be used. Empties thus account for about 10 per cent of existing container assets and 20.5 per cent of global port handling.

The major causes of this problem include:

- Trade imbalances. They are probably the most important source in the accumulation of empty containers in the global economy. A region that imports more than it exports will face the systematic accumulation of empty containers, while a region that exports more than it imports will face a shortage of containers. If this situation endures, a repositioning of large amounts of containers will be required between the two trade partners, involving higher transportation costs and tying up existing distribution capacities.
- Repositioning costs. They include a combination of inland transport and international transport costs. If they are low enough, a trade imbalance could endure without much of an impact as containers get

repositioned without much of a burden on the shipping industry. Repositioning costs can also get lower if imbalances are acute as carriers (and possibly terminal operators) will offer discounts for flows in the reverse direction of dominant flows. However, if costs are high, particularly for repositioning container inland, shortages of container may appear on export markets.

- Revenue generation. Shipowners allocate their containers to maximize their revenue, not necessarily the economic opportunities of their customers. In view of trade imbalances and of the higher container rates they impose on the inbound trip for transpacific pendulum routes, shipowners often opt to reposition their containers back to Asian export markets instead of waiting for the availability of an export load. For instance, while a container could take 3 to 4 weeks in the hinterland to be loaded and brought back to the port and earning an income of about $800, the same time can be allocated to reposition the container across the Pacific to generate an return income of $3,000.
- Manufacturing and leasing costs. If the costs of manufacturing new containers, or leasing existing units, are cheaper than repositioning them, which can be possible over long distances, then an accumulation can happen. Inversely, higher manufacturing or leasing costs may favour the repositioning of empty containers. Such a condition tends to be temporary as leasing costs and imbalances are correlated.
- Usage preferences. A large number of shipping lines uses containers as a way of branding the company name and to offer readily available capacity to their customers. This observation combined with the reluctance of shipping lines and leasing companies to share market information on container positions and quantities for competitive reasons, makes it very difficult to establish container pools or to widely introduce the 'grey box' concept. Still, as demonstrated by the North American rail system (TTX rail equipment pool), it is possible for transport companies to distinctly separate container assets from modal assets so that the efficiency (such as the turnover rate) can be improved.
- Slow steaming. Excess capacity and rising bunker fuel prices have incited maritime shipping companies to reduce the operational speed of their containerships from 21 knots to 19 knots, a practice known as slow steaming. The resulting longer transoceanic journeys tie more container inventory in transit, incite transloading in proximity of port terminals and reduce the availability of containers inland.

REPOSITIONING SCALES

Container repositioning can take place at three major scales, depending on the nature of the container flow imbalances.

Each of these scales involves specific repositioning strategies:

- Local (Empty interchange). Occurs regularly as containers are reshuffled between locations where they are emptied to those where they are filled. They are of short duration with limited use of storages facilities since containers are simply in queue at the consignee or the consigner, especially if they are managed by the same freight distributor. This problem is compounded by the availability of chassis.
- Regional (Intermodal repositioning). Involves industrial and consumption regions where there are imbalances, often the outcome of economic specialization. For instance, a metropolitan area having a marked service function may be a net importer of containers while a nearby area may have a specialization in manufacturing, implying a status of net exporter. The matter then becomes the repositioning of the surplus containers from one part of the region to the other. This may involve a longer time period, due to the scale and scope of repositioning and often requires the usage of specialized storage facilities. This scale offers opportunities for freight forwarders to establish strategies such as dedicated empty container flows and storage depots (or inland ports) at suitable locations. However, locating empty depots near port facilities consumes valuable real estate.
- International (Overseas repositioning). Is the outcome of systematic macro-economic imbalances between trade partners, as exemplified by China and the United States. Such a repositioning scale is obviously the most costly and time consuming as it ties up substantial storage capacity, in proportion to the trade imbalance. Significant inland freight distribution capacities are also wasted since long distance trade, especially concerning manufactured goods, tend to involve a wide arrays of destinations in a national economy. This is paradoxical as maritime container shipping capacity will be readily available for global repositioning, but high inland freight transport costs could limit the amount of empty containers reaching the vicinity of a container port. It may even force an oversupply of containers as the trade partner having a net deficit of containers (exporter) may find more convenient to manufacture new containers than to reposition existing units, which disrupts the container leasing market.

Empty container repositioning costs are multiple and include handling and transshipping at the terminal, chassis location for drayage, empty warehousing while waiting to be repositioned, inland repositioning by rail or trucking towards a maritime terminal and maritime repositioning. An empty container takes the same amount of space in a truck, railcar or containership slot than a full container. Shipping companies spend on average $110 billion per year in the management of their container assets (purchase, maintenance, repairs), of which $16 billion for the repositioning of empties. This means that repositioning accounts for 15 per cent of the operational costs related to container assets. To cover these costs, shipping companies have imposed surcharges on full containers on a number of export routes. These surcharges can amount between $100 and $1,000 per TEU and are thus an important share of shipping costs towards developing countries in Africa, Asia and the Caribbean. The outcome is higher costs for imported goods, which is economically damaging for countries having a low level of income.

REPOSITIONING STRATEGIES

Within large commercial gateways, containerized distribution and empty repositioning are facing numerous challenges:

- Transport companies must cope with access and storing charges at terminals as well as wear and tear on equipment.
- Truck drivers are losing hours waiting to access terminal gates and distribution centers to return empty containers and chassis.
- Terminal operators lose productivity because of congestion and are facing pressures from localities to reduce the number of idle trucks at their gates.
- The fundamental reason behind the repositioning of a container is the search for cargo to insure the continuity of paid movements. A container is an asset which usage level is linked with profit and thus must constantly be in circulation. Its velocity involves higher turnover rates and three main options are available to promote this velocity:
- If there are few opportunities to load empty containers on the backhaul trip, an efficient repositioning system must be in place to insure the overall productivity of the distribution system. Transloading is part of such a strategy as it frees maritime containers by moving loads into domestic containers. There are therefore less risks that shipping companies would impose surcharges because of imbalanced containerized flows.
- Improve the efficiency of existing cargo rotation with a better link between import and export activities through a synchronization of flows. Instead of returning directly to the rail or maritime terminal, an empty container can be brought right away to an export location to be loaded. However, asymmetry between import and export-based logistics make this a difficult proposition.
- Develop an export market taking advantage of filling empty containers with new cargo, notably commodities. This can imply a variety of strategies such as a substitution from bulk to containers or the setting of consolidation centers enabling to regroup small cargo batches into

container loads. This particularly benefits small companies and enables them to access new global markets.

The case of the United States is particularly eloquent. For 100 containers entering the United States, half will be repositioned empty to foreign markets. Of the 50 that remains, most return empty to port terminals awaiting for export cargo to become available. When so, the empty container is picked up from the port terminal to a distribution center to return to the terminal once loaded. Only 5 of the 50 containers will be loaded with export cargo shortly after being unloaded of import cargo and without coming back empty first to the maritime terminal. Cargo rotation appears as a simple repositioning strategy but requires a fairly complex coordination. It can take place if import and export activities are located nearby and thus enable a quick rotation. Otherwise, an intermediary stage implying the usage of an empty container depot is required. Thus, cargo rotation is an operational process for repositioning that can be supported by empty container depots, which are physical infrastructures. Those two elements require a management system where involved actors in supply chains interact to combine movements needs and the availability of containers.

In recent years, a new concept was brought forward to help connect the various commercial needs (imports and exports) with the availability of containers, which came to be known as thevirtual container yard. This system implies an online market where information about container availability is displayed without the necessity for the container to be in a physical storage depot. The container can as well be in circulation or in a distribution center, but the important point is that its availability, both geographically and temporarily, for a new load is known.

The main goals of a virtual container yard are:

- Display status information about containers such as their characteristics, location and availability.
- Improve information exchange between actors involved in supply chain management such as trucking companies, shipping companies, distribution centers and equipment leasing companies.
- Transfer the container lease and the related documentation without bringing back to container to the depot or the terminal.
- Assist the actors in supply chain management in their decision making process about theusage of container assets, namely returns and exchanges.

Therefore, a virtual container yard is a "clearinghouse" where detailed information is made available to the the involved actors. Firms that are the most likely to use a virtual container yard are of small and medium size. They generally have less logistical expertise and available resources in the management of containerized assets. Large logistics firms and maritime shipping companies are less prone to use such a system since they already have substantial expertise and their own management systems. A strategy will therefore be necessary to eventually involve all the actors in a system where a market for the exchange of empties becomes possible. In the case of Southern California, investigations have underlined that while an empty container yard have some potential advantages, they should not be expected to be highly significant. It was assessed that the share of containers returning full to a terminal without initially been picked up empty from that terminal or a depot would shift from 2 to 10 per cent if a virtual container yard was used. Thus, repositioning strategies are important in the management of containerized assets, but effectiveness is a difficult goal to achieve.

7

Tanker Shipping Logistics

TANKER (SHIP)

A tanker (or tank ship or tankship) is a merchant vessel designed to transport liquids or gases in bulk. Major types of tankship include the oil tanker, the chemical tanker, and gas carrier. In the United States Navy and Military Sealift Command, any type of tanker used to refuel other ships is called an oiler.

BACKGROUND

Tankers can range in size of capacity from several hundred tons, which includes vessels for servicing small harbours and coastal settlements, to several hundred thousand tons, for long-range haulage. Besides ocean- or seagoing tankers there are also specialized inland-waterway tankers which operate on rivers and canals with an average cargocapacity up to some thousand tons.

A wide range of products are carried by tankers, including:

- Hydrocarbon products such as oil, liquefied petroleum gas (LPG), and liquefied natural gas (LNG)
- Chemicals, such as ammonia, chlorine, and styrene monomer
- Fresh water
- Wine
- Molasses

Tankers are a relatively new concept, dating from the later years of the 19th century. Before this, technology had simply not supported the idea of carrying bulk liquids.

The market was also not geared towards transporting or selling cargo in bulk, therefore most ships carried a wide range of different products in different holds and traded outside fixed routes. Liquids were usually loaded in casks—hence the term "tonnage", which refers to the volume of the holds in terms of how many tuns or casks of wine could be carried. Even potable water, vital for the survival of the crew, was stowed in casks.

Fig. The Thomas W. Lawson (1902), Converted in 1906 into the World's First Sailing Tanker.

Carrying bulk liquids in earlier ships posed several problems:

- *The holds:* On timber ships the holds were not sufficiently water, oil or air-tight to prevent a liquid cargo from spoiling or leaking. The development of iron and steel hulls solved this problem.
- *Loading and discharging:* Bulk liquids must be pumped - the development of efficient pumps and piping systems was vital to the development of the tanker. Steam engines were developed as prime-movers for early pumping systems. Dedicated cargo handling facilities were now required ashore too - as was a market for receiving a product in that quantity. Casks could be unloaded using ordinary cranes, and the awkward nature of the casks meant that the volume of liquid was always relatively small - therefore keeping the market more stable.
- *Free Surface Effect:* A large body of liquid carried aboard a ship will impact on the ship's stability, particularly when the liquid is flowing around the hold or tank in response to the ship's movements. The effect was negligible in casks, but could cause capsizing if the tank extended the width of the ship; a problem solved by extensive subdivision of the tanks.

Tankers were first used by the oil industry to transfer refined fuel in bulk from refineries to customers. This would then be stored in large tanks ashore, and subdivided for delivery to individual locations. The use of tankers caught on because other liquids were also cheaper to transport in bulk, store in dedicated terminals, then subdivide. Even theGuinness brewery used tankers to transport the stout across the Irish Sea.

Fig. A US Navy T2 Tanker in 1943.

Different products require different handling and transport, with specialised variants such as "chemical tankers", "oil tankers", and "LNG carriers" developed to handle dangerous chemicals, oil and oil-derived products, and liquefied natural gas respectively. These broad variants may be further differentiated with respect to ability to carry only a single product or simultaneously transport mixed cargoes such as several different chemicals or refined petroleum products. Among oil tankers, supertankers are designed for transporting oil around the Horn of Africa from the Middle East. The supertanker Seawise Giant, scrapped in 2010, was 458 meters (1,503 ft) in length and 69 meters (226 ft) wide. Supertankers are one of the three preferred methods for transporting large quantities of oil, along with pipeline transport and rail.

Despite being highly regulated, tankers have been involved in environmental disasters resulting from oil spills.

DESIGN CONSIDERATIONS

Many modern tankers are designed for a specific cargo and a specific route. Draft is typically limited by the depth of water in loading and unloading harbors; and may be limited by the depth of straits along the preferred shipping route. Cargoes with high vapor pressure at ambient temperatures may require pressurized tanks or vapor recovery systems. Tank heaters may be required to maintain heavy crude oil, residual fuel, asphalt, wax, or molasses in a fluid state for offloading.

TANKER CAPACITY

Tankers used for liquid fuels are classified according to their capacity.

In 1954, Shell Oil developed the average freight rate assessment (AFRA) system which classifies tankers of different sizes. To make it an independent instrument, Shell consulted the London Tanker Brokers' Panel (LTBP). At first, they divided the groups as General Purposefor tankers under 25,000 tons deadweight (DWT); Medium Range for ships between 25,000 and 45,000 DWT and Large Range for the then-enormous ships that were larger than 45,000 DWT.

Fig. The Small Coastal Tanker Pegasuson the River Weser.

Fig. The Very Large Crude Carrier (VLCC) MV Sirius Star in 2008 After Her Capture by Somali Pirates.

The ships became larger during the 1970s, and the list was extended, where the tons are long tons:

- *10,000–24,999 DWT:* General Purpose tanker
- *25,000–54,999 DWT:* Medium Range tanker
- *55,000–79,999 DWT:* Long Range 1 (LR1)

- *80,000–159,999 DWT:* Long Range 2 (LR2)
- *160,000–319,999 DWT:* Very Large Crude Carrier (VLCC)
- *320,000–549,999 DWT:* Ultra Large Crude Carrier (ULCC)

Petroleum Tankers					
Class	**Length**	**Beam**	**Draft**	**Typical Min DWT**	**Typical Max DWT**
Seawaymax	226 m (741 ft)	24 m (79 ft)	7.92 m (26.0 ft)	10,000 t DWT	60,000 t DWT
Panamax	228.6 m (750 ft)	32.3 m (106 ft)	12.6 m (41 ft)	60,000 t DWT	80,000 t DWT
Aframax	253.0 m (830.1 ft)	44.2 m (145 ft)	11.6 m (38 ft)	80,000 t DWT	120,000 t DWT
Suezmax			16 m (52 ft)	120,000 t DWT	200,000 t DWT
VLCC (Malaccamax)	330 m (1,080 ft)	60 m (200 ft)	20 m (66 ft)	200,000 t DWT	315,000 t DWT
ULCC				320,000 t DWT	550,000 t DWT

Very Large Crude Carrier Size Range There are more ships smaller in size. At nearly 380 vessels in the size range 279,000 t DWT to 320,000 t DWT, these are by far the most popular size range among the larger VLCCs. Only seven vessels are larger than this, and approximately 90 between 220,000 t DWT and 279,000 t DWT.

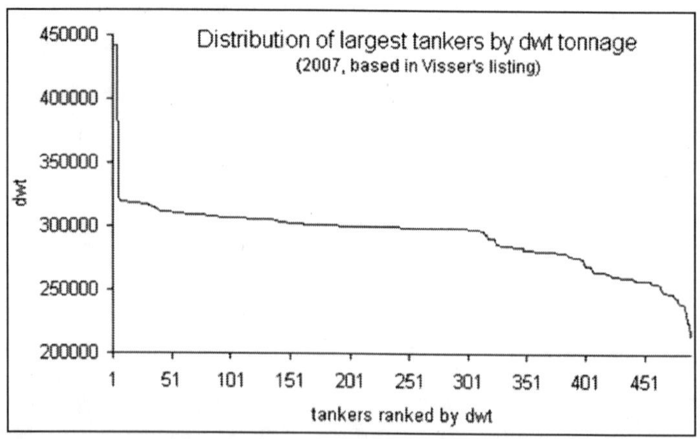

FLEETS OF THE WORLD

Flag States

As of 2005, the United States Maritime Administration's statistics count 4,024 tankers of 10,000 LT DWT or greater worldwide. 2,582 of these are double-hulled. Panama is the leading flag state of tankers with 592 registered ships. Five other flag states have more than two hundred registered tankers: Liberia (520), The Marshall Islands (323), Greece(233), Singapore (274) and The Bahamas (215). These flag states are also the top six in terms of fleet size in terms of deadweight tonnage.

Largest Fleets

Greece, Japan, and the United States are the top three owners of tankers (including those owned but registered to other nations), with 733, 394, and 311 vessels respectively. These three nations account for 1,438 vessels or over 36 per cent of the world's fleet.

Builders

Asian companies dominate the construction of tankers. Of the world's 4,024 tankers, 2,822 or over 70 per cent were built in South Korea, Japan or China.

HYDROGEN TANKER

A hydrogen tanker is a tank ship designed for transporting liquefied hydrogen.

Research

The World Energy Network research programme of the Japanese New Sunshine Project was divided into 3 phases during the period 1993 to 2002, its goal was to study the distribution of liquid hydrogen with hydrogen tankers based on the LNG carrier technology of self-supporting tank designs such as the prismatic and spherical tank. Further research on maritime transport of hydrogen was done in the development for safe utilization and infrastructure of hydrogen project (2003–2007). Similar to an LNG carrier the boil off gas can be used for propulsion of the ship.

HYDROGEN SHIP

A hydrogen ship is a hydrogen-fueled ship, power-assisted by an electric motor that gets its electricity from a fuel cell.

HISTORY

In 2000, the 22-person Hydra ship was demonstrated, and in 2003 the Duffy-Herreshoff watertaxi went into service. 2003 saw the debut of Yacht No. 1, as well Hydroxy3000.The AUV DeepC and Yacht XV 1 were shown in 2004. In 2005 the first example of the Type 212 submarine, which is powered underwater by fuel cells, went into service with the German navy. In 2006 the 12-person Xperiance was debuted, as well as the Zebotec. In 2007 both the 8-person Tuckerboot and the Canal boat Ross Barlow debuted, and in 2008 the 100-passenger Zemships project Alsterwasser went into service in Hamburg. Also, in 2009 the Nemo H2 and the Frauscher 600 Riviera HP went into service. In 2013 the Hydrogenesis Passenger Ferry project went into service.

Economy

Hjalti Pall Ingolfsson from Icelandic New Energy has commented that ships are fast becoming the biggest source of air pollution in the European Union. It is estimated that by 2020 emissions of sulfur dioxide and nitrogen oxides from ships will exceed land-based emissions in Europe.

Fig. Electrolysis of Water Ship Hydrogen Challenger.

A big issue to be dealt with would be the storage of hydrogen on ships, given that there would be no opportunity to refill them when out at sea, although one can use wind power and solar panels to generate electricity from the ocean while they are far from the shores and produce onboard hydrogen.

INFRASTRUCTURE

The need for a hydrogen infrastructure varies, where the Yacht No. 1 was fueled by a mobile hydrogen station, the prototype HaveblueYacht XV 1 was intended to have onboard hydrogen generation, the Xperiance and Tuckerboot have exchangeable high-pressure hydrogen tanks which can be refilled at a localhydrogen station, the canal boat Ross Barlow uses fixed onboard low-pressure solid-state metal hydride storage tanks and depends on a refilling station on the waterside, the Zemships Alsterwasser refills at a fixed waterside storage tank with 17,000 liters of hydrogen which is refuelled by a compressed hydrogen tube trailer.

CODES AND STANDARDS

Hydrogen codes and standards have repeatedly been identified as a major institutional barrier to the deployment of hydrogen technologies and the development of a hydrogen economy. To enable the commercialization of hydrogen in consumer products, new model building codes and equipment, as well as other technical standards are developed and recognized by federal, state, and local governments. The Germanischer Lloyd guidelines for fuel cells on ships and boats is used for the Hydra, Tuckerboot, Yacht No. 1, Zebotec and Zemships.

Research

The NEW H SHIP project was a 15-month project that started February 2004. FC-SHIP was funded by the European Commission under FP5 - GROWTH from 2002 to 2004. The Viking Fellowship is a Nordic project. The SMART H2 project started in 2007 by placing a fuel cell in the existing whale-watching ship Elding. Other studies have also considered various ways of combining fuel cell operations on board with air conditioning systems for operations while in harbour.

CHEMICAL TANKER

Fig. The Chemical Tanker GINGA FALCONon the Columbia River.

Fig. The Deck of a Chemical Tanker has a Complicated Piping System. This is the Saudi Chemical Tanker of 43,851 Tonnesdead Weight (DWT) 1986 Built Al Farabi, Carrying Molasses, in Brest.

The MV Golden Nori at sea.

A chemical tanker is a type of tanker ship designed to transport chemicals in bulk. The chemical tanker means a ship constructed or adapted for carrying in bulk any liquid product listed in chapter 17 of the International Bulk Chemical Code. As well as industrial chemicals and clean petroleum products, such ships also often carry other types of sensitive cargo which require a high standard of tank cleaning, such as palm oil, vegetable oils, tallow, caustic soda and methanol. Oceangoing chemical tankers range from 5,000 tonnes deadweight (DWT) to 35,000 DWT in size, which is smaller than the average size of other tanker types due to the specialized nature of their cargo and the size restrictions of the port terminals where they call to load and discharge.

Chemical tankers normally have a series of separate cargo tanks which are either coated with specialized coatings such as phenolic epoxy or zinc paint, or made from stainless steel. The coating or cargo tank material determines what types of cargo a particular tank can carry: stainless steel tanks are required for aggressive acid cargoes such as sulfuric and phosphoric acid, while 'easier' cargoes — such as vegetable oil — can be carried in epoxy coated tanks. The coating or tank material also influences how quickly tanks can be cleaned. Typically, ships with stainless steel tanks can carry a wider range of cargoes and can clean more quickly between one cargo and another, which justifies the additional cost of their construction.

CLASSIFICATION

In general, ships carrying chemicals in bulk are classed into three types:

1. A 'Type 1' ship is a chemical tanker intended to transport Chapter 17 of the IBC Code products with very severe environmental and safety hazards which require maximum preventive measures to preclude an escape of such cargo.
2. A'Type 2' ship is a chemical tanker intended to transport Chapter 17 of the IBC Code products with appreciably severe environmental and safety hazards which require significant preventive measures to preclude an escape of such cargo.
3. A 'Type 3' ship is a chemical tanker intended to transport Chapter 17 of the IBC Code products with sufficiently severe environmental and safety hazards which require a moderate degree of containment to increase survival capability in a damaged condition.

Most chemical tankers are IMO 2 and 3 rated, since the volume of IMO 1 cargoes is very limited.

MAIN CHARACTERISTICS OF CHEMICAL TANKERS

Chemical tankers often have a system for tank heating in order to maintain the viscosity of certain cargoes, typically by passing pressurized steam through stainless steel 'heating coils' in the cargo tanks, transferring heat into the cargo which circulates in the tank by convection. All modern chemical tankers feature double hull construction and most have one pump for each tank with independent piping, which means that each tank can load a separate cargo without any mixing. Tank cleaning after discharging cargo is a very important aspect of chemical tanker operations, because tanks which are not properly cleaned of all cargo residue can adversely affect the purity of the next cargo loaded. Before tanks are cleaned, they must be properly ventilated and checked to be free of potentially explosive gases. Chemical tankers usually have transverse stiffeners on deck rather than inside the cargo tanks, in order to make the tank walls smooth and easier to clean by fitted tank cleaning machines. Cargo tanks, either empty or filled, are normally protected against explosion by inert gas blankets. Often nitrogen is the inert gas used, supplied either from portable gas bottles or a Nitrogen generator.

Most new chemical tankers are built by shipbuilders in Japan, Korea or China, with other builders in Turkey, Italy, Germany and Poland. Japanese shipbuilders now account for the large majority of stainless steel chemical tankers built, as welding stainless steel to the accuracy required for cargo tank construction is a skill which is difficult to acquire. Notable major chemical tanker operators including Stolt-Nielsen, Odfjell, Tokyo Marine and Eitzen Chemical. Charterers, the end users of the ships, include oil majors, industrial consumers and specialist chemical companies.

TANK VESSEL DESIGN, OPERATION, AND REGULATION

Before embarking on a technical analysis of alternative tank vessel designs, standard design and operational practices related to pollution prevention should be understood. This chapter will discuss the evolution of these practices, as well as the legal and regulatory framework governing the tank vessel industry. The discussion applies primarily to tankers, although some sections, as noted, apply to barges.

TANK VESSEL DESIGN AND OPERATION

Tanker Design

Crude oil and petroleum products have been carried in ships for more than 100 years. The practice of carrying the oil directly inside the single hull of a ship has been common since this type of ship was first built in 1886. The hull provided far better security for the cargo than barrels, or casks, which could split and spill oil, creating fire and explosion hazards.

Tanker designs established in the late 1880s remained virtually unchanged until shortly after World War II. Tankers commonly were of 10,000 to 15,000 DWT, with a single skin, the engine to the stern, and multiple compartmentation with either two or three tanks across. Cargoes were usually refined products, most often light or "white" oils, which were not considered polluting as they rapidly evaporated if spilled. The non-polluting cargo meant that tanks could be rinsed out with water (which then was dumped at sea), and the same tanks could be used for ballast (sea water). Separate ballast tanks, other than the peak tanks (at the ends of the ship), were virtually unheard-of until after World War II.

After the war, the world economy expanded with a resulting huge increase in demand for energy in the form of oil. At the same time, a new shipping pattern evolved: Crude oil often was transported from distant sources, such as the Persian Gulf, to major marketing areas, notably North America, Northern Europe, and Japan, where the crude was refined and redistributed as product. These long voyages set the stage for a dramatic increase in ship size, which started about 1950. Between 1950 and 1975, the largest tanker in the world grew from about 25,000 DWT to over 500,000 DWT. The numbers of tankers in the world fleet also multiplied many times over.

Meanwhile, significant technical developments were afoot, including the following:

- Welding replaced riveting, a major benefit to the tanker industry in assuring tightness of tanks. The practice initially led to some cracking, and ships breaking in half, but these problems were solved with better materials, welding, and design.
- The empirical, or rule-of-thumb, design approach was augmented and partially supplanted by theoretical techniques. This trend was facilitated by the introduction of computers in the 1950s and 1960s, and, in fact, was necessitated by the growth in ship size from vessels of around 500 feet to over 1,400 feet, with an increase in deadweight of over twenty-fold in less than 20 years.
- While the basic types of static and dynamic forces acting on ship structure had been known in general for years, it was not until the 1960s that naval architects were able to quantify the loads precisely and to carry out the stress analysis needed to design ships on a theoretically sophisticated basis. By the 1970s, reliable theoretical quantification of loads and structural response was common for tankers; however, practical service experience remains vital to verify structural integrity and detail design.
- As newer design techniques were introduced, "safety factors" (design allowances for unknown factors) were reduced, in the desire to keep costs down and to get maximum deadweight for minimum draft (the depth of water a vessel draws). The significant reduction in ratio of lightweight (ship weight without cargo, crew, fuel, or stores) to deadweight directly reduces the cost of a ship per ton of cargo; this

means a ship can carry more cargo for a given draft. It also implies more efficient structure, and, in general, less margin to tolerate construction or maintenance errors or unusual operational events.

- Structural weight reductions were accompanied by a reduction in the number (and resulting increase in size) of compartments; the intent was to lower construction cost and simplify operations. While this change has

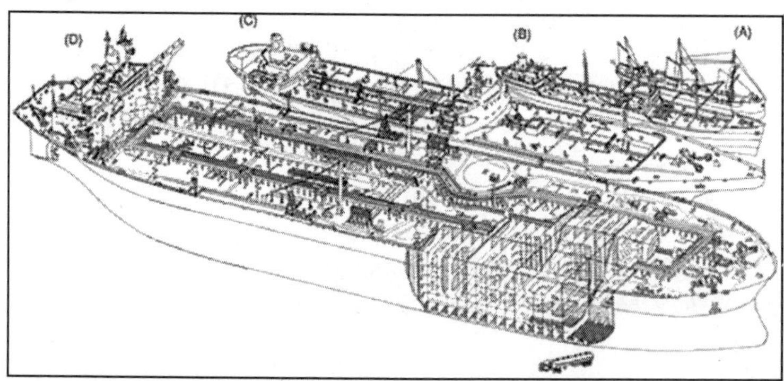

Fig. Evolution of the tanker. Sources: National Geographic Magazine, July 1978, and Tanker Advisory Center. (A) 1886, GLUCKAUF—First prototype tanker, 3,000 DWT. (B) 1945, T-2, World War II workhorse, 16,500 DWT, 525 built. (C) 1962, MANHATTAN—115,000 DWT (after conversion to an ice-breaker in 1969), the largest U.S.-flag ship at time of building. (D) 1977, KAPETAN GIANNIS—(formerly ESSO ATLANTIC) 517,000 DWT, length: 1,334 ft., third largest tanker in the world.

Table. Reduction in Tanker Lightweight to Deadweight Over Time.

Years	Deadweight	Approximate lightweight	LW/DW
1940s	16,500 (T-Z)	6,000	.36
1950s	50,000	12,000	.24
1960s	100,000	27,000	.27
1960s	200,000 (VLCC)	30,000	.15
1970s	300,000	40,000	.13
1970s	500,000	65,000	.13

been criticized on safety grounds, large tankers (with two or three longitudinal bulkheads, multiple transverse bulkheads, and a nearly continuous upper deck) seldom have stability problems experienced by other types of ships with much larger (relative to the size of the ship) open spaces. A valid concern with larger compartments is the increased amount of oil that could be spilled if the tank were breached.

As tanker design practices evolved, problems, of course, periodically surfaced. Among the more significant problems was buckling of internal structures, encountered in larger tankers in the late 1960s and early 1970s. The solution was use of more precise finite element and more sophisticated frame analysis techniques. The most dramatic problem from the industry standpoint was explosions, especially after three VLCCs exploded (two were total losses) in one week in 1969. The solution was inert gas systems, which were mandated by international agreement for progressively smaller ships during the 1970s.

In sum, there are two key features of modern structural design of tankers. First, introduction of new stress analysis techniques (employing finite element analysis and three-dimensional frame analysis) have permitted reductions in the structural weight. This in turn has led to a substantial reduction in cost (steel, measured by weight, is a major component in ship cost), and a modest increase in cargo-carrying capability. Second, improved welding and steel-making techniques have led to increased use of high-strength steel in tanker hulls, with attendant economic benefits. Even with these more sophisticated methods, however, ship design still must be conservative because loads never can be precisely predicted for all environments.

The exact design of a particular tank vessel depends on many factors. *There are 10 basic ship characteristics that must be considered:*

- Ship dimensions
- Hull form
- Machinery size, type, and location
- Speed and endurance
- Cargo capacity and deadweight
- Accommodations arrangements
- Cargo/ballast tanks arrangements
- Subdivision and stability accommodations
- Relative amounts of mild or high-tensile steel
- Basic scantling and structural arrangement

Irrespective of any specific design chosen, however, the technical advances in the design process have fostered a number of difficulties. These concerns, involving corrosion resistance, design margins, and fatigue resistance. Suffice to say at this point, advancements in design techniques and analyses unquestionably have made modern tankers more vulnerable to failure under conditions of unusual stress, or less-than-diligent maintenance. This matter has been of considerable interest to the committee.

The committee also has noted that prevention of damage or rupture of structure due to collisions or groundings heretofore has not been a design consideration for merchant ships, except in rare cases (*e.g.*, barriers to nuclear reactors and, to a lesser degree, chemical carriers and liquified natural gas carriers). In attempting to reduce pollution risk, incorporation of these additional criteria into tanker design practices warrants serious attention. Finally, it should be noted that design practices, while technically oriented, have a direct bearing on cost, and this is a factor in design decisions. The process is essentially circular, for the following reasons.

Because the structural rules, which are developed by classification societies, determine the weight and thus a major component of the cost of the ship, "class" decisions to a large degree control cost. The differences among classification societies—non-profit groups in competition—are factors that attract clients (shipowners who pay fees to "class" their ships). At the same time, classification societies are managed fundamentally through boards of directors composed mainly of shipowners but with some representation from shipbuilders, insurers, and government. This situation offers the potential for conflict of interest, in that it makes this aspect of the industry essentially self-regulating.

The owners' interest in maintaining reliable ship structure has kept class rules, in the majority view, to a high technical standard. non-etheless, it must be acknowledged that competition among classification societies and among shipyards has produced strong pressure to produce a minimum cost ship that will perform to an adequate structural standard.

Barge Design

Ocean-going barges have been used in the shipping industry for many years. In the United States especially, barges have become extremely important in coastal transportation, particularly since World War II. There are two principal reasons. First, under U.S. manning regulations, a non-propelled cargo section pushed or pulled by a tugboat requires a much smaller crew than a tanker, thus offering a major economic savings. Second, structural and safety requirements have been less stringent for barges. Until recently, unmanned barges could be built to lesser scantling (dimensions of structural members) requirements than ships with cargo sections of the same size. In addition, the absence of a crew meant that unmanned barges could escape many of the safety requirements (related to fire fighting, life-saving, anchoring, etc.) imposed on tankers. Similarly, barges had more liberal (lower) freeboard assignments than ships and usually could be operated without ballast, thus providing substantial economic advantages.

In recent years, many of the differences in technical standards between tankers and barges have been eliminated, and the U.S. Coast Guard has applied structural provisions of international tanker conventions to larger barges. However, the manning requirements remain quite different, and this—besides encouraging the continued use of barges—influences vessel design, including the choice of appropriate alternative for pollution control.

The basic design process for offshore barges carrying petroleum products is similar to that for tankers. Structurally, barges are somewhat different in that they tend to have heavier side structure (to accommodate loads from contact with piers, locks, and tugboats), and they have greater breadth than tankers of the same length.

Tank Vessel Operations

Tankers generally operate between single or multiple loading and discharge ports. When tankers were smaller in the 1950s and early 1960s, they often loaded and discharged alongside a pier, usually in a harbor. As ships got larger, requiring deeper ports, new port complexes were constructed, principally in the Middle East, Europe, and Japan. While many of these facilities were essentially conventional, with a sheltered port and a permanent fixed pier, the tanker industry also developed offshore multi-buoy moorings (MBMs) and, eventually, single-point moorings (SPMs).

Tankers are loaded near the midship point by shore pumps, or gravity if storage tanks are elevated, through hoses or "hard-arms" (hard pipe structures with swivel connections) connected to the ship's piping system. Tankers commonly have pipes on deck and running down to the ship bottom. When a tanker is discharging, the ship's power drives cargo pumps, usually located in a pump room between the engine room at the stern and the cargo tanks. The cargo is pumped up to the deck, and then ashore through the hoses or hard-arms. The process is essentially identical for the handling of crude oil, fuel oil, or refined products. Most tankers have two, three, or more separate piping and pumping systems, so as not to intermingle cargoes of different grades or characteristics. These systems are powerful enough to transfer cargo in an emergency, provided they remain intact; however, setting up the system to drain cargo from a damaged tank quickly is difficult, because the installed transfer piping suction is on the tank bottom and the oil remaining normally will float above the suction.

Tankers operate on many different trade routes and serve thousands of delivery points. Most tankers load cargo in one area, take it to another area for discharge, and then return empty to a loading area. Thus, tankers typically are loaded roughly half the time, and otherwise are "in ballast." To deal with buildup of sludge, and to clean tanks between switches of grades in product trades, cargo tanks are cleaned periodically. For many years this was done with either cold or hot water. And, until the late 1960s, sea water often was placed in some empty cargo tanks for the ballast voyage. These practices, of course, led to some mixing of oil and water, and discharge of rinsing or ballast water inevitably caused some pollution of the seas. Concern about this "operational pollution" led to a series of new practices mandated by international conventions in the 1970s.

Lightering

Another measure adopted widely by the tanker industry in the post-war years was lightering (or lightening), the process of transferring cargo from one floating vessel directly to another. Lightering is used principally to remove cargo from larger vessels to make them lighter (and to reduce their draft), to allow them either to enter a harbor or to approach a pier to discharge remaining cargo. Sometimes the entire cargo is removed offshore ("lightering to extinction"). Lightering is relevant to the present study because its use may be encouraged by the Oil Pollution Act of 1990, which prohibits some tank vessels from approaching U.S. shores.

Nearly all types of dry and liquid cargo, in bulk or in containers, can be transferred by lightering.

Crude oil often is moved in this manner, at least in the following areas:

- The English Channel;
- Argentina;
- The Mediterranean, Middle East, and Far East;
- The lower Delaware Bay (where barges are commonly used to take some cargo out of larger arriving tankers, to allow them to proceed to refinery terminals farther up the Delaware River);
- The U.S. Gulf of Mexico; and
- San Francisco Bay.

Lightering became common in the U.S. Gulf of Mexico in the early to mid-1970s, when crude oil imports increased rapidly along with the size of ships. With no resolution of the debate on the wisdom of deepwater ports, lightering was the industry solution for accommodating the largest tankers, which could not be berthed in shallow U.S. harbors even in lightened condition. Lighters in the 50,000 to 80,000 DWT size range were employed; at times, probably six to eight of these vessels were engaged full-time in the Gulf of Mexico and the Caribbean. Then, as oil imports declined and the first—and still only—U.S. deepwater port (LOOP, 18 miles off the coast of Louisiana) came on stream in early 1982, use of lightering dwindled.

Now, with crude oil imports increasing again, imports of refined products rising, and the LOOP operating at full capacity, tanker activity in the Gulf—including lightering—will intensify once more. Another offshore facility, TexPort, is under consideration by an oil company consortium; it would be located 27 miles off Freeport, Texas, where there are no depth constraints to even the largest tankers. At its greatest proposed capacity, TexPort could handle nearly a third of the present U.S. oil import volume (about 100 million tons per year). The consortium estimates that this facility will be operable five years after local, state, and federal regulatory hurdles are overcome.

Reliability and Safety of Lightering. The industry took several steps in the early 1970s to assure the reliability and safety of lightering. Special techniques involving large fenders, special mooring arrangements, and ship handling techniques were explored at both model and full-scale levels, to develop the best methods for mooring and maneuvering two ships together. Lightering with both ships underway was found to be, in many instances, the preferred method, as the best course could be determined with regard to wind and waves, thus simplifying ship handling. Also, with both ships underway the mooring of the smaller vessel alongside the VLCC could be accomplished with full control over the lighter. The procedures for maneuvering vessels, mooring, and handling cargo were codified in a detailed Ship To Ship Transfer Guide (International Chamber of Shipping, 1978).

The committee is unaware of specific records kept on the safety of lightering, but, based on inquires to concerned industry organizations, there is no evidence of any major accident or pollution incident stemming from lightering of tankers.

ECONOMIC CONSIDERATIONS

Tank vessel design is an important factor in the economics of tanker transportation, and this should be taken into account when considering future design changes. The basic principles involved are described here; a fuller explanation, including the economic impact of specific design alternatives.

There are three basic categories of costs that comprise the total cost of carrying oil by tanker. These are:

- Capital cost, the predominant component of overall cost for tankers of nearly all sizes. It may be expressed either as the vessel price or as a down payment plus loan payments, just as with a house. Tankers are expected to last 15 to 30 years, so operators must think in terms of depreciation or capital recovery.
- Operating costs, covering the crew, maintenance and repair, stores, supplies, insurance, overhead, and administration. This is the second largest component of overall cost and is heavily influenced by vessel cost (which affects insurance rates), the complexity of the vessel (which affects maintenance and repair), and the size and nationality of the crew.
- Voyage costs, including fuel, port charges, piloting, and berthing tugs.

There are economies of scale in the tanker industry. In other words, a large tanker nearly always can carry oil at a substantially cheaper rate than a smaller tanker, assuming there is adequate cargo to fill the ship and that the ports can accommodate large vessels.

There are three main reasons for the economy of scale: (1) The amount of steel needed to contain a given quantity of cargo does not increase in proportion to the deadweight of the ship; (2) The horsepower needed to propel the ship at service speed does not increase nearly in proportion to the increase in ship size (offering economies in both vessel price and subsequent voyage cost for bunkers); and (3) The size of tanker crews seldom is related to vessel size. Thus, a crew of 20 to 25 will suffice for both a small tanker (20,000 to 30,000 DWT) and a ship 5 to 10 times larger. Of course, tanker economics depends on more than cost structure, because tankers in international trade are essentially regarded as commodities. This is because tankers of similar size and characteristics are essentially interchangeable. Thus, market factors driven by supply and demand will play a dominant role in the actual shipping rates ultimately earned by tanker owners. In summary, when considering possible design changes, the impact on capital costs, operating expenses, and the marketplace should be borne in mind.

Safety Considerations

As economic concerns drove the tanker world to increasingly larger ships, the size increase resulted in two important safety improvements. First, the number of ships needed to carry the world's ever-growing demand for petroleum was far less than it would have been with smaller ships. The increase in traffic and congestion would have been enormous if maximum ship size had remained at the World War II level (16,500 DWT); about three times the roughly 6,000 ocean tankers (over 5,000 DWT) now sailing the world seas would be needed.

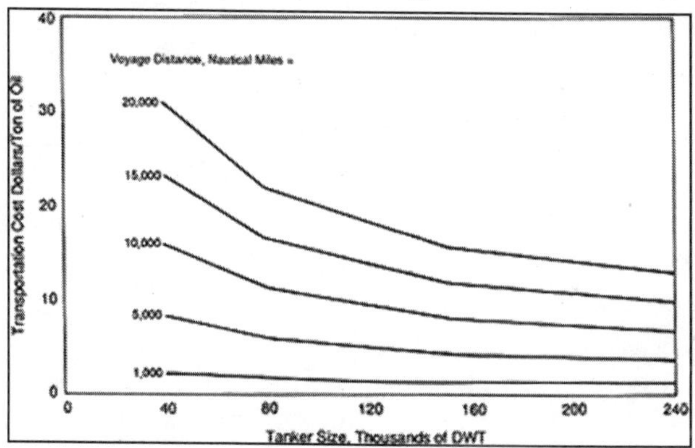

Fig. Tanker Transportation Economics.

Second, larger ships generally discharge cargo at remote locations. This has kept them at distance from some, though not all, of the world's busiest harbors. However, the United States was very slow to adopt deepwater ports, offshore SBMs, and other new facilities to accommodate the largest tankers. Thus, it remains common in the United States to see tanker drafts limited to roughly 40 feet, which restricts tanker size to a maximum of roughly 60,000 to 80,000 DWT. By contrast, most of the rest of the world deals with much larger ships at more remote locations. These changes may have helped control the incidence and impact of pollution, albeit indirectly. The industry also took other steps in its continuing concern for the consequences of groundings and collisions. Structural solutions (*i.e.*, "crash-proofing") were studied, although they never achieved prominence or widespread adoption.

Instead, the industry concentrated on:

- Radar and electronic navigation, which became important for ships of all types but particularly tankers;

- Harbor and coastal traffic control systems, which became prominent in much of Europe and were adopted to a lesser degree in the United States;
- Ship handling and bridge team simulator training, which were promoted by some tanker operators and were adopted in a number of prominent fleets, though by no means universally;
- Research on ship maneuverability, to the point that prediction of ship maneuvers became commonplace in tanker design and operation; and
- An international agreement covering crew training and licensing, ratified by many nations though not yet by the United States.

The effectiveness of these measures, either individually or collectively, is difficult to assess. Data on serious tanker casualties do seem to show that tanker accidents have decreased over the last 10 years, based on the ratio of accidents to the number of tankships in service worldwide. However, a comparison of accidents to a general measure of exposure—ton-miles per year of oil and products shipped—while demonstrating a decrease in casualties since the mid-1980s, does not show such a clear safety improvement.

LEGAL REQUIREMENTS FOR VESSEL DESIGN AND POLLUTION PREVENTION

This section discusses the evolution of international conventions and laws related to tank vessel design and pollution prevention, as well as the current status of enforcement activities related to tankers operating in U.S. waters. Tankers must satisfy a substantial number of design requirements when initially constructed, for purposes of safety and pollution prevention. These requirements fall into three broad categories: international legal requirements, domestic legal requirements, and classification society requirements.

INTERNATIONAL LEGAL REQUIREMENTS

The International Maritime Organization (IMO) is the United Nations agency responsible for maritime safety and environmental protection of the oceans. All of the world's major shipping nations are members of IMO. Each member nation is encouraged to accept the international agreements adopted by IMO. These include 22 full conventions or treaties and 17 codes (as of December 31,1989) as well as numerous resolutions containing recommendations and guidelines.

Regulation of ship design for safety and pollution prevention is achieved primarily through three international conventions:

- The International Convention on Load Lines (1966), or ICLL;
- The International Convention for the Safety of Life at Sea (1974) and its 1978 Protocol (SOLAS); and
- The International Convention for the Prevention of Pollution from Ships (1973) and its 1978 Protocol (MARPOL).

The ICLL establishes the deepest draft to which a ship can be safely loaded. These "loadlines" are commonly seen as the "Plimsoll Mark" line on a ship's side. Historically, the objective of the loadline was to assure that ships were not so overloaded as to run undue risk of sinking, or to create unsafe working conditions. The overall objective of SOLAS is to assure safety of the crew, ports, passengers, ships, and cargo, and, indirectly, the environment. Among the more important provisions are: (1) subdivision and stability requirements, to prevent ships from capsizing, and to ensure survival under specified collision and grounding damage circumstances; (2) general construction principles, to ensure the ship is strong enough for its intended trade; (3) safety equipment requirements, to assure the carriage of sufficient life-boats and other safety equipment; (4) fire protection requirements, to ensure that ships could withstand certain fire damage and fight fires effectively; and (5) radio telegraphy requirements, specifying the communications and navigation equipment ships must carry.

Both ICLL and SOLAS have the indirect effect of preventing oil spills and consequent marine pollution. The MARPOL convention seeks to prevent pollution directly, both from normal operational discharges and accidents. MARPOL specifies design, equipment, and procedural requirements to prevent pollution of the seas from oil, chemicals carried in bulk, harmful substances carried in packages, sewage, and garbage. Each of these five potential sources of pollution is addressed in regulations set out in an annex to MARPOL.

MARPOL addressed the prevention of pollution from oil, and it and certain SOLAS provisions include these major requirements:

- Segregated Ballast Tanks (SBT). Oil carriers over 20,000 DWT built after dates specified in MARPOL '78, and tankers over 70,000 DWT built after dates specified in MARPOL '73, are required to carry ballast in SBT. Only in severe weather can additional ballast be carried in cargo tanks. In such cases, this water must be processed and discharged in accordance with specific regulations.
- Protective location of SBT. The required SBT must be arranged to cover a specified percentage of the side and bottom shell of the cargo section. Thus, the protectively located segregated ballast tanks (PL/SBT) are intended to provide a measure of protection against oil outflow in a grounding or collision. To be credited, each wing tank or double-bottom tank must meet certain minimum width or depth requirements, respectively (generally 2 meters).
- Draft and trim requirements. To assure safe operation of the vessel in ballast condition, the SBT must be of sufficient capacity to permit full submergence of the propeller. They are to provide a molded draft (d) amidships of not less than $d = 2.0 + 0.02\ L$, and a trim (horizontal tilt) by stern not greater than $0.015L$, where L is the ship length in meters.

- Tank size limitations. To minimize pollution in case of side or bottom damage, the maximum length of cargo tanks is limited to values between 10 meters and 0.2 L, depending on tank location and longitudinal bulkhead arrangement. The maximum volume of each cargo tank may vary up to 22,500 m3 for side tanks and up to 50,000 m3 for center tanks, depending on tank arrangement and location.
- Hypothetical outflow of oil. Formulas establish the maximum allowable hypothetical outflow of oil in case a cargo tank is breached at any location on the ship. For the purposes of these calculations, the regulations specify certain assumed longitudinal, transverse, and vertical damage. The key damage assumptions, where B is the ship's beam or breadth, are:

Side transverse extent: B/5 or 11.5 meters, whichever is less
Bottom vertical extent: B/15 or 6 meters, whichever is less

- Subdivision and stability. For a specified assumed shell damage, the regulations require that tank subdivision and ship features be such that, under certain specific damage conditions: The final water line is below any opening leading to progressive down-flooding, and the heeling angle (tilt to one side) does not exceed 25 degrees (or 30 degrees if the deck edge is not submerged).
- Crude Oil Washing (COW). New crude oil tankers must be fitted with an effective tank cleaning procedure that uses cargo oil as the washing medium. COW is a superior system of cleaning cargo tanks using the dissolving action of crude oil to reduce clingage and sludge. Furthermore, elimination or reduction of water washing has helped reduce operational oil pollution of the seas.
- Inert Gas System (IGS). This system supplies the cargo tanks with an atmosphere lacking in oxygen so that combustion cannot take place. Treated flue gas from main or auxiliary boilers, inert gas generators, or other sources may be used for that purpose.
- Slop tanks. Tankers must be fitted with slop tanks of specified capacity to retain on board all slop, cargo drainage, sludge, washings, and other oil residues. Their discharge then is monitored in accordance with the regulations.

THE SIGNIFICANCE OF MARPOL

The IMO Conferences of 1973 and 1978 together produced fundamental changes in the way tankers are designed and operated. The significance of these changes in relation to the present study will be summarized here. Most important is the fact that the "MARPOL vessel" represents the current standard, against which any further design changes should be measured. MARPOL also set a precedent by establishing major retrofitting requirements for tankers, applying new equipment requirements (IGS and either SBT or COW) to existing tankers for the first time. The following other points may be less obvious.

Historically, control of pollution from operations had been accomplished through the "load on top," or LOT, system. This method was highly dependent on the vigilance of the crew and was difficult to monitor; MARPOL introduced structural means of achieving the same goal, clearly an advantage. However, these provisions involved inherent difficulties. The introduction of segregated ballast basically changed tankers from deadweight-limited carriers to cubic-limited carriers, and this in turn tended to increase the amount of oil outflow in groundings. This drawback was noted by the drafters of MARPOL; the result was increased pollution risk in some accidents for newly built SBT crude carriers, and even most "black fuel" carriers. The time frame for implementation of MARPOL and SOLAS requirements, including SBT/PL. Even now, the world fleet remains a mix of carriers, many of which are exempt from these SBT and SBT/PL regulations due to age or year of construction. About 35 percent of the world tanker fleet over 10,000 DWT has SBT, and about half of these ships have SBT protectively located, thus meeting full MARPOL requirements.

In new vessels, the attempt to satisfy MARPOL requirements in the most economical way has led to two changes in ship proportions. First, to make up for cubic lost to SBT, tankers became deeper in relation to their length; the length to depth ratio (L over D) is now lower, and the ratio of draft to depth (H/D) has decreased, because freeboard is increased. Second, in the interests of economy and with improving hull form design, ships generally were made broader and shorter, as breadth is a cheaper dimension to increase than length. Thus the ratio of length to beam (L/D) generally has decreased. In comparing pre-MARPOL to SBT ship designs, four general observations can be made (U.S. Coast Guard, 1973) that are relevant to the present study: (1) Depth must be increased in SBT ships to obtain sufficient volume for ballast; (2) for a given cargo volume, the ballast volume increases a great deal in SBT ships—in the range of 234 to 334 percent, which is indicative of the additional area that must be protected from corrosion; (3) expected oil outflow in groundings increases by up to 90 percent in many SBT designs; and (4) the greater depth (for a given draft and deadweight) in SBT designs means that deck and bottom plate thickness can be reduced significantly.

IMPLEMENTATION OF INTERNATIONAL LAW

Implementation of IMO conventions is not straightforward, because the procedures—and their effectiveness—can vary. Requirements are imposed on a vessel through its flag state. (The flag usually is carried at the stern with the city of registry and ship's name.) Each tankship therefore is governed in design, arrangements, and construction by the international agreements ratified by its flag state.

Nations that have formally ratified or approved IMO conventions usually implement the requirements through legislation. When a vessel is judged to have been designed and built to international standards, the flag state issues a certificate for each convention to which the vessel complies. Each certificate is valid for five years, provided an annual inspection—afloat—demonstrates that the ship has been maintained in accordance with convention requirements. After five years, the ship undergoes a major inspection and, as deemed necessary, renovation, prior to renewal of the certificate.

In traditional maritime nations, the inspection of vessels for compliance with both international and domestic requirements usually is carried out by government agencies, such as the Department of Transport in the United Kingdom, the Coast Guard in the United States, and the Coast Guard in Canada. Increasingly, with open registry or "flag of convenience" ships, however, enforcement and inspection is conducted on a contract basis, in which the flag state contracts for all these services to be handled by a classification society.

DOMESTIC LEGAL REQUIREMENTS

In addition to complying with international convention requirements, ships must adhere to any additional requirements imposed by the flag state. Compliance becomes further complicated when nations, as port states, impose unilateral requirements. There are very few unilateral port state requirements related to basic ship design and construction that represent a variance or extension of the international standards. Unilateral regulations imposed by port states usually deal with matters such as employment of pilots, hours in which ships can operate particular channels, use of tugs, and other issues peculiar to a certain locale. The United States, however, has imposed several requirements that vary significantly from international standards, as described in the following pages. Each flag state may require its own vessels to meet any set of regulations deemed appropriate. The regulations may apply as vessels travel anywhere in the world. However, each port state may require foreign-flag vessels entering its territorial waters to meet its own set of regulations. Foreign-flag ships have the option of either abiding by port state requirements or not traveling in those waters.

Flag state requirements are subject to continual monitoring. Basically, this is handled by yearly inspections, which are fairly routine, and with more thorough inspections occurring at five-year intervals. No extension can be granted for five-year surveys. IMO conventions do not specify penalties for noncompliance, other than removal of the current certificate. They direct that penalties (by indictment, warning, fine, or imprisonment of the person(s) responsible for the violation) be imposed by the flag state.

CLASSIFICATION REQUIREMENTS

Classification societies establish standards, guidelines, and rules for the design, construction, and survey of ships. There are eleven leading classification societies, as represented by the membership of the International Association of Classification Societies (IACS). A ship that has been constructed in accordance with the rules of a society is issued a classification certificate. To maintain their classification, vessels must be presented for survey at regular intervals.

Class requirements essentially are concerned with the structural integrity of the ship and its propulsion and steering systems; they do not address safety equipment or crew qualifications. Class requirements embrace: (1) materials for hull and key machinery components; (2) structural design requirements including scantlings (dimensions of structural elements) and details of all structure and key machinery components (*i.e.*, main engine, shafting, propeller, etc.); and (3) supervision, inspection and certification of manufacture of steel, welding, machinery components, hull structure, etc.

These requirements must be met for the ship to comply fully with international convention requirements and to obtain more favorable insurance rates. The requirements are not statutory in nature; however, under the SOLAS Convention, each ocean-going ship must have a Safety Construction Certificate attesting to the adequacy of the construction. Being "in class" does not, in itself, satisfy SOLAS requirements, but, when authorized, a classification society may issue a SOLAS certification on behalf of a flag state.

Survey Procedures

Once a ship has been delivered, it can maintain its "in class" status only by meeting continuing survey requirements of the classification society. Essentially, the ship has to satisfy the society of its suitability to continue trading by passing both hull and machinery surveys at various intervals. Surveys can be of either a continuous or periodic nature, or a combination thereof.

Historically, periodic surveys were set up based on a system of annual and special surveys. Annual surveys do not include in-depth inspection of the ship's machinery and structure, unless there is cause for concern. Special surveys of hull and machinery are spaced at four-year intervals, although the society often grants a "year of grace" unless there is a compelling reason to deny it. Therefore, special surveys tend to fall at age 5, 10, 15, etc. The basic purpose of the special survey system is to assure the vessel's ability to trade successfully until the next scheduled special survey.

Special surveys become increasingly rigourous, at least in theory, as a ship gets older. The first special hull surveys will include, for example, a general examination of the most critical parts of the ship structure. By the second special survey, a more thorough examination is conducted, including measurement of the thickness of certain key structural members. The third special survey includes a comprehensive examination of the ship's structure and measurement of thickness of structure.

Continuous surveys, in lieu of special surveys, are applied particularly to machinery, and sometimes to the hull. Under this system, various parts of the ship are inspected by classification surveyors during port calls, while the vessel remains in service. One approach to conducting structural surveys on large tankers. The inspection of the vast structural areas of a modern VLCC requires more time than is usually available while a tanker is in port, making operator inspection while the ship is underway and in ballast an attractive and economically efficient option.

When significant damage has occurred, or is suspected, which might affect the vessel's seaworthiness, the ship's owner is required to call in classification surveyors to inspect the damaged area. The surveyor then has three options: To allow the ship to continue trading "in class," to specify temporary repairs, or to require permanent repairs before the vessel can again be regarded "in class."

HOW REQUIREMENTS ARE IMPLEMENTED IN THE UNITED STATES

The U.S. implementing legislation of MARPOL applies not only to seagoing ships of U.S. registry, but also to foreign-flag seagoing ships while in U.S. waters. The law authorizes the inspection of such ships, while in a port or terminal under U.S. jurisdiction, for compliance with the requirements of MARPOL. If a violation is found, the ship may be detained until authorities determine that it can proceed without undue threat of harm to the environment.

In some respects, U.S. law exceeds the requirements of MARPOL. For example, in U.S. waters, crude tankers between 20,000 and 40,000 DWT were required to have SBT or COW by 1986, or upon reaching 15 years of age, whichever occurred later. Product tankers in the same range were required to retrofit to SBT or operate dedicated clean ballast tanks by 1986, or upon reaching 15 years of age. Neither of these measures were required under MARPOL. Only one example of a flag-state requirement going beyond international requirements related to tanker design (other than for ice-navigation capability) has been identified outside of the United States: Finland's imposition of a large surcharge in imports of crude oil carried in single-hull ships. The Oil Pollution Act of 1990, enacted on August 18, requires that all ships trading to U.S. waters meet standards that exceed the construction and design requirements of MARPOL in compliance with a phase-in schedule. Specifically, all new tank vessels (contracted after June 30, 1990 or delivered after January 1, 1994) operating in U.S. waters or the Exclusive Economic Zone must be fitted with double hulls. Existing single hull tank vessels are permitted to operate until the time limits set forth in the Act; the timetable ends January 1, 2010. Existing tank vessels with a double bottom or double sides meet a separate schedule that ends in 2015.

A number of exceptions are provided to the requirements for double hulls. Tankers used exclusively for responding to oil spills, and tank vessels under 5,000 gross registered tons (about 10,000 DWT) fitted with a double containment system, are exempt. Also exempt until January 1, 2015, are tank vessels unloading or discharging at a deepwater port, off-loading in a lightering operation more than 60 miles from U.S. coasts, and under 5,000 GRT.

COAST GUARD RESPONSIBILITIES

In the United States, the Coast Guard is responsible for regulations and enforcement related to tank vessel design, construction, and safety. Specifically, the Coast Guard is responsible for safety of life and property at sea and protection of the marine environment under provisions of Title 46 of the U.S. Code, Part B—Inspection and Regulation of Vessels, and 33 U.S. Code—Prevention of Pollution from Ships, respectively, and other laws. Regulations prescribed by the Coast Guard incorporate American Bureau of Shipping (ABS) rules. In carrying out inspections and vessel design plan reviews, the Coast Guard may rely on ABS reports, documents, and certificates (46 USC 3316).

New Construction

Vessel design plans are subject to Coast Guard approval, and inspection and review of plans and construction is a Coast Guard responsibility. The Coast Guard has delegated selected parts of its responsibility in this regard to the ABS, except for major safety aspects such as stability and fire fighting. The Coast Guard accepts ABS plan review and inspection as part of the certification process for new vessels, or vessels undergoing a major modification without review or attendance by Coast Guard personnel. The Coast Guard maintains an oversight programme, overseeing approximately 20 percent of all ABS plan approval and inspection activities (U.S. Coast Guard, 1989b).

Vessel Maintenance

The Coast Guard is also responsible for ensuring that vessels are maintained to the appropriate standards. For this purpose, the Coast Guard requires inspection of U.S.-flag tank vessels every two years. Tankers, however, are often on a five-year operating and drydock cycle, conforming to most classification society survey intervals. In practice, this can mean that in a five-year period, the Coast Guard may have to conduct more than two biennial inspections on the vessel. The Coast Guard is also required to determine whether foreign-flag tank vessels can operate safely in U.S. waters. Regulations require that each foreign-flag tankship be inspected or examined at least once a year, with detailed inspections for vessels over 10 years of age. In practice, Coast Guard inspections of foreign-flag tank vessels do not routinely include internal inspection of the cargo or ballast tanks. The Coast Guard relies on the flag state or classification societies to conduct internal tank inspections.

8

Port Management

PORT MANAGEMENT IS THE MANAGEMENT OF PORTS.

According to a syllabus at the United Nations University:

Large ports need to deal with a number of disparate activities: the movement of ships, containers, and other cargo, the loading and unloading of ships and containers,customs activities. As well as human resources, anchorages, channels, lighters, tugs, berths, warehouse, and other storage spaces have to be allocated and released. The efficient management of a port involves managing these activities and resources, managing the flows of money involved between the agents providing and using these resources, and providing management information. A port is a location on a coast or shore containing one or more harbors where ships can dock and transfer people or cargo to or from land. Port locations are selected to optimize access to land and navigable water, for commercial demand, and for shelter from wind and waves. Ports with deeper water are rarer, but can handle larger, more economical ships. Since ports throughout history handled every kind of traffic, support and storage facilities vary widely, may extend for miles, and dominate the local economy. Some ports have an important military role.

HISTORICAL

One of the world's oldest known artificial harbors is at Wadi al-Jarf on the Red Sea. Along with the finding of harbor structures, ancient anchors have also been found.

Ancient China

Guangzhou was an important port during the ancient times as far back as the Qin Dynasty.

Ancient Egypt

Canopus was the principal port in Egypt for Greek trade before the foundation of Alexandria.

Ancient Greece

Athens' port of Piraeus was the base for the Athenian fleet and this played a crucial role in the battle of Salamis against the Persians in 480 BC.

Ancient India

Lothal is one of the most prominent cities of the ancient Indus valley civilization, located in the Bhal region of the modern state of Gujarat and dating from 3700 BCE.

Ancient Rome

Ostia Antica was the port of ancient Rome with Portus established by Claudius and enlarged by Trajan to supplement the nearby port of Ostia.

DISTRIBUTION

Ports often have cargo-handling equipment, such as cranes (operated by longshoremen) and forklifts for use in loading ships, which may be provided by private interests or public bodies. Often, canneries or other processing facilities will be located nearby. Some ports featurecanals, which allow ships further movement inland. Access to intermodal transportation, such as railroads and highways, is critical to a port, so that passengers and cargo can also move further inland beyond the port area. Ports with international traffic have customsfacilities. Harbor pilots and tugboats may maneuver large ships in tight quarters when near docks.

TYPES

The terms "port" and "seaport" are used for different types of port facilities that handle ocean-going vessels, and river port is used for river traffic, such as barges and other shallow-draft vessels.

Inland Port

An inland port is a port on a navigable lake, river (fluvial port), or canal with access to a sea or ocean, which therefore allows a ship to sail from the ocean inland to the port to load or unload its cargo. An example of this is the St. Lawrence Seaway which allows ships to travel from the Atlantic Ocean several thousand kilometers inland to Great Lakes ports like Duluth-Superior and Chicago.

Fishing Port

A fishing port is a port or harbor for landing and distributing fish. It may be a recreational facility, but it is usually commercial. A fishing port is the only port that depends on an ocean product, and depletion of fish may cause a fishing port to be uneconomical. In recent decades, regulations to save fishing stock may limit the use of a fishing port, perhaps effectively closing it.

Dry Port

A dry port is an inland intermodal terminal directly connected by road or rail to a seaport and operating as a centre for the transshipmentof sea cargo to inland destinations.

Warm-Water Port

A warm-water port is one where the water does not freeze in wintertime. Because they are available year-round, warm-water ports can be of great geopolitical or economic interest. Such settlements as Dalian in China, Vostochny Port, Murmansk and Petropavlovsk-Kamchatsky in Russia, Odessa in Ukraine, Kushiro in Japan and Valdez at the terminus of the Alaska Pipeline owe their very existence to being ice-free ports. The Baltic Sea and similar areas have ports available year-round thanks to icebreakers beginning in the 20th century, but earlier access problems prompted Russia to expand its territory to the Black Sea.

Seaport

A seaport is further categorized as a "cruise port" or a "cargo port". Additionally, "cruise ports" are also known as a "home port" or a "port of call". The "cargo port" is also further categorized into a "bulk" or "break bulk port" or as a "container port".

Cruise Home Port

A cruise home port is the port where cruise-ship passengers board (or embark) to start their cruise and disembark the cruise ship at the end of their cruise. It is also where the cruise ship's supplies are loaded for the cruise, which includes everything from fresh water and fuel to fruits, vegetable, champagne, and any other supplies needed for the cruise. "Cruise home ports" are a very busy place during the day the cruise ship is in port, because off-going passengers debark their baggage and on-coming passengers board the ship in addition to all the supplies being loaded. Currently, the Cruise Capital of the World is the Port of Miami, Florida, closely followed behind by Port Everglades, Florida and the Port of San Juan, Puerto Rico.

Port of Call

A port of call is an intermediate stop for a ship on its sailing itinerary. At these ports, cargo ships may take on supplies or fuel, as well as unloading and loading cargo while cruise liners have passengers get on or off ship.

Cargo Port

Cargo ports, on the other hand, are quite different from cruise ports, because each handles very different cargo, which has to be loaded and unloaded by very different mechanical means. The port may handle one particular type of cargo or it may handle numerous cargoes, such as grains, liquid fuels, liquid chemicals, wood, automobiles, etc. Such ports are known as the "bulk" or "break bulk ports". Those ports that handle containerized cargo are known as container ports. Most cargo ports handle all sorts of cargo, but some ports are very specific as to what cargo they handle. Additionally, the individual cargo ports are divided into different operating terminals which handle the different cargoes, and are operated by different companies, also known as terminal operators or stevedores.

ACCESS

Ports sometimes fall out of use. Rye, East Sussex, was an important English port in the Middle Ages, but the coastline changed and it is now 2 miles (3.2 km) from the sea, while the ports of Ravenspurn and Dunwich have been lost to coastal erosion. Also in the United Kingdom, London, on the River Thames, was once an important international port, but changes in shipping methods, such as the use of containers and larger ships, put it at a disadvantage.

ENVIRONMENTAL EFFECT

There are several initiatives to decrease ports' environmental effect. These include SIMPYC, the World Ports Climate Initiative, theAfrican Green Port Initiative and EcoPorts.

WORLD'S MAJOR PORTS

Africa

The busiest port in Africa is Port Said in Egypt.

Asia

The port of Shanghai is the largest port in the world in both cargo tonnage and activity. It regained its position as the world's busiest port by cargo tonnage and the world's busiest container port in 2009 and 2010, respectively. It is followed by the ports of Singapore and Hong Kong, both of which are in Asia.

Europe

Europe's busiest container port and biggest port by cargo tonnage by far is the Port of Rotterdam, in the Netherlands. It is followed by the Belgian Port of Antwerp or the GermanPort of Hamburg, depending on which metric is used.

North America

The largest ports include the ports of Los Angeles and South Louisiana in the U.S., Manzanillo in Mexico and Vancouver in Canada. Panama also has the Panama Canal that connects the Pacific and Atlantic Ocean, and is a key conduit for international trade.

PORT AUTHORITY

In Canada and the United States, port authority (less commonly a port district) is a governmental or quasi-governmental public authority for a special-purpose district usually formed by a legislative body (or bodies) to operate ports and other transportation infrastructure. Most port authorities are financially self-supporting. In addition to owning land, setting fees, and sometimes levying taxes, port districts can also operate shipping terminals, airports, railroads, and irrigation facilities. Port authorities are usually governed by boards or commissions, which are commonly appointed by governmental chief executives, often from different jurisdictions. In Canada, the federal Minister of Transport selects the local chief executive board member and the rest of the board is appointed at the recommendation of port users to the federal Minister; while all Canadian port authorities have a federal or Crown charter called Letters Patent.

In Mexico, the federal government created sixteen port administrations in 1994–1995 called Administración Portuaria Integral (API) in Spanish, as result of the Ley de Puertos of 1993. These are organized as variable capital corporations (Sociedad Anónima de Capital Variable or S.A. de C.V.), with the intent of creating more private investment in a state owned sector. Numerous Caribbean nations also have port authorities, including those of Aruba, British Virgin Islands, Bahamas, Jamaica, Cayman Islands, Trinidad and Tobago, St. Lucia, St. Maarten, St. Vincent and the Grenadines. Central and South America also have port agencies such as autoridad and consorcio (authority and consortium).

PORT SECURITY

Port security refers to the defence, law and treaty enforcement, and counterterrorism activities that fall within the port and maritime domain. It includes the protection of the seaports themselves, the protection and inspection of the cargo moving through the ports, and maritime security. Internationally, port security is governed by rules issued by the International Maritime Organization and its 2002 International Ship and Port Facility Security Code. Additionally, some United States-based programmes have become de facto global port security programmes, including theContainer Security Initiative and the Customs Trade Partnership against Terrorism.

PORT SECURITY IN THE UNITED STATES

In the United States, port security is handled jointly by the Coast Guard and U.S. Customs and Border Protection, both components of the Department of Homeland Security. Local law enforcement agencies and the FBI also have a role in port security at the local and regional level. Port security gained prominence politically in 2006 due to the sale of British company P and O Ports (including its American port assets) to Dubai Ports World. The ensuing controversy led to charges that the purchase would pose a national security risk. In March 2006, Dubai Ports World announced that it would sell off its American assets, and they were sold to AIG in December 2006. The new attention to port security that the controversy generated led to the passage of the SAFE Port Act (H.R. 4954) in Congress in 2006.

Vulnerabilities

The importance of the container shipping industry is equally matched by its vulnerabilities to terrorist attack. The U.S. maritime system consists of over 300 sea and river ports with more than 3,700 cargo and passenger terminals. The United States and global economies depend on commercial shipping as the most reliable, cost efficient method of transporting goods, with U.S. ports handling approximately 20 per cent of the maritime trade worldwide. The volume of trade throughout the U.S. and the world creates a desirable target for terrorist attack. An attack on any aspect of the maritime system, mainly major ports, can severely hamper trade and potentially affect the global economy by billions of dollars.

The security of ports and their deficiencies are numerous and leave US ports vulnerable to terrorist attack. The vulnerabilities of our ports are many, leading to potential security breaches in almost all aspects of the container shipping industry. With the sheer volume of maritime traffic, there is serious concern of cargo/passenger ship hijackings and pirate attack, as well as accountability of the millions of shipping containers transported worldwide. Given the overwhelming number of ships and containers, there are many areas of concern regarding the security of U.S. ports.

Cargo containers represent the largest area of concern in terms of security and vulnerability. With an estimated global inventory of over 12 million, the securing, tracking, and inspection of all shipping containers is a difficult task. The largest obstacle to overcome with cargo and port security is cost: the cost of inspecting the containers, and the cost of shipping delays from those inspections. A large container ship has the capacity to carry in excess of 3,000 containers, making inspection impossible without disrupting shipment. More than 6 million cargo containers enter U.S. seaports annually, of which only 2 per cent are physically inspected by Customs.

Terrorists can, and eventually may, exploit the shipping industries deficiencies in cargo security. Potential threats include the smuggling of weapons of mass destruction (WMD), a radiological "dirty" bomb, a conventional explosive device, and transportation of terrorist operatives, as well. Studies have claimed a Hiroshima sized nuclear detonation at a major seaport would kill fifty thousand to one million people. The container shipping system is an attractive outlet for terrorist activities.

It is common knowledge within the industry that security measures of major ports cannot have a significant effect on the movement of goods, thereby allowing exploitation of the system for terrorist use. Container shipping is an amalgam of many different actors: the exporter, the importer, freight forwarder, customs broker, excise inspectors, truckers, railroad workers, dock workers, and the crews of the vessels themselves. Greenberg (2006) states "that whenever and wherever a container is handled during movement represents a potential vulnerability for the security and integrity of the cargo". This produces many different windows of opportunity for terrorist infiltration of containers.

There are other areas of vulnerability that terrorist may infiltrate. The geographical/physical layout of the ports themselves is of concern. The protection and security of the landside perimeter of a port is difficult due to their large size. Ports located in highly urbanized areas allow terrorists a densely populated area in which to hide while infiltrating or escaping the port area at their perimeter. The high volume of trucks entering and exiting port facilities pose a threat to the port, as well as surrounding geographical areas. Exiting trucks may contain WMD or terrorist operatives that are to infiltrate a surrounding metropolitan area, *i.e.*, transporting a chemical explosive device (from the Port of Los Angeles) to a more densely populated area (downtown Los Angeles). Container ships anchored at port facilities are particularly vulnerable to both highjacking and explosive devices as they are stationary targets. Most crews of cargo ships are unarmed, and would be defenseless to an armed attack. The disabling of a ship at port is enough to halt all activity at that port for an extended period of time, especially if the disabled ship is blocking a throughway for other vessels.

The economic impact of such an attack would be disastrous on a global scale. An example of such an economic impact can be drawn from a labour-management dispute that closed ports along the west coast of the United States. These port closures cost the U.S. economy approximately $1 billion per day for the first 5 days, and rose exponentially thereafter. When the International Longshore and Warehouse Union strike closed 29 West Coast ports for 10 days, one study estimated that it cost the United States economy $19.4 billion. Many manufacturing companies of the world employ a just-in-time distribution model, allowing for lower inventory carrying costs and savings from warehouse space. The shipping industry is essential to this method, as its speed and reliability allow new inventory to be shipped and received precisely when it is needed. The adopting of the just-in-time method has dropped business logistics cost from 16.1 per cent of U.S. GDP to 10.1 per cent between 1980 and 2000. Although this method has dropped costs significantly, it has put a stranglehold on security options, as the shipping times of these shipments are exact and cannot afford delays from inspection. Other aspects of economic impact include costs of altering shipping routes away from a disabled port, as well as delays from ports operating over capacity that receive the rerouted ships. Most ports operate at near capacity and can ill afford an attack of this nature.

Although there are many government sponsored agencies involved with port security, the responsibility of providing that security is of state and local governments. Allen (2007) states that "under the protective principle, a state has jurisdiction to prescribe and enforce laws against acts that threaten vital state interests". The protective principle "recognizes that a state may apply its laws to protect vital state interests, such as the state's national security or governmental functions". Some ports may enact their own police forces in addition to city law enforcement.

Federal agencies that are involved with port security include the Coast Guard, U.S. Customs and Border Protection, and the Transportation Security Administration (TSA). These three agencies are now under the jurisdiction of the Department of Homeland Security. The Maritime Administration (MARAD) is also, while the Coast Guard and Customs are the two prominent agencies at ports.

The Coast Guard is responsible for evaluating, boarding, and inspecting commercial ships as they approach U.S. waters, for countering terrorist threats in U.S. ports, and for helping to protect U.S. Navy ships in U.S. ports. CBP's primary responsibility is the inspecting of cargo, including containers that commercial ships bring into U.S. ports. CBP is also responsible for the inspection of ship crews and passengers aboard the vessel. The TSA's focus was initially focused on air transportation, but now has the authority of all modes of transportation. MARAD is a civilian agency that is part of the Department of Transportation. MARAD publishes Maritime Security Reports and national planning guides on port security.

There have been proposals to consolidate federal agencies responsible for border security. The consolidation may offer some long-term benefits, but three challenges may hinder a successful implementation of security enhancing initiatives at the nations ports: standards, funding, and collaboration.

The first challenge involves implementing a set of standards that defines what safeguards a port should have in place. Under the Coast Guard's direction, a set of standards is being developed for all U.S. ports to use in conducting port vulnerability assessments. However, many questions remain about whether the thousands of people who have grown accustomed to working in certain ways at the nation's ports will agree to, and implement, the kinds of changes that a substantially changed environment will require. The second challenge involves determining the amounts needed and sources of funding for the kinds of security improvements that are likely to be required to meet the standards. Florida's experience indicates that security measures are likely to be more expensive than many anticipate, and determining how to pay these costs and how the federal government should participate will present a challenge.

The third challenge is ensuring that there is sufficient cooperation and coordination among the many stakeholders to make the security measures work. Experience to date indicates that this coordination is more difficult than many stakeholders anticipate, and that continued practice and testing will be key in making it work. The September 11 attacks demanded a new initiative be taken in maritime security efforts. The Coast Guard is initializing an approach that will improve the quality and timing of shipping and carrier information so that it may be properly evaluated for terrorist threats. This allows more time for proper recognition of vessels, and will aid in the flow of legitimate shipping vessels. Together with the Navy, the Coast Guard has developed the use of maritime domain awareness, which is essentially the collection of all intelligence gathered from government agencies, and assembled to provide a common operating picture. CBP has initiated new programmes to aid in counter terrorist efforts by creating the Container Security Initiative (CSI) and the Customs Trade Partnership against Terrorism (C-TPAT). The CSI consists of four core elements: Using intelligence and automated information to identify and target containers that pose a risk for terrorism, pre-screening those containers that pose a risk at the port of departure before they arrive at U.S. ports, using detection technology to quickly pre-screen containers that pose a risk, and using smarter, tamper-evident containers. Under C-TPAT, shippers commit to improving the security of their cargo shipments, and in return, they receive a variety of benefits from the government.

Policing

Whilst the threat of terrorism cannot be totally be dismissed the day-to-day operations of port and harbour police more often deals with more mundane issues, such as theft (including pilferage by dock workers), smuggling, illegal immigration; health and safety with regards to hazardous cargoes, safe docking of vessels, and safe operation of vehicles and plant; environmental protection *e.g.* spillages and contaminated bilge water.

PORT STATE CONTROL

Port State Control (PSC) is the inspection of foreign ships in other national ports by PSC officers (inspectors) for the purpose of verifying that the competency of the master and officers on board, and the condition of the ship and its equipment comply with the requirements of international conventions (*e.g.* SOLAS, MARPOL, STCW, etc.) and that the vessel is manned and operated in compliance with applicable international law.

HISTORY

In 1978, a number of European countries agreed in The Hague on a memorandum that agreed to audit whether the labour conditions on board vessels were in accordance with the rules of the ILO. After the Amoco Cadiz sank that year, it was decided to also audit on safety and pollution. To this end, in 1982 the Paris Memorandum of Understanding(Paris MoU) was agreed upon, establishing Port State Control, nowadays 26 European countries and Canada. In practice, this was a reaction to the failure of the flag states - especially flags of convenience that have delegated their task to classification societies - to comply with their survey and certification duties. Following on the foundation built by the Paris MOU, several other regional MOUs have been signed, including the Tokyo MOU (Pacific Ocean), Acuerdo Latino or Acuerdo de Viña del Mar (South and Central America), the Caribbean MOU, the Mediterranean MOU, the Indian Ocean MOU, the Abuja MOU (West and Central Atlantic Africa),the Black Sea MOU, and the Riyadh MOU (Persian Gulf). The United States Coast Guard verifies that all foreign vessels operating in United States waters are in substantial compliance with international conventions, as well as all applicable U.S. laws, regulations and treaties. The U.S. is not a member of any Port State Control MOU.

DETENTION OF SHIP UNDER PORT STATE CONTROL

Under Port State Control (PSC), inspection of ships in port would be taken by Port State Control Officer (PSCO). Annual report of Paris MoU reported a total of 74,713 deficiencies were recorded during port state control inspections in 2007. These deficiencies resulted in 1,250 detentions in the same year. Detention of the ship is the last course of action that a PSCO would take upon finding deficiencies aboard the vessel.

Courses of action a PSCO may impose on a ship with deficiencies (in order of ascending gravity):

1. Deficiencies can be rectified within 14 days for minor infractions
2. Under specific conditions, deficiencies can be rectified when the ship arrives at the next port
3. Deficiencies must be rectified before the ship can depart the port;
4. Detention of the ship

CONTRACT BEING DISCHARGED UNDER DETENTION

Ships taking visit to port are usually under a certain kind of contract, chartered or responsible for carrying goods as a carrier. Detention means the ship and the cargo would not be able to perform the contract according to what is agreed. Ships under detention cannot continue the voyage and arrive at the destination port as stated in the contract in the specific time assigned in the contract. As a result of detention the contract is discharged, and it may or may not be discharged by frustration.

Contract Discharged by Frustration

A contract discharged by frustration is well defined in Taylor v Caldwell, where the contract between Taylor and Caldwell is held frustrated. It is because the concert hall which is hired by Taylor from Caldwell is destroyed without fault of either party and the contract is therefore discharged by frustration.

Discharged by Frustration for Being Out of Control

A voyage contract can be discharged by frustration if the ship is beyond the control of the party involved in the contract. According to Texas Company v. Hogarth Shipping Corp, a voyage charter is carrying out in 1915 while the British government take control of the vessel while the vessel is in British waters. This requisition resulted in another vessel being hired to perform the contract. The court held that the original contract is being frustrated as the original vessel is beyond the control of the party involved.

The case demonstrated the contract can be discharged by frustration while the control of the subject vessel is under control of a third party which has no relation with the contracted parties.

Discharged by Frustration for Extremely Long Time Delay

The contract can be discharged by frustration if the detention lasts long enough for the frustration doctrine to be invoked. In Jackson v Union Marine Insurance Co, the contract is held frustrated. When the vessel went aground and require a time of 8 months to repair the ship, the delay is too long, the cargo can be shipped by another charter in a much shorter time. The length of the delay is long enough to provoked the frustration doctrine.

SELF-INDUCED DETENTION CANNOT DISCHARGE THE CONTRACT THROUGH FRUSTRATION

The contract cannot be discharged by frustration if it is caused by self-induced detention.

Criteria for Detaining a Ship by PSCO

The main criteria for detention is that the ship is deemed unsafe to proceed to sea and that the deficiencies on a ship are considered serious by the inspector. These deficiencies must be rectified before the ship may sail again.

In the annual report of Paris MOU, it stated that the major deficiencies are:

1. Certification of crew
2. Safety
3. Maritime Security
4. Marine Pollution and Environment
5. Working and Living Condition
6. Operational
7. Management

These deficiencies are the most common concern of a PSCO. When these deficiencies are clearly hazardous to safety, health, or the environment, the

PSCO would require the hazard to be rectified before the ship can sail or detain the vessel or even issue a formal prohibition of the ship to operate. As these deficiencies are self-induced by the ship operator or the ship owner, detention under PSC for the reasons listed above is not able to reach a frustration to discharge the contract on the vessel.

SHORT PERIOD OF DETENTION CANNOT DISCHARGE THE CONTRACT THROUGH FRUSTRATION

The contract cannot be discharged by frustration if the time under detention is not long enough to provoked the frustration doctrine.

PSC Requirement Upon Detaining a Ship

The PSC require a ship being detained to remedy the deficiencies which caused the detention. If the deficiencies cannot be remedied in the port of inspection, the port state would allow the ship to proceed to another port under special condition. The ship become free of detention only when all the fee induced by the inspection and detention is paid by the ship-owner.

No Party Wants a Long Detention

Rationally, both the port state and the ship-owner do not want the ship to be detained for a long time. For the port state, the hazard of the ship might affect the condition of the port, and the ship-owner understand the vessel can only make money when it is sailing. Neither party would have the intention to keep the vessel being detained for an extremely long period of time. Therefore, the time of detention is normally not long enough to provoke the detention doctrine to discharge a contract.

DISCHARGE OF CONTRACT UNDER DETENTION IN PSC USUALLY DO NOT FRUSTRATE THE VOYAGE CONTRACT

In conclusion, a voyage contract can be frustrated when: The vessel is beyond the control of the parties in the contract The time delayed is long enough to provoke the frustration doctrine Under PSC, detention is mostly caused by self-induced deficiencies which is neither unforeseeable and unexpected, and the time for detention is not likely being long enough to provoke the frustration doctrine. Therefore, detention of a ship by PSC cannot discharge a voyage contract by frustration.

PORT OPERATOR

A port operator is port authority or company that contracts with the port authority to move cargo through a port at a contracted minimum level of productivity. They may be state-owned (particularly for port authorities) or privately run. The work involves managing the movement of cargo containers between cargo ships, trucks and freight trains and optimizing the flow of goods through customs to minimize the amount of time a ship spends in port. Maintaining efficiency involves managing and upgrading gantry cranes, berths, waterways, roads, storage facilities, communication equipment, computer systems and dockworkers' union contracts. The port operator also manages paperwork, leases, safety and port security.

PORT OPERATIONS SIMULATOR

Fig. Port Operations Simulations are Used to Model and Simulate Conditions at Large Ports, Such as the Port of Miami.

Port operations simulators are applications of simulation technology used to determine the outcomes of potential changes to factors affecting ports, security policies, traffic patterns, port expansion or growth, natural disasters, inclement weather, or terrorist activity.

NISAC PORT OPERATIONS SIMULATOR

The National Infrastructure Simulation Analysis Center, a programme within the Department of Homeland Security, has developed a Port Operations Simulator, which is designed to model, simulate, and analyze the effects on port economic health as a result of potential shipping container and port security policies. There is also a companion programme, the Economic Simulator, which analyzes the long term economic impact of security policies in the port. The simulator was originally designed specifically for ports in Portland, Seattle, and Houston, but it can be modified to apply to other ports as well. The Houston adaptation has built-in scenarios, including loss of electric power, loss of telecommunications, labour disruptions, and major security threats. Users have the ability to direct controls in order to determine the best response and recovery plans to these types of scenarios.

SIMPORT

SimPort is a serious game simulation in which the users must plan and manage a port expansion called the SecondMaasvlakte at the Port of Rotterdam in the Netherlands. Each team in the game is given three laptops and each user is given a role from the options of General Director, Commercial Director, or Director of Infrastructure and Management. The game consists of four one-hour rounds: Round 1 consists of defining strategies and creating an allocation plan; the subsequent rounds each represent ten years of management of the site. The game is targeted primarily at actual Port of Rotterdam staff, but is considered applicable to others in training and education settings.

According to the official web site, the Port of Rotterdam has three aims in the use of this game:

1. Gain better insight into any unforeseen, undesirable and unintentional effects of one or more development strategies and design variations in the medium term (10–30 years) as a result of exogenous uncertainties (economic, market, technological) and due to strategic behaviour of the parties involved.
2. Stimulate holistic and multidisciplinary thinking within the Port of Rotterdam on commercial and technical/infrastructural considerations, interests and choices.
3. Improve the results of negotiations with respect to contracts (customers) and equipment (infrastructure) in the port area.

9

Dry Port: Concept and Practice

As we know, sea port is situated near sea. If the importer or exporter is far away from sea port, it will be an inconvenience to co-ordinate and handle the goods properly. So government has allowed CFS (container freight station) to handle export and import formalities under customs supervision. The cargo will be moved by rail or road from the sea port to CFS.

The exporter can complete customs formalities in CFS and ship the goods without moving cargo to sea port. Likewise, importer can take delivery of cargo near his place after completing procedures at dry port. If the buyer insist for 'on board bill of lading', as a proof of export, the buyer waits to get the shipment reached at sea port and once cargo loaded in to vessel, the on board bill of lading is obtained from shipping line. If the buyer needs only a proof of shipment, the exporter can obtain 'Received for shipment Bill of Lading' from the carrier who is a multi model transporter. A multi model transporter is a carrier who carries goods in two or more modes of transport like road, rail, air, or sea.

A dry port (sometimes inland port) is an inland intermodal terminal directly connected by road or rail to a seaport and operating as a centre for the transshipment of sea cargo to inland destinations. In addition to their role in cargo transshipment, dry ports may also include facilities for storage and consolidation of goods, maintenance for road or rail cargo carriers and customs clearance services. The location of these facilities at a dry port relieves competition for storage and customs space at the seaport itself.

DRY PORT CONCEPT

Dry port concept is a way to improve intermodal transport system's cost-efficiency and environmental friendliness. Dry port concept is a rather recent concept that aims at increasing cost-efficiency and environmental friendliness of transportation system. It has been researched since the late last century, although the most dry port researc is conducted during the last five or ten years.

Roso (2009b, p.308) has defined the dry port concept as:

'The dry port concept is based on a seaport directly connected by rail to inland intermodal terminals, where shippers can leave and/or collect their goods in intermodal loading units as if directly at the seaport. In addition to the transshipment that a conventional inland intermodal terminal provides, services such as storage, consolidation, depot, maintenance of containers and customs clearance are also available at dry ports.'

In the dry port concept majority of freight is transported by rail from seaport to inland intermodal terminals, which are called dry ports and vice versa. Only the final leg of transportation is accomplished by road *i.e.* main transport type of dry port concept is rail. The dry port concept is a way to improve the capacity and cost-efficiency of a transport system; especially seaport's inland access. The dry port concept also improves transport system's environmental friendliness. The concept decreases external costs of the transport system, since railroad is environmentally friendlier transport mode than road. There are also other benefits of the dry port concept such as reduced congestion, noise and accidents at the whole transportation system.

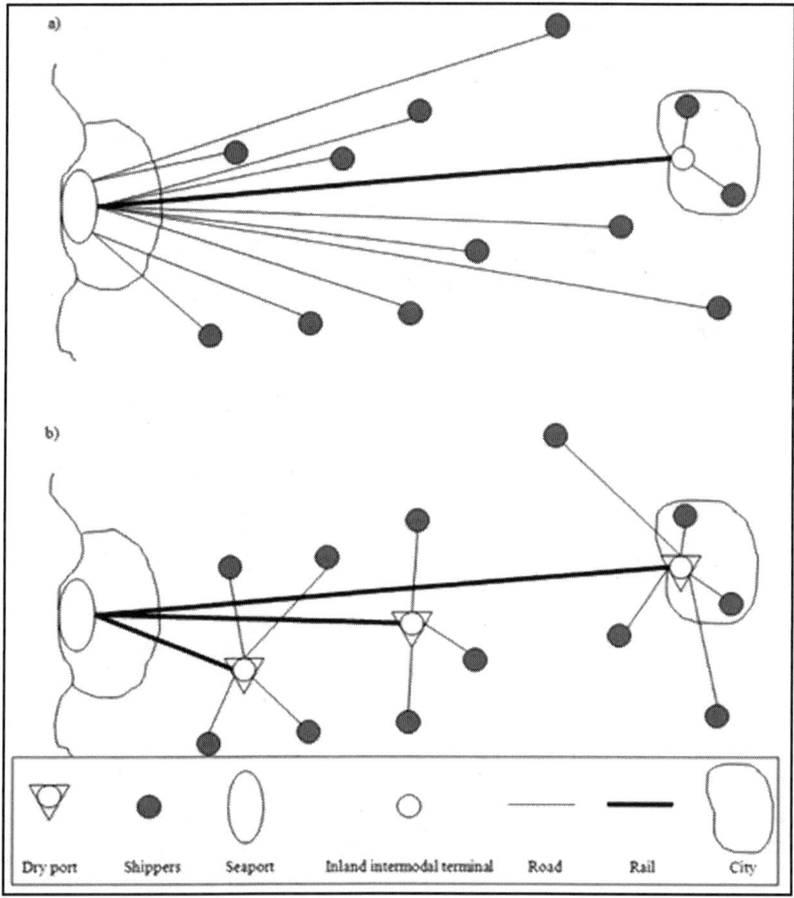

Fig. Comparison of a Conventional Hinterland Transport and an Implemented Dry Port Concept.

The dry port concept is an intermodal transportation system. The dry port itself is an inland intermodal terminal with additional services located inland. It is directly connected by rail to seaport or in some cases two or more seaports. In a dry port concept the maximum possible amount of freight transportation is accomplished by rail between the dry port and the seaport. Only the final leg of the door-to-door transportation is carried out by road transport. In an optimal dry port implementation the whole freight transportation between seaport and dry port is carried out by rail. However, that is usually not possible due to capacity of rail connection. (Roso, 2009a, b)

The dry port offers value-creating services (*e.g.* consolidation, storage, depot, maintenance of containers and customs clearance) to actors which operate within the transportation system *i.e.* there is a whole range of administrative activities that could be moved inland with implementation of a dry port. Outsourcing activities from seaport to dry port relieves seaport, and hence seaport can concentrate in its core tasks and competencies. According to most recent literature, dry ports are categorized into three different categories. They are close dry port, mirrange dry port and distant dry port. The difference in different dry port are the location from seaport. Close dry ports are located approximately 50 kilometers from seaport. Distant dry ports are located 500 km or over from seaport. Midrange dry ports are situated between close and distant dry ports. All the different dry port categories. In addition, a comparison of a conventional hinterland transport and an implemented dry port concept.

Table. Impacts Generated by Dry Ports for the Actors for the Transportation System.

	Distant	Midrange	Close
Seaports	Less congestion Expanded hinterland Interface with hinterland	Less congestion Dedicated trains Depot Interface with hinterland	Less congestion Increased capacity Depot Direct loading ship-train
Seaport cities	Less road congestion Land use opportunities	Less congestion Land use opportunities	Less road congestion Land use opportunities
Rail operators	Economies of scale Gain market share	Day trains Gain market share	Day trains Gain market share
Road operators	Less time in congested roads and terminals	Less time in congested roads and terminals	Less time in congested roads and terminals Avoiding environmental zones
Shippers	Improved seaport access "Environment marketing"	Improved seaport access "Environment marketing"	Improved seaport access
Society	Lower environmental impact Job opportunities Regional development	Lower environmental impact Job opportunities Regional development	Lower environmental impact

From Figure above it can be seen that the distance travelled by road transport shortens, because shippers can use the nearest dry port instead of always carrying freight to seaport city. Also the number of freight connections to seaports lessens. There are 10 road connections and one rail connection to and from seaport in the upper part. With dry port solutions there are only three rail connections to and from seaport. Dry ports relieve the transportation system. Different benefits that dry ports create according.

THE DRY PORT CONCEPT – THEORY AND PRACTICE

Driven by the long-term stimulus of increasing worldwide trade and globalisation, the international freight transport industry thrives on continuous change and development, as reflected in managerial, regulatory and technological innovations within the sector. For container ports, in particular, the dynamic nature of such an environment has been most acutely felt in terms of considerable increases in the size of containerships, the rationalisation of cargo handling operations in pursuit of greater efficiency, the devolution of port governance and the need to reorient the marketing of port services for strategic positioning within inherently competitive supply chains, rather than simply within essentially captive hinterlands.

For the most part, the container port industry itself and the agencies (both governmental and otherwise) which influence its performance, have responded in a most positive and successful manner to this constantly changing environment and the challenges it poses; international trade has continued to expand virtually unabated, despite the many occurrences of congestion and bottlenecks in and around ports that must interfere with the pace of what is otherwise an inexorable trend. It is inevitably the case, however, that the development of transport corridors and associated infrastructure to facilitate access to ports lags behind the response of the ports themselves to the difficulties they are sometimes faced with. In addition, the availability of sufficient container storage space within ports is a matter of significant concern, especially for those ports in traditional locations – close to, or even within, suburban or urban areas.

For facilitating the future evolution of container ports, therefore, it is crucially important that a viable solution is found that overcomes the potential multifaceted conflicts which may exist between the need for capacity expansion, environmental considerations, community restrictions (not least those imposed by the geography of a port) and the continued embedding of freight transport and logistics functions within integrated supply chains. One prospective solution that is emerging more and more often, both in practice and as an identifiable field of research in the relevant literature, is the 'dry port' concept.

As originally conceived, a 'dry port' was defined as an inland terminal to and from which shipping lines could issue their bills of lading, with the concept being initially envisaged as applicable to all types of cargo (UNCTAD, 1982). In both theory and practice, however, the concept has evolved not only to be closely associated with the rapid expansion of containerisation and related changes in cargo handling (UNCTAD, 1991), but also to be applied in a variety of different contexts having the common characteristic of relating simply to 'a place inland that fulfils original port functions'. As a consequence, usage of the term 'dry port' has become rather vague, with numerous different definitions appearing in the literature. In contrast, there does seem to exist a common understanding that the successful implementation of the 'dry port' concept will have the joint effects of lessening congestion, alleviating pressure on storage space and reducing handling operations in port, as well as delivering lower transaction costs to shippers.

Cullinane and Wilmsmeier (2011) have aligned port development and, specifically, the 'dry port' concept to the Product Life Cycle. In their exposition, where a port has evolved to attain the maturity phase, the space required for container storage and other port-related activities approaches, and eventually encounters, either a physical constraint on further expansion, or possibly a competitive constraint from other activities and land use in areas adjacent to the port. It is for this reason that much investment during the maturity stage of the port development cycle focuses on the rationalisation of port services, as well as on process innovations primarily aimed at capacity effects (for example, conversion to more effective storage technologies), particularly as land becomes a scarce commodity and commands premium prices or rents.

The argument continues that ports enter the decline phase of the Product Life Cycle once the point has been reached when the limits to feasible rationalisation, investment and access are reached and it is then that port activity reduces. At this point, the supply of port capacity becomes fixed, since neither further expansion of the physical port area nor any other efficiency gains are possible. With an inevitable increase in the level of congestion within the port, market share is lost to competing ports with overlapping hinterlands and this soon manifests itself as declining throughput and sales volume.

In accordance with this alignment of port development to the Product Life Cycle, the 'dry port' concept can be implemented to extend the product life cycle of a port; specifically, by elongating thematurity phase and deferring a port's entry into a state of decline. In consequence, any required expansion of a port is redirected from the seaward to an inland location (UNCTAD, 1991). Of course, for this to work, the 'dry port' option must be practically feasible, with available and suitable physical site locations and the appropriate means of connectivity to the port itself either already present or potentially implementable.

In the final analysis, however, it is the outcome of an economic appraisal of feasible capacity expansion alternatives which informs the ultimate decision taken. The implementation of the 'dry port' option may, thus, be justified purely and simply on the basis of the private profit motive, even to the extent that it becomes economically desirable before some of the more conventional approaches to capacity expansion are considered. While this might imply that the 'dry port' concept may be more relevant during periods of economic expansion or boom periods than during times of recession or depression, capacity expansion is not the only reason why the dry port concept might be implemented.

There are also benefits in terms of accessing the existing hinterland, expanding a port's hinterland and the capturing of cargo closer to source and/ or further up the supply chain. It is also reasonable to recognise, however, that on some occasions, the economic case may require the receipt of some form of subsidy (for example, large infrastructure grants are sometimes available from public sector authorities and agencies) and that, of course, there also certain sets of circumstances where there exists no realistic level of subsidy that will prompt the adoption of the concept.

In order to provide a suitable forum for disseminating the current state-of-the-art in dry port theory and practice, but also with the intention of gaining a common understanding of the definition of the term 'dry port', the South-East of Scotland Transport Partnership and the Transport Research Institute at Edinburgh Napier University jointly organised the 'Dryport Conference' in Edinburgh in October 2010. The event formed an integral part of a multinational project partly funded under the European Union's Interreg IVb North Sea Region programme and to which the glitterati of the 'dry port' world were invited to deliver their perspective. Although, unsurprisingly, no consensus was arrived at on a definition of the term 'dry port', numerous interesting and illuminating papers were presented on both the theory and practice of 'dry port' implementation. This Special Issue presents just some of the excellent papers to emerge from that conference.

CONTENT OF THE SPECIAL ISSUE

In terms of private sector developments of dry ports in practice, there are perhaps several motives underpinning ECT's investments in dry port projects in Venlo, Duisberg and Willebroek. In the first of the papers in this Special Issue, Veenstra et al (2011) suggest, however, that the major prompt for ECT's actions was the unpredicted and unprecedented surge in demand in all the ports of the Hamburg-Le Havre range in 2004/2005, on the back of a steep rise in Europe's trade with China and the resulting congestion which emerged. This was particularly acutely felt at the port of Rotterdam.

As an innovative response to the problems being faced, the authors describe the implementation within ECT's Rotterdam operation of what is referred to as the 'Extended Gate' concept, whereby a container terminal operator might unilaterally and independently push blocks of containers back into hinterland locations without the involvement of other interested third parties. Although the authors go to some effort to distinguish the 'Extended Gate' concept from the more generic 'dry port' concept, the existing literature on the topic and the contents of most of the papers delivered at the Edinburgh Dryport Conference in 2010 would suggest that the term 'dry port' covers an extensive range of potential configurations, including the specific form of an 'Extended Gate'. As the authors provide evidence for, however, the 'Extended Gate' concept, certainly as applied by ECT, can be considered to lie at one end of the 'dry port' continuum of possible configurations.

Following a detailed description of ECT's implementation of its 'Extended gate' concept, the authors provide us with their vision of hinterland networks into the future. This vision encompasses the selective development of preferred transport and logistics hubs within port hinterlands that share common, though as yet undefined, characteristics; not least of which is their direct connection to one or more seaports. The authors assert that it is the location and connectivity of these hinterland hubs that will define the strategic freight transport network within Europe, with seaports becoming intimately bound to these networks in order to move cargo into the hinterland, primarily by barge and rail. The possible impacts of this emergent strategic freight network within Europe are described as being: a reduction in road freight transport into and out of ports; the loss of value-added logistics activities from seaport locations and the reversion of seaports to focusing solely on port-related activities; the relocation of many ancillary activities back into the hinterland – most critically, customs clearance and; greater externalities (particularly, congestion and pollution) occurring in and around the inland location of hinterland hubs.

The authors go on to finally suggest that whether this vision ultimately comes to fruition will depend upon the future decisions and actions of both logistics practitioners and policymakers. For instance, the efficiency of hinterland terminals will need to be improved to a level expected from terminals in a seaport; local governance structures in hinterland hub locations should be fit for the purpose of meeting the challenges that will arise; administrative systems for freight cargoes should be pushed back further along the supply chain – possibly even to the countries of origin of shipments and; novel business partnerships between terminal operators and multimodal transport service providers will need to be facilitated by changes to the legislative environment so that greater flexibility and integration can be provided within the multimodal hinterland network.

Iannone (2011) presents an analysis of container logistics within the Southern Italian region of Campania. Its main focus lies with import and export container movements between the coastal seaports of Naples and Salerno and the inland dry ports at Nola and Marcianise. The analysis involves the development of a comprehensive and large-scale linear programming model of the spatial network under scrutiny, given the assumption of capacitated transhipment. The objective function is specified as the minimisation of aggregate generalised logistics costs, defined as comprising transportation costs (by both road and rail), terminal handling and storage costs, customs control costs, in-transit inventory holding costs and container leasing costs. As such, this equates to the objectives and perspective of a generic multimodal operator that takes its own decisions with respect to hinterland container transport and other logistics choices.

In converging to an optimum network solution, the model yields simultaneous solutions to: (a) the optimal routing of import and export containers throughout the hinterland, including distinguishing between full and empty containers and identifying appropriate transhipment locations; (b) the associated subsidiary problem of allocating demand to infrastructure nodes within the network (that is seaports, dry ports and other inland nodes); (c) estimating modal split between rail and road flows and; (d) determining whether customs clearance takes place at dry port or seaport locations.

The outcomes from the model point to several shortcomings in port-hinterland container logistics within the Campania region, such as low utilisation rates on existing railway capacity linking seaports and dry ports, high container dwell times at the port of Naples because of customs-induced congestion and the general dearth of modern customs and intermodal procedures. The author suggests, however, that the numerical solution to the model also provides direction as to how to improve upon current performance levels. In particular, he advocates that Campania's existing dry ports should be developed as extended gates of the regional seaport system, following a similar development path to that of Rotterdam as described in the previous paper by Veenstra et al (2011).

Although the author asserts that the potential savings from rerouting customs clearance activities from the region's ports to its dry ports are significant, he also recognises that improved customs facilitation at dry ports will be of little help as long as railway connections between seaports and dry ports remain inadequate.

The outcomes from the model lead the author to conclude that rail and dry port capacity utilisation needs to be improved through the imposition of more streamlined regulation and by better organisation and administration, all of which should be supported by logistics marketing initiatives that disseminate the improvements achieved. All of these recommendations clearly have implications for political leaders in the region. In addition, the answer to the question of how they are to be implemented, if at all, will depend upon the nature of the existing governance structure underpinning logistics provision within the Campania region and whether the appropriate incentives exist to prompt the taking of such decisions by either the public or private sector players. What is predictable, however, is that any improvement in capacity utilisation will obviously mean a reduction in aggregate logistics costs, but will also bring with it associated benefits such as the mitigation of the environmental impact of logistics in the region and increased local value-added and employment.

There is ample and obvious evidence that China's container ports have developed dramatically in the past two decades as a response to rapidly increasing demand for Chinese exports. However, inland transport and other logistics costs are high and there exists significant pressure, as well as the political will, to improve matters so that the economic benefits of China's container trade are extended to all parts of the country, not just the areas in and around the nation's major ports. There are also obvious implications for both national and port competiveness. As such, China is proving to be a dynamic and fertile arena for the implementation of the dry port concept where, as attested to in the paper by Beresford et al (2011), they are used primarily as 'extended gates' through which flows can be better managed (Roso and Lumsden, 2010).

On the basis of considerable evidence collected through a variety of different means, Beresford et al (2011) classify existing dry port developments in China into three spatial categories – 'Seaport-based', 'City-based' and 'Border-based' and go on to provide detailed case studies of specific dry port locations within China that are representative of each of the three categories. As might be expected, the authors' analysis reveals that different dry ports in China are at different stages of development, as determined by their core functions and institutional expectations.

Perhaps what is more surprising is that, whatever the stage of their development, this paper is generally critical of the dry port concept as implemented in China, with the case study analysis revealing numerous problems and inefficiencies within the sector.

The most damning assertion is that, in many cases, shippers are actually very reluctant to use dry ports; suggesting, therefore, that China's dry port operations are simply failing to fulfil the role or potential for which they were established.

As an outcome of their case-study analysis, the authors attribute the ultimate raison d'être for this performance malaise on the inadequacy of the governance and regulatory framework within which China's dry ports have to operate. More specifically, they are critical of the current institutional arrangements whereby: (a) responsibility for planning, operating and regulating inland intermodal transport systems is fragmented between three central government ministries, each of which operates independently and has a different role and priorities and; (b) local government has considerable autonomy to interpret central government policy decisions according to local need.

The authors conclude that, given the current variations in institutional structures and the way that they operate in practice, central government intervention has become necessary in order to systematise the policy framework within which dry ports are operated and developed and to implement universally applied standards in governance. They envisage this involving the establishment of an overarching coordinating and regulatory institution or body and the development of an associated comprehensive regulatory framework for dry port development.

All of which is predicated, of course, upon the development of a precise, easily interpreted and legally recognised standard definition of what constitutes a 'dry port'; one of the fundamental problems alluded to in an earlier part of this introduction.

Brazil, another of the world's fastest developing economies. Similar to the Chinese context addressed, Padilha and Ng (2011) suggest that it is also the case in Brazil that the role of dry ports goes far beyond simply providing a route to greater port competitiveness by improving hinterland access. In support of the work of Do et al (2011), Ng and Tongzon (2010) and UNESCAP (2006), they point out that the political and economic significance of dry ports to the promotion of regional integration and development is also of critical importance within the context of developing economies.

Setting the scene with a review of port development theory and basing their analysis on archival research and in-depth interviews with key stakeholders, Padilha and Ng (2011) analyse the spatial evolution of dry ports in the state of Sao Paulo. Their specific focus rests with relating and linking the current spatial configuration of the state's dry ports to the parallel evolution of the major port of Santos. Their pivotal finding is that the spatial pattern of port development implied by accepted theory may vary significantly from the practice in Brazil and, by imputation, in other developing countries; where key phases in the established evolution of ports may be observed to be poorly developed and/or to occur late, out of sequence or even not at all. In the specific case of Brazil, the authors identify the relative absence of intermodal systems (particularly involving the use of rail), the continuous concentration of freight flows within ports (particularly at Santos) and the de-concentration of flows through inland freight facilities (particularly dry ports) as manifestations of this phenomenon.

In seeking to explain their fundamental finding that port evolution within the state of Sao Paulo has deviated from what might be expected from established theory, Padilha and Ng (2011) argue that institutional inefficiencies are pervasive within the developing economy context and have led to this distortion of expected outcomes in the case of Brazil. As such, they reaffirm the conclusions of the preceding paper by Beresford et al (2011) and the previous work of Garnwaet al (2009), Ng and Cetin (2011), Ng and Tongzon (2010) and Ng and Gujar (2009), all of which suggest that institutional factors are pivotal to dry port performance within the developing economy context. In order to eliminate the institutional inefficiencies which exist within the state of Sao Paulo, the authors advocate: (a) the implementation of integrated planning – though do not go so far as to suggest that this should be centralised; (b) greater clarity in regulations to incentivise infrastructure investment and; (c) new legislation to encourage collaboration between ports and dry ports and the efficient use of inland logistics infrastructure in order to reap both economic and environmental benefits. At the same time, it is explicitly acknowledged that, particularly within the developing economy context, such key changes in policy are likely to prove difficult to implement (if not impossible) in the face of what the authors themselves refer to as 'entrenched vested interests and political forces'.

Again addressing the particular problems of a rapidly developing economy, the focus of the final paper in this Special Issue is dry ports in India, by Haralambides and Gujar (2011). This geo-political context, however, is very different from that which applied to the two previous studies. In India, a recent deregulatory shift in government policy has resulted in what was intended – the positive promotion of private sector participation in dry ports and the railway sector. This has prompted the injection of significant new investment capital into the dry port sector, the immediate short-term effect of which has been a surfeit of surplus supply over and above what is demanded in the market. This is a situation that, of course, places considerable pressure on prices in what is a highly competitive market and, ultimately, this phenomenon will become reflected in the bottom lines of the organisations involved.

The current disequilibrium in the market is clearly unsustainable and, inevitably, the market mechanism will come into play to ensure a resolution is arrived at. The detailed evolution of the marketplace in terms of which of the current participants will actually continue to survive into the long-term future and with what market share, will be largely a function of the relative operational efficiency of each of the market players. The authors suggest that the particular nature of production and operations associated with any industry will relate very closely to the definition of efficiency which should be applied and that, in the specific case of dry port operations, this should cater equally for intangible factors as it does for the more obvious tangible aspects. Thus, they advocate that the inevitable, but undesirable, 'negative output' of carbon emissions from the productive activities of dry ports should also be taken into consideration in any evaluation of efficiency within the sector; a view supported in the research undertaken by Growitsch and Wetzel (2009).

In pursuit of this objective, the paper describes the empirical estimation of the efficiency of dry ports in the North Capital Region of India using data covering the period 2006–2009.

The widely accepted technique of Data Envelopment Analysis is chosen as the preferred approach to the empirical application but, in line with the recommendation ofDyckhoff and Allen (2001), is further refined to account for the associated complexity of the 'negative output' of carbon emissions from the sample of dry ports. As the authors themselves suggest, therefore, the efficiency scores that are derived really represent some measure of social or eco-efficiency.

On the basis of their empirical analysis and in stark contrast to conventional approaches, the authors conclude that their proposed eco-model provides decision makers with unequivocal and transparent information on the efficiency effects of carbon emissions and allows them to assess the direct efficiency effect of ameliorative actions on emissions. As environmental impacts gain greater emphasis in logistics decisions, it is certainly the case that this capability is becoming increasingly important.

This is particularly the case as greater recognition is given to the potential of 'green-gold' solutions for the industry, whereby actions taken (and investments made) to reduce environmental damage can exert a positive influence on sales figures, especially through the appropriate marketing of 'green credentials'. As a final aside on this issue, from a methodological perspective, establishing and dealing with any prospective functional relationship which may be hypothesised to exist between both desirable and undesirable outputs (in any dynamic context for efficiency estimation) brings its own modelling challenges that, while not insurmountable, can hardly be described as trivial.

A second major conclusion of the paper is that the pursuit of technical efficiency cannot be unconstrained and that environmental impacts and consequences also need to be taken into consideration within India's dry port operations. There are important implications of this for the governance of the sector.

The authors propose, for example, that given their fundamentally social, rather than commercial, objectives, the public sector dry port operators in India should be leading on environmental initiatives. However, the government has not provided them with any such remit, objectives or incentives. Since they are competing head-to-head with private sector dry ports that are intent on profit maximisation and cost minimisation, it is difficult to envisage how this might even be attempted in the absence of any greater stringency in environmental regulation and while national economic development through a strategy of export-led growth remains a priority.

INLAND PORT

Fig. Duisburg Inner Harbour, the World's Largest Inland Port.

The term inland port is used in two different but related ways to mean either a port on an inland waterway or an inland site carrying out some functions of a seaport.

AS A PORT ON AN INLAND WATERWAY

Fig. Port of Bratislava at Night.

An inland port in the wide sense, as used in common speech, is simply a port on an inland waterway such as a river, lake or canal. TheUnited States Army Corps of Engineers publishes a list of such locations and for this purpose states that "inland ports" are ports that are located on rivers and do not handle deep draft ship traffic. The list includes familiar ports such as St. Louis, Cincinnati, Pittsburgh, Kansas City, and Memphis. A network of inland waterways including ports is developed also in Europe (France, Germany, Poland, Russia, UK, Netherlands, Belgium), China and Brazil.

AS AN INLAND SITE WITH SEAPORT FUNCTION

The term inland port is also used in a narrow sense in the field of transportation systems to mean a rather more specialized facility that has come about with the advent of the intermodal container (standardized shipping container) in international transport. Rather than goods being loaded and unloaded in such ports, shipping containers can just be transferred between ship and road vehicle or ship andtrain. The container may be transferred again between road and rail elsewhere and the goods are only loaded or unloaded at their point of origin or final destination.

Shipping containers allow some functions traditionally carried out at a seaport to be moved elsewhere. Examples are the functions of receiving, processing through customs, inspecting, sorting, and consolidating containers going to the same overseas port. Container transfer at the seaport can be sped up and container handling space can be reduced by transferring functions to an inland site away from the port and coast.

Distribution may also be made more efficient by setting up the link between inland site and seaport as, say, a high-capacity rail link with a lower unit cost than sending containers individually by road. The containers are still collected from their origins or distributed to their ultimate destinations by road with the transfer happening at the inland site.

An inland port is just such an inland site linked to a seaport. This kind of inland port does not require a waterway. Key features of an inland port are the transfer of containers between different modes of transportation (intermodal transfer) and the processing of international trade. This differentiates an inland port from a container depot or transport hub.

The term inland port may also be used for a similar model of a site linked to an airport or land border crossing rather than a seaport. The definition of inland port in the jargon of the transportation and logistics industries is: An inland port is a physical site located away from traditional land, air and coastal borders with the vision to facilitate and process international trade through strategic investment in multi-modal transportation assets and by promoting value-added services as goods move through the supply chain. Inland ports may also be referred to as dry ports or intermodal hubs.

Fig. Port of Montreal, Canada's Second Busiest Port.

Advantages of an Inland Port

Fig. North River Port in Moscow.

An inland port can speed the flow of cargo between ships and major land transportation networks, creating a more central distribution point. Inland ports can improve the movement of imports and exports, moving the time-consuming sorting and processing of containers inland, away from congested seaports.

A NEW ROLE FOR INLAND TERMINALS

In many places around the world bimodal and trimodal inland terminals have become an intrinsic part of the transport system, particularly in gateway regions having a high reliance on trade. Transport development is gradually shifting inland after a phase that focused on the development of port terminals and maritime shipping networks. The complexity of modern freight distribution, the increased focus on intermodal and co-modal transport solutions and capacity issues appear to be the main drivers behind a renewed focus on hinterland logistics. While trucking tends to be sufficient in the initial phase of the development of inland freight distribution systems, at some level of activity, diminishing returns such as congestion, energy consumption and empty movements become strong incentives to consider the setting of inland terminals as the next step in regional freight planning. Also the massification of flows in networks, through a concentration of cargo on a limited set of ports of call and associated trunk lines to the hinterland, have created the right conditions for nodes to appear along and at the end of these trunk lines.

The evolution of inland freight distribution can be seen as a cycle in the ongoing developments of containerization and intermodal transportation. The geographical characteristics linked with modal availability, capacity and reliability of regional inland access have an important role to play in shaping this development. As maritime shipping networks and port terminal activities become better integrated, particularly through the symbiotic relationship between maritime shipping and port operations, the focus shifted on inland transportation and the inland terminal as a fundamental component of this strategy. Thus, after a phase that relied on the development of port terminals and maritime shipping networks, the integration of maritime and inland freight distribution systems has favored the setting of inland ports.

Inland port. A rail or a barge terminal that is linked to a maritime terminal with regular inland transport services. An inland port has a level of integration with the maritime terminal and supports a more efficient access to the inland market both for inbound and outbound traffic. This implies an array of related logistical activities linked with the terminal, such as distribution centers, depots for containers and chassis, warehouses and logistical service providers.

Since the inland terminal is essentially an extension of some port activities inland, the term "dry port" has gained acceptance. However, using this term to define an inland terminal is subject to debate since many inland terminals are in fact 'wet' given their direct access to inland waterway systems. Moreover, the inland location can effectively be a port if a barge service is concerned, but fundamentally cannot be considered a port if it involves a rail terminal or more simply truck depots. Thus, there seems to be no consensus on the terminology resulting in a wide range of terms including dry ports, inland terminals, inland ports, inland hubs, inland logistics centers, inland freight villages, etc. The reason for this lies in the multiple shapes, functions and network positions these nodes can have. A similar issue applies with the inclusion of airport terminals, mainly the freight component, as an element of an inland port. A whole array of transport terminal infrastructures is therefore often presented as a dry port. Therefore, the concept of inland port is polymorphic, implying that it can have different meaning depending on its location, connectivity, role and function. *Regardless of the terminology used, three fundamental characteristics are related to an inland node:*

- An intermodal terminal, either rail or barge that has been built or expanded.
- A connection with a port terminal through rail, barge or truck services, often through a high capacity corridor.
- An array of logistical activities that support and organize the freight transited, often co-located with the intermodal terminal.

The functional specialization of inland terminals has been linked with cluster formation of logistical activities. Inland terminals in many cases have witnessed a clustering of logistics sites in the vicinity, leading to a process of logistics polarization and the creation of logistic zones. They have become excellent locations for consolidating a range of ancillary activities and logistics companies. In recent years, the dynamics in logistics networks have created the right conditions for a large-scale development of such logistics zones.

DRIVING FORCES

Each inland port remains the outcome of the considerations of a transport geography pertaining to modal availability and efficiency, market function and intensity as well as the regulatory framework and governance. Their emergence underlines some deficiency in conventional inland freight distribution that needed to be mitigated. This mitigation includes:

- Input costs. Land and labour costs are among the most significant logistics costs. Many deep sea terminal facilities have limited land available for expansion, implying higher land costs, while inland locations tend to have land available. Many port areas are also facing higher labour costs since they are located within large metropolitan areas. High input costs favors the intensification of activities at the main terminal and the search of lower value locations supporting less intensive freight activities.
- Capacity and congestion. Capacity issues appear to be the main driver of inland port development since a system of inland terminals increases the intermodal capacity of inland freight distribution. While trucking tends to be sufficient in the initial phase of the development of inland freight distribution systems, at some level of activity, diminishing returns such as congestion, energy and empty movements become strong incentives to consider the setting of inland terminals as the next step in regional freight planning.
- Hinterland market. Through long distance transport corridors, inland ports confer a higher level of accessibility because of lower distribution costs and improved capacity. These high-capacity inland transport corridors allow ports to penetrate the local hinterland of competing ports and thus to extend their cargo base. In such a setting, the inland port becomes a commercial and trade development tools that jointly increase imports, exports and intermodal terminal use. It is thus better placed to support regional and international trade patterns.
- Supply chain management. An inland port is a location actively integrated within supply chain management practices, particularly in view of containerization. It is reflective of the level of vertical

integration between the port and hinterland actors such as transport companies and supply chain managers. This takes many forms such as the agglomeration of freight distribution centers, custom clearance, container depots and logistical capabilities. The inland terminal can also become a buffer in supply chains, acting as a temporary warehousing facility.

- Policy and regulations. Economic development strategies, land use policy, and financial incentives by port authorities and economic development agencies can lead to the development of inland ports. This can be supported by policies related to foreign trade zones and customs procedures, enabling a transfer of functions that were previously taking place at the port to an inland location. This is commonly as significant hurdle since many national trade regulations only enables containers to be cleared for imports or exports at a port. A similar trend applies to cargo safety and security procedures where the inland port becomes a component of a chain of cargo integrity.

The geographical characteristics linked with modal availability and the capacity of regional inland access have an important role to play in shaping the emergence and development of inland ports. Each inland market has its own potential requiring different transport services. Thus, there is no single strategy for an inland port in terms of modal preferences as the regional effect remains fundamental. In developed countries, namely North America and Europe, which tended to be at the receiving end of many containerized supply chains, a number of inland ports have been developed with a focus on inbound logistics.

The setting of global supply chains and the strategy of Pacific Asian countries around the export-oriented paradigm have been powerful forces shaping contemporary freight distribution. Indirectly, this has forced players in the freight transport industry (shipping companies, terminal operators, logistics providers) to examine supply chains as a whole and to identify legs where capacity and reliability were an issue. Once maritime shipping networks and port terminal activities have been better integrated, particularly through the symbiotic relationship between maritime shipping and port operations, inland transportation became the obvious focus and the inland terminal a fundamental component of this strategy. This initially took place in developed countries, namely North America and Europe, which tended to be at the receiving end of many containerized supply chains. The focus has also shifted to considering inland terminals for the early stages of global supply chains (outbound logistics), namely in countries having a marked export-oriented function.

Inland terminals have evolved from simple intermodal locations to their incorporation within logistic zones. Rail terminals in particular have historically been locations from which specific market coverage was achieved.

Containerization has impacted this coverage through the selection of terminals that were servicing a wider market area. This spatial change also came with a functional change as intermodal terminals began to experience a specialization of roles based on their geographical location but also based on their 'location' within supply chains.

FUNCTIONS WITHIN TRANSPORT CHAINS

A functional and added value hierarchy has emerged for inland terminals as they try to replicate inland several services performed at a port terminal, namely customs clearance, container storage, cargo consolidation and deconsolidation. In many instances, freight transport terminals fit within a hierarchy with a functionally integrated inland transport system of gateways and their corridors, where they service three major functions:

- Satellite terminals. They tend to be close to a port facility, but mainly at the periphery of its metropolitan area (often less than 100 km), since they mainly assume a service function to the seaport facilities. They accommodate additional traffic and serves functions that either have become too expensive at the port such as warehousing and empty container depots or are less bound to a location near a deep sea quay. A number of satellite terminals only have a transport function transshipping cargo from rail/barge to trucks and vice versa, as is the case for the 'container transferium' concept of the port of Rotterdam or the Gateway Access Point (GAP) concept in Belgium. Satellite terminals can also serve as load centers for local or regional markets, particularly if economic density is high, in which case they form a multi-terminal cluster with the main port they are connected to through regular rail or barge shuttle services. For gateways having a strong import component, a satellite terminal can also serve a significant transloading function where the contents of maritime containers are transloaded into domestic containers or truckloads.
- Freight distribution clusters (load centers). A major intermodal facility - load center - granting access to well defined regional markets that include production and consumption functions. It commonly corresponds to a metropolitan area where a variety of terminals serve concomitantly intermodal, warehousing, distribution and logistics functions. These tend to take place in logistics parks and free trade zones (or foreign trade zones). The inland terminal is thus the point of collection or distribution of a regional market. The more extensive and diversified the market, the more important is the load center. If the load center has a good intermediary location, such as being along a major rail corridor, then freight distribution activities servicing an extended market will be present.

- Transshipment facilities. Link large systems of freight circulation either through the same mode (*e.g.* rail-to-rail) or through intermodalism (rail-to-truck, or even rail-to-barge). In the later case, the inland terminal assumes the role of a load center. The origin or the destination of the freight handled is outside the terminal's market area, a function similar to that of transshipment hubs in maritime shipping networks. Such transshipment terminals are often found near country borders in view of combining administrative processes linked to cross border traffic to value-added logistics activities. Although this function remains marginal in most parts of the world, ongoing developments in inland freight distribution, where the scale and scope of intermodal services are increasing, are indicative that transshipment services are bound to become more prominent.

These functions are not exclusive, implying that inland terminals can service several functions at once. Therefore, there is no single model for an inland port. For inbound or outbound freight flows, the inland terminal is the first tier of a functional hierarchy that defines its fundamental (activities it directly services) and extended (activities it indirectly services) hinterlands. *Considering the potential mix of the functions of inland ports, five major criteria insure that they fulfill efficiently their role as an interface between global and regional freight distribution systems:*

- Site and situation. Like any transport facility of significance, an inland port requires an appropriate site with good access to the rail or the barge terminal as well as available land for development. Access to an area of significant economic density, such as large population base, is of importance since it will be linked to the level of import and export activities handled by the inland port. Transportation remains the most significant logistics cost, underlining the importance of an accessible location. Several inland ports also have an airport in proximity which can help support a variety of freight activities.
- Massification. The hinterland massification opportunities offered by inland ports are associated with lower transport costs and a better accessibility. It takes place over two interdependent dimensions. The first concern the massification of flows between the port terminal and the inland port through a high capacity corridor. Intermodal rail and barge services represent the dominant means over which this process is achieved. The second relates to the consolidation and deconsolidation of cargo flows depending if it concerns inbound or outbound logistics.
- Reconciling cargo flows. Since most long distance trade (and some domestic) is supported by containerization, there are numerous instances where a regional market imports more than it exports (or

vice-versa). Under such circumstances, an inland port must provide the physical and logistical capabilities to insure that empty containers are repositioned efficiently to other markets if local cargo cannot be found. This can take the form of empty container depots and arrangements with freight forwarders to have slots available for repositioning. Whether there are imbalances in container flows or not, an inland port must insure that the inbound and outbound flows are reconciled as quickly as possible. A common way involves a cargo rotation from imports activities where containers are emptied to exports activities where containers are filled with goods. For container owners, let them be maritime shipping or leasing companies, a rapid turnover of their assets is fundamental and will secure a continuous usage of the inland port. Effective repositioning and cargo rotations strategies insure higher revenue for both the container owners and the inland port operators.

- Trade and transactional facilitation. An inland port can also be a fundamental structure promoting both the import and export sectors of a region, particularly for smaller businesses unable to achieve economies of scale on their own. Through these, new market opportunities become possible as both imports and exports are cheaper. The setting of a Foreign Trade Zone (FTZ) is also an option to be considered as a trade facilitation strategy. The functional pairing of inland ports is a transactional strategy where an inland port is activity seeking agreements with other inland ports so that reciprocal supply chains are established or reinforced.
- Governance. The way an inland port is owned and operated is indicative of its potential to identify new market opportunities and invest accordingly. In many cases, the commitment of a large private investor such as a terminal operator or a real estate developer can be perceived as a risk mitigation strategy in addition to provide expertise in the development of facilities and related activities. Sections of an inland port can be shared facilities (*e.g.* distribution centers) so that smaller players can get involved by renting space and equipment. This also applies to the appropriate strategies related to each stage in the life cycle of an inland terminal from its construction to its maturity where its potential has essentially been taped off.

THE REGIONAL IMPACTS OF INLAND PORTS

Regional issues, namely how inland ports interact with their regional markets, remain fundamental as it defines their modal characteristics, their regulatory framework and their commercial opportunities. Depending on the geographical setting and the structure, governance and ownership of inland transport systems, inland terminals have different levels of development and integration with port terminals. They are part of a port regionalization strategy supporting a more extensive hinterland.

It is in Western Europe that the setting of inland terminals is the most advanced with a close integration of port terminals with rail shuttles and barge services. Rail-based dry ports are found throughout Europe, often linked to the development of logistics zones. Depending on the European country considered, these logistics zones are known under different names: 'platformes logistiques' in France, the Güterverkehrszentren (GVZ) in Germany, Interporti in Italy, Freight Villages in the UK, Transport Centres in Denmark, and Zonas de Actividades Logisticas (ZAL) in Spain. The rail liberalization process in Europe is supporting the development of real pan-European rail services on a one-stop shop basis. All over Europe, new entrants are emerging while some large former national railway companies have joined forces. Rail terminals in Europe are mostly built and operated by large railway ventures. The largest rail facilities have bundles of up to 10 rail tracks with lengths of maximum 800m per track. Rail hubs are typically equipped to allow simultaneous batch exchanges (direct transshipment) through the use of rail-mounted gantry cranes that stretch over the rail bundles.

In northwest Europe, barge transport is taking up a more prominent role in dealing with gateway traffic. Barge container transport has its origins in transport between Antwerp, Rotterdam and the Rhine basin, and in the last decade it has also developed greatly along the north-south axis between the Benelux and northern France. Antwerp and Rotterdam together handled nearly 5 million TEU of inland barge traffic in 2010 or about 95 per cent of total European container transport by barge. Promising barging developments are also found on the Seine between Le Havre and the Paris region, in the Rhône/Seine basin between Marseille, Lyon and Dijon, on the Elbe and the Weser in Northern Germany and on the Danube River out of the port of Constantza. Barge services have also been initiated on the Po River connecting the Port of Venice with Mantua and Cremona near Milan.

European integration processes have permitted the setting of more natural (commercially based) hinterlands that did not exist before. Since a good share of the European market is inland, a growth in international trade required the setting of intermediary locations inland to help accommodate larger flows between ports and their hinterland. A large concentration of inland terminals can be found around the Rhine/Scheldt delta, which is Europe's most important gateway region with a total container throughput of 22.2 million TEU in 2010, and where the function of satellite terminals is prominent. Almost every European port has an inland terminal strategy as a way to secure hinterland traffic.

There have been large inland terminals in North America since the development of the continental railway system in the late 19th century. Their setting was a natural process where inland terminals corresponded to large inland market areas, commonly around metropolitan areas commanding a regional manufacturing base and distribution system. Although exports were significant, particularly for agricultural goods, this system of inland terminals was mostly for domestic freight distribution. With globalization and intermodalism two main categories of inland terminals have emerged in North America.

The first is related to ocean trade where inland terminals are an extension of a maritime terminal located in one of the three major ranges (Atlantic, Gulf and Pacific) either as satellite terminals and more commonly as inland load centers (*e.g.* Chicago or Mexico). The second category concerns inland terminals mainly connected to NAFTA trade that can act as custom pre-clearance centers. Kansas City can be considered the most advanced inland port initiative in North America as it combines intermodal rail facilities from four different rail operators, foreign trade zones and logistics parks at various locations through the metropolitan area. There is even the world's largest underground warehousing facility, Subtropolis, where temperature stable space can be leased. Like Chicago, the city can essentially be perceived as a terminal.Several recent logistic zones projects in North America are capitalizing on the planning and setting of a new intermodal rail terminal done concomitantly with a logistics zone project. This co-location partnership fundamentally acts as a filter for the commercial potential of the project as both actors must make the decision to go ahead with their respective capital investment in terminal facilities and commercial real estate. Compared to Europe, North American dry ports tend to be larger, but covering a much more substantial market area.

For Asia, inland terminals are almost unknown, so they can be considered to be in their infancy. Geographical characteristics, namely coastal population concentrations, and export oriented development strategies have not been prone to the setting of inland terminals. Several container depots have appeared inland as a way to improve the availability of export containers within manufacturing clusters (*e.g.* South Korea, Thailand, India), but containers are mainly carried by truck.

It is in the case of China that resides the largest potential for the emergence of a network of inland terminals, with three main types emerging:

- The first are satellite facilities in the vicinity of port terminals. They assume the conventional role of accommodating activities decongesting port operations, such as container deports, as well as performing customs clearance.
- The second type concerns inland facilities located at major metropolitan areas to provide better connectivity to port terminals

along the coast as well as to support the logistics of a growing internal consumption market. Significant dry port development is taking place on the Yangtze river all the way up to the upper stretches near Chongqing, some 2,400 km upstream from Shanghai. Intermodal rail development faces the challenge of the strong focus of the existing rail network on passengers and dry bulk commodities. As the Chinese economy moves towards a more extensive internal market intermodal rail and barge traffic will increase, and so the usage of inland ports.

- The third type are border facilities that play the function of custom clearance, consolidation and deconsolidation of cargo as well as emerging trans-modal functions of linking different systems or circulation. The setting of Asia-Europe rail connections may promote this function.

Another system of inland terminals is likely to emerge in Southeast Asia, particularly along the Mekong. In light of the North American and European experiences, the question remains about how Pacific Asia can develop its own inland port strategy and regionalism. The unique geographical characteristics of the region are likely to rely much on the satellite terminal concept and inland load centers in relative proximity. For this context, the European example is more suitable. However, the setting of long distance intermodal rail corridors within China and through Central Asia is prone to the development of the inland load center system common in North America.

FUTURE PROSPECTS

The setting of dry ports (inland ports) have been a dominant paradigm in the development of hinterland transportation as the growth of maritime transportation and its economies of scale have placed pressures on the inland segment of freight distribution. The prospects for inland ports remain positive with large continental markets like North America and Europe relying on a network of satellite terminals and load centers as a fundamental structure to support hinterland freight movements, particularly their massification. This entailed the emergence of extended gates and with them extended forms of supply chain management in which inland terminals play an active role. As congestion increases, inland terminals will be even more important in maintaining efficient commodity chains.

It can also be expected that resources will play a greater role within containerized trade with inland terminals, again underlining unique regional characteristics. This implies a set of repositioning strategies where inland terminals play a fundamental role either to improve the efficiency of this repositioning, by providing better cargo rotation opportunities, or by acting as an agent that can help promote containerized exports. Inland ports will take part of the ongoing intermodal integration between ports and their hinterland through long distance rail and barge corridors. They are likely to be more important elements within supply chains, particularly through their role of buffer where containerized consignments can be cheaply stored, waiting to be forwarded to their final destinations.

Like several stages in intermodal transport development, such as in port infrastructure, there is a potential of overinvestment, duplication and redundancy as many inland locations would like to claim a stake in global value chains. This appears to be the case in Western Europe where an abundance of inland terminals, particularly within the Rhine / Scheldt delta, is indicative of an over competitive environment and the waste of resources it implies.

In North America, because of a different ownership and governance structure, the setting of an inland port, at least the intermodal terminal component, is mostly in the hands of rail operators. Each decision thus takes place with much more consideration being placed on market potential as well as the overall impact on their network structure. The decision of a rail company to build a new terminal or to expand existing facilities commonly marks the moment where regional stakeholders, from real estate developers to logistics service providers, readjust their strategies. In some instances, local governments will come with inland port strategies adjusting to existing commercial decisions in the hope to create multiplying effects.

The development of dry ports around the world has clearly underlined an emerging functional relation of port terminals and their hinterland. Based upon their regional setting, dry ports assume a variety of functions with co-location with logistical zones a dominant development paradigm. While the interest in dry ports has increased we have to be aware that no two dry ports are the same. Each dry port is confronted with a local/regional economic, geographical and regulatory setting which not only define the functions taken up by the dry port, but its relations vis-à-vis seaports. Best practices can only be applied successfully if one takes into account the relative uniqueness of each dry port setting.

Bibliography

Alan Rushton, Phil Croucher and Peter Baker: *The Handbook of Logistics and Distribution Management*, Viva Books, Delhi, 2010.

Alan Rushton, Phil Croucher and Peter Baker: *The Handbook of Logistics and Distribution Management*, Kogan Page India, 2007.

Alpana Bhatnagar: *Retailing Logistics and Fresh Food Packaging: Managing Change in the Supply Chain*, Surendra Publication, Delhi, 2010.

B. Khetrapal: *Logistics and Supply : Chain Management*, Alfa Publication, Delhi, 2009.

Baldev Raj Nayar: *The State and Market in India's Shipping : Nationalism, Globalization and Marginalization*, Manohar Publication, Delhi, 1996.

Dinesh Kumar Popli: *Research and Analysis in Logistics Management*, Cyber Tech Publication, Delhi, 2012.

Dinesh Tomar: *Export Management*, Vista International Publication, Delhi, 2008.

Dyckhoff: *Supply Chain Management and Reverse Logistics*, Springer, India, 2003.

FRAZELLE: *Supply Chain Strategy: The Logistics of Supply Chain Management*, Tata McGraw-Hill, Delhi, 2003.

John Fernie and Leigh Sparks: *Logistics and Retail Management*, Viva Books, Delhi, 2010.

Justin Paul and Rajiv Aserkar: *Export Import Management*, Oxford University Press, Delhi, 2008.

La. Na. Swamy: *Some Aspects of South Indian Shipping*, Bharatiya Kala Prakashan, Delhi, 2012.

M.A. Shewan: *Export Management*, Sonali Publication, Delhi, 2008.

P.P. Singh: *Logistics Strategy Management*, ALP Books, Delhi, 2011.

P.S. Senguttuvan: *Fundamentals of Air Transport Management*, Excel Books, Delhi, 2006.

Prashant Chaturvedi: *Shipping Laws*, Global India Publications, Delhi, 2011.

Rameshwar Prasad: *The Army Logistics and War Equipments*, Cyber Tech Publications, Delhi, 2011.

S K Sinha: *Logistics and Supply Chain Management*, Shree Publication, Delhi, 2007.

S. Anthony Raj and S. Sudalaimuthu: *Logistics Management For International Business: Text And Cases*, PHI Learning, Delhi, 2006.

Seema Gupta and Krishna Kumar: *Logistics Management*, Knowledge Book, Delhi, 2010.

Shardul Chaubey: *Logistics Management*, Discovery Publishing, Delhi, 2011.

Simchi-Levi: *The Logic of Logistics: Theory, Algorithms, and Applications for Logistics and Supply Chain Management, 2e*, Springer, India, 2001.

Sushil Mahajan: *Export Management and Export Marketing*, Pearl Books, Delhi, 2011.

T.D. Koshy: *Silk Production and Export Management : Silkmans Companion for the New Millennium*, A.P.H Publication, Delhi, 2011.

Vijay Kumar: *Logistics Management*, Print Media Publication, Delhi, 2007.

Index